D0856205

THE MAJORITY OF ONE

THE MAJORITY OF ONE

Towards a Theory of Regional Compatibility

Minerva M. Etzioni

With a Preface by RICHARD A. FALK

WITHDRAWN
FROM
UNIVERSITY OF PENNSYLVANIA
LIBRARIES

SAGE Publications, Inc. Beverly Hills, California

Copyright © 1970 by Sage Publications, Inc.

All rights reserved. No part of
this book may be reproduced or utilized
in any form or by any means, electronic
or mechanical, including photocopying,
recording, or by any information
storage and retrieval system, without
permission in writing from the
Publisher.

For information address:

SAGE PUBLICATIONS, INC.
275 South Beverly Drive
Beverly Hills, California 90212

JX
1979
E78
cop. 2

First Printing

Printed in the United States of America

Standard Book Number 8039-0042-2

Library of Congress Catalog Card No. 71-92351

DESIGNED BY HANFT/LAGARDERE/HOFFMAN

UNIVERSITY
OF
PENNSYLVANIA
LIBRARIES

E., M. M.

For Amitai

VJ C15937

ACKNOWLEDGMENTS

The author is indebted to Leland M. Goodrich and Bryce Wood for detailed comments on the ideas expressed in this volume. I am also grateful to my students at the Mexico City National University, El Colegio de México and at the New School for Social Research, for penetrating questions they raised when I discussed sections of this book with them.

The writing of this book was begun at the Center of El Colegio de México. A Fellowship of the Rockefeller Foundation allowed me to continue and complete my research at the United Nations Library and at Columbia University. I am also deeply grateful to Charles Wagley, Director of the Institute for Latin American Studies at Columbia University, and to the staff of the Institute, for facilities, support, and the opportunity to exchange views with colleagues and visiting professors.

I am grateful to Linda Hoeschler and Nancy Gertner for their research assistance. I also want to acknowledge Mary West's assistance in copy editing.

Finally, my gratitude to my husband, whose loving support and expert assistance made this book possible, is exceeded only by my love and admiration for him.

WASHINGTON, D.C.   M.E.

CONTENTS

PREFACE

In the period since World War II no international development has been more baffling than the progress and regress of the regional movement. It remains a matter of controversy as to whether regionalism has had a beneficial influence upon the overall quest for world order. Has it protected or jeopardized the economic destinies and political independence of smaller states? Has the claim of regional authorization been used by the most powerful states, especially the United States and the Soviet Union, to disguise their control over political developments in their respective spheres of influence? Does the growth of regional institutions reinforce or undermine the role of the United Nations in matters of peace and security? Do strong regional institutions facilitate or inhibit a transition toward a safer system of world order in which national governments are substantially disarmed and more peaceful procedures are relied upon to resolve international disputes?

The literature devoted to regionalism has not cast much light upon these fundamental lines of inquiry. The valuable scholarship in the area has been devoted mainly to the study of the dynamics of supranational integration at the regional (or subsystemic) level. Much of this literature has concentrated upon regional integration in the European context, partly because it was in Europe that the most ambitious steps toward integration were being taken in the years after 1945. Other less influential work on regionalism has consisted of a series of case studies of particular regional projects such as the Arab League, the Organization of Africa Unity, or the Organization of American States. These case studies treat a particular regional organization by examining its underlying constitutional structure, by narrating the main events in its organizational career, and by appraising its successes and failures. Generalizations about regionalism are rarely attempted in these case studies and no very clear conceptual categories are used to depict the history of the regional movement under scrutiny. As will be evident, then, neither the integration literature nor case studies in depth deal with regional organizations as an aspect of world order.

Against this scholarly background, Minerva Etzioni's *The Majority of One* is a pathbreaking book of great interest. It is a major effort to examine the OAS in the wider context of world order. It builds far beyond the earlier inquiry of Inis Claude in his 1964 monograph "The OAS, the UN, and the United States." Mrs. Etzioni carries the inquiry much further, both conceptually and by her detailed presentation and analysis of empirical material. She makes very effective use of a central distinction between compatible and incompatible regionalism to explore the relationship between the OAS and the UN. The method of inquiry can serve in many ways as a model for an entire field of regional studies, hitherto virtually unexplored. The distinguishing feature of this method is to approach the UN-OAS relationship in several ways: as a matter of constitutional history (how was the relationship conceived at the drafting stage of the UN Charter?), as a matter of organizational history (how did the League of Nations relate to the Pan American Movement that preceded the OAS?), as a matter of juridical analysis (what does the language of the relevant Charter provisions have to say about the UN-OAS relationship?), and as a matter of diplomatic history (what has been the relationship between the OAS and the UN in critical periods of violent conflict?). One of the fascinating features of her study is to show the extent to which United States diplomacy within the OAS has undermined the expectations of the drafters and the language of the Charter.

In this respect, *The Majority of One* is an illuminating study in the use of regional institutions as a contemporary vehicle of great-power diplomacy. The book reveals, in its analysis of principal incidents of peaceful settlement and enforcement, the extent to which American foreign-policy-makers have succeeded in using the OAS to legitimate more or less unilateral uses of force in the Western Hemisphere in such a fashion as to contradict UN purposes and to defeat the intended jurisdiction of the world organization. As a consequence, the UN-OAS relationship is properly characterized as an illustration of "incompatible regionalism." Mrs. Etzioni documents this conclusion by her careful recitation of the facts on those principal occasions (Guatemala, Cuba, Dominican Republic) where the United States succeeded both in having the OAS endorse its conduct and in preventing the UN from acting to uphold the principal commitments of its own Charter. Such an experience is peculiarly ironic in view of the vigor with which Latin American countries had themselves struggled in the Charter-drafting stages against the United States to secure a high degree of automony for the OAS within the UN structure. The United States changed its own posture from championing universalism during World War II to claiming the prerogatives of hegemonial intervention to prevent a Latin American country from falling into or staying in radical hands. Castro has survived in Cuba because the United States has not been prepared to use direct military force to overthrow his regime and was thwarted in its effort to reach this result indirectly by its sponsorship of the exile invasion at the Bay of Pigs in April of 1961.

Since *The Majority of One* was written the OAS has apparently enjoyed the greatest success in its twenty-one-year history—bringing the war of July, 1969, between El Salvador and the Honduras to a prompt and satisfactory end. The OAS role in this settlement process seems to have been both constructive and decisive. The essential bargain reached has led to the withdrawal of the soldiers of El Salvador, who had penetrated up to twenty-five miles into Honduran territory, in exchange for guarantees by the Honduras to uphold the rights of 300,000 Salvadorians living within her territory, the abuse of whom had incited the invasion. It is doubtful whether the two countries could have negotiated such a settlement alone or whether the United Nations could have been used nearly as effectively as was the OAS. The specific support of the Latin American setting seems to have been what led to such a creative and successful experience of peacemaking at the regional level. Significantly, the United States maintained only a quiet presence throughout the entire period of the conflict, having neither interests at stake nor the cultural affinity with the disputants of the sort enjoyed by a Latin American country. One supposes that, had the United States played a more active role, it would have been more difficult for the OAS to achieve a mutually acceptable, if tentative, solution. The OAS threat to impose economic sanctions on El Salvador if it did not withdraw carried the moral weight of a genuinely collective judgment; it also appeared to be economically intimidating to El Salvador. The so-called "soccer war" then provides us with a case of what the OAS can do when its "majority-of-one" character is absent, that is, if the United States behaves as one of twenty-one members rather than as a hegemonial actor.

It is too soon to evaluate the role of the OAS in light of the brief, but serious, war between Honduras and El Salvador. But the war serves to suggest that, even within the Western Hemisphere, there may be crucial peacekeeping roles for a regional organization that implement, rather than contradict, the authority and objectives of the UN. From a historical perspective, we need to weigh the benefits of compatible regionalism against the burdens of incompatible regionalism in assessing the experience of the OAS over the years. From a policy perspective, we should explore tactics and devices by which the operations of compatible regionalism might be strengthened in the OAS-UN nexus, while those of incompatible regionalism are weakened. And finally, from an analytical perspective, it would seem worthwhile to isolate the conditions under which the OAS might be expected to act to uphold the mandate of the UN and those conditions under which it would not.

The normative criterion that could guide such inquiries is that regionalism is beneficial for world order only so long as it does not impair the regulatory claims or authority of the United Nations. If this criterion is used in the OAS-UN context, then the OAS would appear beneficial only to the extent that the United States fails to exercise either its capacity to dominate the OAS or its ability to keep hemispheric disputes off the agenda of the Security Council and General Assembly. Such an assessment encourages us to contemplate the potentialities of compatible regionalism in the Latin American setting if the United States were to withdraw altogether from the OAS. But, given the realities of power politics and the actualities of spheres of influence, it is unlikely that the United States would withdraw; even if it did withdraw one supposes that other modes of domination would be discovered to sustain the hegemonial role of the United States, especially in the Caribbean area. Perhaps, then, a better question, even granting a distaste for hegemonial diplomacy, is whether the OAS moderates the behavior of the United States so as to make its conduct *less* incompatible with UN Charter expectations than if the OAS did not exist. Concerns such as these take shape as a result of the analytical clarity that animates the sweep of argument in *The Majority of One.*

Mrs. Etzioni has initiated an entire tradition of systematic inquiry into the relationship between regional actors and the United Nations. Such inquiry can be usefully extended to other regions and it can be used eventually as the basis of a comprehensive theory of optimal and suboptimal relationships between regional organizations and the UN both within the various partial international systems of the world and in relation to principal matters of international concern. The boundary between compatible and incompatible regionalism may shift depending on whether the subsystem is South Asia, the Middle East, Europe, or Africa and on whether the subject is peace and security, human rights, or economic welfare. In any event, Mrs. Etzioni's book should be read and studied, not only as a seminal account of the OAS-UN relationship, but as the intellectual foundation for an entirely new approach to the place of regionalism in the international political system.

–RICHARD A. FALK

Stanford, California
August 1969

1

TOWARDS A NEW THEORY OF INTERNATIONAL ORGANIZATION

IN THE AGE OF international organization, of developing patterns of institutions above and beyond that of the nation-state, many critics have pointed to the incompatibility of universal and regional organizations: the opposing assumptions of collective security under the United Nations and of military alliances such as NATO and the Warsaw pact, the conflict between the community of man and communities of men. However, in reality, regional and universal organizations do not only coexist and interact; it is our central thesis that the two approaches to international relations may in fact be made complementary. Unlike those who advocate either an exclusively regional or universal approach to international organization, we hold that the principles which underlie these two types of international organization are not mutually exclusive. International experience of the twentieth century suggests that both universalism and regionalism have useful applications; that both are partial characterizations of a more realistic international organizational web which is neither universalist nor confined to the regional setting.

This book is a study of relations established over the last twenty years in the handling of political and security matters between a universal and a regional international organization, the United Nations and the Organization of American States.

The primary purpose of the examination is to explore the specific conditions under which a harmonious relation between the regional and universal organizations can be attained, although—as we shall see—this must of necessity be mainly an "exercise in inversion": that is, we are inferring a likeness of compatible relations from instances of incompatibility. The analysis depicts the organizational, legal, and political mechanisms used in the process of articulating the regionalist approach with the universalist one, and discusses the varying degrees of compatibility which result.

BETWEEN UNIVERSALISM AND REGIONALISM

A variety of writings have argued that the conflict between universalism and regionalism is manifold. Adherents of *universalism* assert the need for international organizations built upon bases which are broad in scope. Looking primarily to the concerns of the world community, universalists argue that world peace is indivisible and that the major problems concerning peace and security are of *world*wide importance. Partisans of this theoretical approach assert that a harmonious relationship between the national aspirations of individual countries and the broader objectives of the international community can and must be achieved. They assert that universal institutions can be made to channel the interests of individual states in order that international and national aims may be simultaneously realized.

The universalist approach, however, has been widely challenged on the grounds that it is premature, abstract, and doctrinaire in the present international situation. More specifically, adversaries have accused universalists of being too general, too ambitious, and of failing to consider the heterogeneity of political, economic, social, and geographical circumstances of the modern world.

Among the regionalists, two main views may be distinguished. On the one hand, some advocates consider regional organizations as a permanent feature of international life, while other supporters view them solely as an intermediate stage. Those in the first category, "hardnosed" regionalists, consider regionalism a substitute for universalism; they believe that the world should be organized exclusively in regional compartments or—that this is the only way it can be organized, whatever the virtues of a world government. Those in the second group, the less doctrinaire regionalists, accept regionalism as a preliminary stage, a stepping-stone towards an effective global organization in a politically more propitious future. But for the present time, in spite of the differences, both regionalist views involve a limitation of the scope of international organization.

However, regionalists, like universalists, are not immune to criticism. Objections to regionalism revolve around the fact that the world cannot be neatly divided into regional units. Regional divisions are hard to draw precisely and are, as a rule, useful only for some specific purposes, the region being redefined as the nature of the purpose changes, say, from trade to defense. Critics point out that in the majority of instances intraregional affinities have proved to be chimerical. Beneath the surface of regional harmony, animosities frequently pose insurmountable obstacles to the regional solution of problems.

Yet, despite the fact that the actual relationship between these two kinds of approach is often seen as antagonistic, it can be shown that this is not necessarily the case. The dichotomizing theories that assume institutional partitions between universalism and regionalism are unsatisfactory; they cannot explain the occasions in which the two organizations interact harmoniously and effectively, nor can they understand in detail why they come into conflict when they do. Analysis of both universalism and regionalism is necessary in order to approach a fuller understanding of international organization. A new theoretical perspective which combines regional and universal approaches is needed, one which focuses on all the possible mechanisms for coordinating regional and universal organizations and the conditions under which they evolve. This study is conducted in the hope of contributing to an integrated theory of this kind.

THE CONCEPT OF COMPATIBILITY

By *compatibility* we mean that the relationship between two organizations is such that the activities of one do not undermine those of the other and vice versa; we are specifically interested here in the circumstances under which regional organizations may be strengthened without undermining the universal organization, or the circumstances under which *compatible* regional organizations may be set up.

In reality, the approaches to international relations which should be distinguished are not universalism versus regionalism but universalism and *compatible* regionalism, on the one hand, versus universalism and *incompatible* regionalism, on the other. The extent of compatibility of regional organizations with a universal body should be judged according to the conflicts between the two and the degree to which such conflicts are minimized. Universal organizations and compatible regional organizations complement each other; there is an interest in maintaining harmonious relation in the sharing of international tasks. Incompatible regional organizations tend to prefer independence of action and oppose control by universal organizations. Consequently, incompatible regional organizations create obstacles to the development of effective universal organizations. Compatible and incompatible features can be distinguished by identifying the divisions of *jurisdiction* and *function* among the regional and universal organizations. Clearly there are several ways in which international duties can be divided between the two organizations. However, only some of these divisions, the cases of *compatible* regionalism, allow for the harmonious functioning of the two. Alternatively, there are specific instances, the cases of *incom-*

patible regionalism, when the devolution of responsibility onto the regional level is incompatible with the maintenance of the universal organization.

Thus, several divisions of jurisdiction occur between the two organizations, either allowing for or detracting from their compatibility. For instance, the charters of regional organizations are compatible when they explicitly defer to the greater authority of constitutions of universal organizations, or when the privileges and obligations they set forth do not diminish those rights or duties of their members that derive from universal organizations. On the contrary, their members may undertake to act in ways that are consonant with their accepted obligations toward universal organizations; conceivably, there could be a Latin American Association for the Advancement of the United Nations, which would clearly be a compatible regional organization. Moreover, if questions of jurisdiction do arise, despite the specific constitutional provisions that attempt to clarify the legal relationship of the two, universalistic commitments legally prevail over any others assumed by the regional organization members. For example, Article 103 in the United Nations Charter asserts that in the event of conflict between the obligations of the members of the United Nations and other international agreements, the obligations of the United Nations Charter prevail. In addition, a regional organization may become compatible by making itself accountable to a universal organization in the sense that it is committed to report its actions to, and be supervised by, the universal organization.

Incompatible regional organizations, on the other hand, assume as their prerogative the right to act independently. Their charters reveal an attempt to avoid the restrictive legal requirements demanded by the universal organization and thus they repudiate universal supervision and remain unaccountable to universal control while engaging in their international activities. While not all incompatible regional organizations explicitly challenge the universal organization, it is apparent that they all carefully avoid its control.

In addition to the division of *jurisdiction,* the *division of function*—political, economic, or military—is significant in determining the extent to which regionalism is compatible or incompatible. The analysis here, however, is more complicated; a compatible division of function may occur either when the regional organization and the international organization share the *same* function, or when the exercise of a particular function devolves predominantly on one level or the other. The determination of which distribution of function is compatible with the existence of both organizations depends to a great extent upon the nature, range, and impact of the problem to be dealt with. In general, compatible regionalism characterizes a regional organization that asserts its jurisdiction only over problems whose consequences remain within regional boundaries. The consideration of problems with extraregional consequences will, as a rule, be transferred to the universal level if the regional organization is to maintain its compatibility.

It is clear, however, that there may be some difficulty in determining the most compatible division of function in cases which are only superficially regional, that is, regional in geographic terms only, but which are actually universal in implication and influence. The preemptive influence of the cold war in Europe, for example, has transformed many regional problems into universal problems which thus require a forum where the superpowers can be represented. Compatible regional organizations would tend to refer consideration of this kind of issue to the universal level. Incompatible regional organizations, on the other hand, would tend to place in regional channels the solution of difficulties which are universal in range and import.

The compatibility and incompatibility of political functions is most clearly distinguishable in the field of the peaceful settlement of disputes. Compatible regionalism exists only when regional organizations consider that the primary responsibility for the maintenance of peace rests in the hands of universal organizations and that their own decision-making power is derived from this source. Although regional organizations may propose regional schemes for the peaceful settlement of disputes, their activity is compatible only so long as it does not diminish the all-encompassing protective responsibility of the international organizations, and the effectiveness of centralized control at the universalist level. Incompatible regionalism exists when regional organizations seek to settle conflicts, especially armed conflicts, without the intrusion of universal agencies and close the door to recourse to the universal body whenever a member is dissatisfied with the handling of a case at the regional level.

A study of the division of *economic functions* also casts some light on differences between compatible and incompatible regionalism. In the case of compatible regionalism, organizations weigh the impact of action not only in terms of immediate consequences for the region itself, but also in terms of the general effect of such action on world economic growth and stability. Incompatible economic regionalism on the other hand, promotes tight discriminatory policies for countries outside the regional limits.

Differences between compatible and incompatible regionalism are also ostensible in the division of *military* functions. Fundamental to compatible regionalism is the belief that peace is indivisible, and thus, that regional organizations—if they are to have any military power at all—must form an integral part of a system of universal collective security. For incompatible regionalism, on the other hand, the essential premise is that the problem of defending a given group of states can be separated from the problem of preserving peace throughout the international community. Incompatible regional organizations consider the universal collective security system deficient and seek to carry out security functions of their own; in so doing, they clearly threaten the United

Nations system as a whole. Regional organizations that are compatible with the universal security system of the United Nations, although they may be equally well aware of its deficences, in many ways seek to avoid creating additional obstacles to its evolution and work for its advancement. Thus, they support the Security Council in its assumption of primary responsibility for the maintenance of peace and security.

The military responsibilities compatible regional organizations do assume, if any, are usually built upon a foundation of previously existing intraregional, nonmilitary ties; a coherent regional community, whose primary focus is internal, exists prior to the development of an external orientation. Incompatible regional organizations may lack this foundation of previously existing ties; the creation of such ties may be stimulated only as a consequence of the desire to expand military commitments. Organizations which are created for military purposes alone (and which continue to function primarily on this basis) are likely to be incompatible with universal collective security systems in the sense that they resemble alliance systems, rather than reflecting preexisting regional groupings.

Moreover, the compatibility or incompatibility of regional security systems can be shown in terms of their actual operation within a given region. Since compatible regional organizations are prepared to confront aggression anywhere—even within their own membership—their functioning complements that of the general security system, a system which presupposes a more or less automatic response to aggression, wherever it occurs. The Organization of American States, for instance, has provisions for a collective response to aggression of both non-American and American origin, until the Security Council takes the measures necessary to restore international peace and security. In contrast, incompatible regional organizations focus primarily on threats from sources outside the regional group. Their security mechanisms are incompatible in the sense that they are used solely as instruments for selective security: they fulfill the needs of governments for each other's assistance in their own struggles for security, and effectively disregard the needs of the world community. Both NATO and the Warsaw Treaty Organization are examples of this sort; the threat of a Communist penetration is a major unifying factor among the European members of NATO while the unity of the Warsaw Treaty Organization is triggered by the possibility of Western expansionism. Security mechanisms here are preventive or anticipatory in that action precedes the event of an armed attack. Compatible mechanisms, on the other hand, are solely reactive; security measures are taken only when an actual attack has occurred.

Once the divisions of jurisdiction and the divisions of functions have been described it is necessary to point out that various combinations between both divisions might occur. The fact that regional organizations have several functions (political, economic, and military) does not exclude the possibility that some functions may also be served in part by universal organizations, just as a service by a state government does not preclude a federal service. The universal organization might simply operate on a higher authority level with regard to the same functions.

In general, upon closer examination, it appears that every international charter or treaty, every article in international constitutions, is not subject to single unequivocal interpretation. As we shall see later, the meaning of an article derived strictly from the text is not as important for the purposes of this analysis as the interpretation given it in actual use. Interpretation in this sense is dynamic; a single article, for instance, may be differently interpreted by different actors at the same time, or by the same actor at different times. Moreover, in each case, the article may be given either a *universalist* interpretation, or a *compatible regionalist* interpretation, or an *incompatible regionalist* interpretation.

UPWARD AND DOWNWARD TRANSFERS

Dealing solely in terms of jurisdictional and functional divisions may give the impression that international organizations are static in time and space. Actually international organizations are dynamic, revealing a relationship between the universal and regional levels that is marked by continuous transfers of function, authority, and loyalty. These transfers between universal and regional organizations are of two kinds: *upward* and *downward.*

Thus, in evaluating regional and universal organizations, consideration should be given to the more dynamic aspects of their relationship—the extent to which the institutions allow for these transfers, their nature and direction. At a given point in time, for example, one could speak of the delay or acceleration of the process of upward transfer of authority to the universal level by regional organizations. This is likely to be characteristic of compatible regionalism since compatibility demands a willingness to accede to any increase in authority which the universal organization might require. Similarly, incompatible regionalism would involve a tendency to favor a downward transfer of power from the universal to the regional level. Furthermore, one can look at the evolution of this relationship over time; regional organizations may serve as intermediate stages in an evolutionary process of upward transfer that would strengthen the universal organization, or, conversely, they may create obstacles to this development. However, it should be noted that incompatible regional organizations subject to an upward transfer may eventually assume characteristics of compatibility, while compatible regional organizations that, for their own reasons, support a policy of downward transfer may actually develop aspects of incompatibility with universal organizations.

BETWEEN THE UNITED NATIONS CHARTER AND THE OAS

The relationship between regional organizations and universal organizations, the extent to which the former are compatible or incompatible with the latter, will be discussed in this study in terms of those parts of a universal international constitution (the United Nations Charter) which refer to regionalism. However, since no international organization is immune to world social and political forces, restricting ourselves to the formal, legal content of the provisions must necessarily be inadequate. International constitutional charters are, in varying degrees, continually shaped and influenced by these external forces and serve as vehicles for their expression. The parts of the United Nations Charter related to regionalism have undergone the same kind of metamorphosis the charter as a whole has experienced since it was written twenty years ago. While there have been no amendments, additions, or deletions to either the text or the formal content of that part of the charter on which this study will focus,[1] there have been changes of functions, power, and legal primacy, which have evolved pragmatically.

There have been both *broadening* interpretations of the charter's provisions, which have expanded the sense in which they were originally intended, and there have been *constricting* interpretations, which confine the meaning of the provisions to the strictest construction of words involved.

In this perspective, the position of universal and regional organizations as provided for in the United Nations Charter must be analyzed within the context of the actual evolution of a particular regional organization and the actual development of the United Nations. The choice of an organizational arena, in a given case, has consequences for the division of jurisdiction and function between the two and hence, for their compatibility or incompatibility. For the purpose of this analysis, the major focus will be on the developing relationship between the United Nations and the Organization of

American States. Since the formal establishment of the Organization of American States as a regional organization in 1948, its relationship with the United Nations has gradually developed stronger and stronger elements of incompatibility; both the actions of the OAS and the interpretations of its role in world affairs have often belied many of the constitutional provisions set up in 1948.[2] Moreover, this has occurred in conjunction with definite shifts of interpretation of the United Nations Charter by the member states, as the following chapters will show.

THE UNDERLYING POWER RELATIONS

The examination focuses primarily on the changes that have taken place in international organization and international law—specifically, the changed relationship of the UN and the OAS. The major level of analysis is thus an organizational one. Yet, in order to better explain the organizational relationships, the study must include an analysis of the underlying power dynamics. The *power* approach is simply an alternate way of looking at this relationship and, while it is not the basic concern of this study, it clearly cannot be ignored. Rather, the power substructure represents another level that must be considered if the organizational relations are to be fully understood: for example, a power analysis reveals the sources of change in the relative influence of the organization and explains the significance of their relationship in terms of its concrete effects on interstate affairs. One can say that the major emphasis of the study, the relationship of the UN and the OAS, is the particular "stage" on which several national "players" interact. The underlying power relations represent, in effect, the backstage maneuverings—questions of who the "star" of the production will be, and who will be assigned to play secondary roles. While we assume that the "stage" of interaction is important, we recognize that a complete explanation requires a consideration of both "backstage" and "onstage" movements. The intention here is to avoid two traps: on the one hand, regarding international organizations as powerful determinants of international relations, losing sight of the power dynamics involved; on the other hand, regarding international organizations as mere facades, or epiphenomena, that reflect but do not affect world politics.

It is apparent that international organizations have not put an end to the dynamics of power politics but have injected a new force in the world which has altered its political configurations. International organizations attain influence through the support of their members on whose behalf the prestige and resources of the organizations have been invested. Their influence is expressed through the moral and legal force of their purposes and principles, and through the persuasive actions of their administrative organs. Hence, which article is used, or the kinds of interpretations given to it, is of some consequence for world politics.

At a given time, however, the precise impact of international organizations on world affairs cannot be definitively ascertained since this depends on the particular period under study and the specific political environment considered. In general, it can be said that the influence of international organizations is quite secondary, owing to the relative autonomy of the member states. Thus, an adequate treatment of the subject must take into account *both* the independent effect of institutions in setting the context for the national power play, and vice versa, the effect of the national power play in selecting the organizational context.

In particular, this study will demonstrate the change between the relative political importance of the UN and the OAS as scenes for the interaction between the United States and the twenty Latin American republics. This is the political context of our story. The power discrepancies between the United States and the Latin American states have affected the weighting of interests in the international organizations with which they were concerned. In most of the period under study the United States was primarily interested in protecting Latin America from Communist intervention, just as in the earlier period it had been concerned with avoiding Fascist intervention. The Latin American governments, while sharing the same concern in varying degrees, were simultaneously concerned with preventing North American intervention. The extraregional interest of one superpower and the delicate balance between extra- and intraregional concerns of the other member nations lies in the background of much of the following analysis: the effort of the shepherd to guard against the wolf and the mixed fear of both the wolf and the shepherd by those who do not like to be treated like sheep. In this case, it is important to note, the "sheep" themselves were not without disputes. Yet in their attempts to work out differences of views and stem intraregional wars, they always had to keep one eye on how these settlements would affect their relationship to the "colossus of the north."

The United States eventually considered that its political interests might best be served if the forum for conducting its international business with the Latin American states were regional rather than universal; within a regional arena the United States would not be exposed to criticism either from other powerful nations or from nonaligned countries. While, in general, the overwhelming power of the United States enabled it to become a dominant member of any international organization it entered, this was especially true in the case of the OAS. Since the United States could influence the majority of the members to support most of its motions, there was indeed some truth to what is often said in Latin America— that the OAS is governed by "the majority of one ... the minority of twenty."[3] As a result, the OAS, particularly after 1965, was repeatedly called upon to resolve intraregional conflicts; the net effect of this was to increase the importance of the OAS at the expense of the UN, and to transform a compatible regional organization into an incompatible one.

It will be shown that the changes in the relationship between the UN and the OAS can, to a great extent, be
explained by the disjunction between the main power features
of this relationship and the formal arrangements of the organizations involved. Despite the constitutional guarantees of one
vote to each member in the General Assembly and in all the
organs of the OAS, it is clear that the influence of the United
States is effectively greater than any Latin American republic,
and in many ways greater than all of them combined. Moreover, in an important sense, the actual power relations have
altered the compatibility of the institutions; in this instance
the analysis of power relations adds another dimension to the
notion of compatibility or incompatibility considered previously. The choice of a regional area, in which the United
States could more easily dominate, rather than of a universal
arena, where the interests of smaller powers were better protected, upset the preexisting balance of the two. In the past,
the mechanisms of one organization had, in effect, compen-
sated for those of the other; this was no longer true in the
cases under consideration here.

In sum, two levels of analysis—political and organizational
—have been combined in this study. The first level considers:
What effect does the organizational context—the choice of the
UN or the OAS—have on the way in which international
power conflicts are played out? Alternatively, what effect do
the power conflicts have on the selection of the particular
organizational context in each case? On the second level, the
following question is asked: What does the selection of arena
in each particular instance imply about the relationship of the
two? At the same time, several questions which effectively
synthesize the two categories are asked throughout: What
type of relationships would have existed had either the UN or
the OAS existed alone? What type of relationships have
evolved given the coexistence of the two? In particular, in
what ways can the OAS be made compatible with the UN
given the current state of United States-Latin American rela-

tions, and conversely, in what ways will United States-Latin American relations evolve, given the current relationship of the UN and the OAS? Together, these questions can be summarized in a single query that represents a major focus of the analysis: How do the dynamics of one organization affect the dynamics of the other?

PLAN OF THE BOOK

The study includes a brief explanatory flashback into the period of the League of Nations and the interlude between the two world wars. This historical introduction provides a touchstone by which to judge UN-OAS relations. It is in this context that the birth, in 1945, of a new universal organization, the United Nations, is placed. The study proceeds from a discussion of the forces that shaped the framing of the United Nations Charter (Chapter II), to a critical analysis of the resultant provisions and their conflicting interpretations (Chapter III). The formation of a regional organization—the OAS—in 1948 is treated similarly: the historical background surrounding its birth, the intentions and interests of its framers, and the charter provisions that finally emerged (Chapter IV). The dynamic relationship of the two organizations from the time of their inception until 1965 is then discussed: 1965 is selected as a cutoff point since it is at this time that an inter-American peace-keeping force was created and the UN-OAS relationship took a new turn.

In brief, between 1945 and 1965 nations changed sides, regionalists became universalists, universalists became regionalists, compatible regionalists became incompatible regionalists, upward transfer changed its course, and the interpretation of various constitutional provisions was altered. Original provisions in the United Nations Charter were pragmatically expanded or restricted through new interpretations based on changing political circumstances. Broadening interpretations of some provisions of the United Nations Charter and constricting interpretations of others had the same net effect: they increased the independence of regional organizations by either expanding original concessions to regionalism or effectively reducing original limitations.

The final two chapters (V and VI) present specific case studies to illustrate some of the changes that have occurred during this period. In addition, various possibilities are explored in regard to the likelihood of finding workable legal or political mechanisms for coping with the trends, within several regional organizations, towards incompatibility.

2

REGIONAL AND UNIVERSAL
FORCES AT THE FOUNDING OF
THE UNITED NATIONS

TOWARD THE END of World War II, the San Francisco Conference convened to establish the foundations of a universal organization, a thoroughly revised edition of the League of Nations. During the period in which the basis for this new international organization was laid, American, British, and Soviet viewpoints prevailed in many instances, while in others the concerted action of small and middle-sized nations influenced important decisions. Similarly, a handful of regional organizations, functioning at various stages of organizational development, were able to exert a considerable influence on the outcome of the founding conference of the United Nations.

A study of the push and pull of regionalist and universalist forces at this point in time provides a basis for our analysis of the United Nations' subsequent development and helps to explain why the features of the United Nations Charter relevant to this analysis are in the form in which we now encounter them.

The regional organizations that were crucial in the emergence of the United Nations had been developed, even before World War II, to satisfy the political and security needs of various groups of nations as a result of the shortcomings of the League of Nations. The British Commonwealth, the Arab League, and the Inter-American System were the most outstanding but not the only examples of these regional offsprings. As successful survivors of the League, as well as representatives of power groupings, it was natural that these organizations expected some sort of recognition from the League of Nations' successor, some sort of status in the new postwar world. Similarly, countries in the orbit of Soviet influence were anxious to safeguard the position their regional associations had achieved.

Under the Covenant of the League of Nations, constitutional compatibility of regional agencies with the universal organization was vague and ambiguous. Most conspicuously, the covenant contained no provisions specifically regulating its relationship with regional pacts. Nor could consensus on the status of regional organizations be found among the Big Four sponsoring governments (United States, China, Great Britain, or Russia) or among the members of the various regional pacts. These regionalist forces were part of the political context within which the stage for post-World War II international organization was being set.

INCOMPATIBLE REGIONALISM IN
THE EARLY PLANNING STAGES

The earliest conception of the United Nations by the allied powers included granting of primary responsibility in the maintenance of international peace and security to the big powers. But in the early planning stages of the world organization, the framers did not carefully delineate the method by which the major powers would carry out these duties, nor did they clarify the role of regional groupings working within this United Nations framework.

On the part of the United States, President Roosevelt, under the influence of Undersecretary of State Sumner Welles and British Prime Minister Winston Churchill, favored, in

1942, a universal system modeled after the Pan-American Union. The latter, a loosely organized association of states meeting informally at specific times for specific purposes, gave considerable autonomy to the units upon which it was based. Here, the pillars of the system would be regional organizations, each organized around the dominant powers in their respective areas.[1]   Officials in the United States, Great Britain, and the Soviet Union seemed to envisage for their own regions something closely akin to the European Concert of the nineteenth century. Thus, the allied powers maintained that a universal council should only have the authority to deal with those problems which the regional councils failed to solve. Such a universal council would include the Big Four (the United States, Great Britain, the Soviet Union, and China) and other countries representing major regional systems. Subordination to the universal council would be more nominal than real, for regional councils would maintain ultimate authority to handle cases within their geographical and political boundaries.

At a meeting in Washington on March 23, 1943, British and American leaders began to consider seriously the role of regional councils and the predominance of the big powers at both the regional and universal levels.[2] The notion of strong regional councils was further explored and expanded in the United States by an Advisory Committee on Problems on War and Peace which had been created in the State Department on January 8, 1940, by Secretary of State Cordell Hull, to study problems posed by the postwar conditions. Undersecretary of State Sumner Welles headed the subcommittee on international organization which did most of the work on the issues raised by the creation of a new international organization; Welles's efforts in this direction greatly influenced the basic orientation of the subcommittee during 1942 and 1943. Although it is very difficult to determine the precise relationship between the president and the subcommittee's members, since discussions were at this point largely exploratory and informal, it appears that the regionalist bias of the subcommittee's initial plans was basically consonant with Roosevelt's views of international organization.

Furthermore, Welles's inclination toward an incompatible regional approach (similar to that of the Inter-American System), was warmly supported by the Latin American governments. At the same time, in order to satisfy the expected demands of the major military powers for freedom to take security measures, Welles favored the establishment of a universal organization based upon a foundation of regional organizations. The blueprint for a universal council advanced by Welles's subcommittee stipulated that the supreme executive agency of the universal organization be composed of the Big Four and states representing regional systems, elected periodically by the states comprising the region.[3] Only in the event that the latter proved unable to handle disputes or to restrain an aggressor, would the universal authority be asked to intervene. Thus, states from every region would be required and able to contribute to the maintenance of regional and world peace.[4] This was the basic content of the final papers drafted by Welles's subcommittee in mid-1943, of which President Roosevelt heartily approved. Only certain details, such as the method of electing the smaller nations' representatives to the executive branch of the universal agency, were left open for further consideration.

Winston Churchill shared Sumner Welles's enthusiasm for preserving such powerful regional systems and for securing their recognition in the United Nations. Presumably he had in mind the preservation of the British Commonwealth, as well as the creation of some sort of autonomous European organization. Great importance was attached in his views to incompatible types of regionalism, since "only the countries whose interests were directly affected by a dispute could be expected to apply themselves with sufficient vigor to secure settlement."[5]

This was clearly the direction of British influence during the formative stage of the United Nations. For instance, Churchill's message to President Roosevelt of February 2, 1943, envisaged the creation of a new European regional council, one embodying the spirit of the League of Nations but not subject to its weakness. Scandinavian, Danubian, and Balkan blocs would compose this regional European council. In addition there would be Far Eastern and Middle Eastern groups. In March, Churchill made several radio addresses in favor of this conception of regional organizations. During his trip to the United States in May, 1943, he made clear to President Roosevelt his support for nearly autonomous regional councils within the framework of a universal body; his proposals called for American participation in the hemispheric, Pacific, and European councils he expected would be established.

This was in fact the central idea in the Churchillian plan; the future world organization was to rest on a structure of three incompatible regional organizations: the Councils of Europe, the Far East, and the Americas. Later in July, 1943, the British government made initial attempts to create a regional organization in Europe. It proposed to the United States and the Soviet Union the creation of a European commission with a dual purpose: to coordinate the execution of surrender or armistice terms imposed on the enemy and to assume a central role with regard to long range European arrangements in the fields of security and economic integration.[6]

The effect of this proposal on the United States was to bring to a head the regional issue, the issue on which American official opinion was still divided in spite of Roosevelt's regionalist inclinations. After much discussion, and considerable opposition to the plan by the Secretary of State, the United States government did agree to create a European commission. Hull objected very strongly to the idea of entrusting this body with long-range peacetime functions, rather than just the short-term problems of surrender or armistice agreements, for reasons discussed below.

In the meantime, an agreement had virtually been reached with the Soviet Union with regard to regional councils independent of universal control. Like Churchill, Stalin believed in the desirability of promoting independent regional councils which would suit Soviet interests by helping to maintain Russia's role in those areas under its sphere of influence.[7] Consequently, by the spring of 1943 it appeared that postwar international relations would be organized almost completely on an incompatible regional basis; the universal organization would at most serve to coordinate the work of regional organizations.

But soon thereafter, the big powers' preference for incompatible regionalism began to encounter rising objections from the smaller nations, and to generate divisions among and within other superpower governments, particularly the United States State Department. Cordell Hull, well known for his opposition to Welles's incompatible regional approach, engaged in a continuing debate with the president concerning the nature of the international organization to be proposed. On his frequent visits to the White House he surrounded himself with a group of officials and experts favoring his universalist views. Sumner Welles was not invited to join this group and this seems to have exacerbated the split between Hull and Welles which eventually led to the latter's resignation. During these meetings Hull and his team tried to persuade President Roosevelt to recognize the necessity for greater universalist regulation of regional organizations. In Hull's perspective, the wartime harmony that prevailed among the big powers could be transferred to a universal organization whose supremacy could be easily guaranteed. A postwar international organization could develop a system controlled more or less by the former allied command. Initially, however, Hull and his group met with little success in convincing the president; on one occasion, Hull reports, "We asked, 'Aren't you at least in favor of a world secretariat? We'll need some such organization to handle international conferences.' " Roosevelt laughed and replied: "I'll give you the Pentagon or the Empire State Building. You can put the world secretariat there."[8]

THE RISE OF UNIVERSALISM

By June, 1943, the report of Welles's subcommittee on international organization had been made public. Its clear advocacy of incompatible regionalism was critically received by Cordell Hull, who felt that:

> *I could not go along with the regional feature; hence I started the subcommittee upon a detailed consideration of international organization in the spring of 1943 on the basis of the fundamental issues rather than on the special subcommittee's draft. The subcommittee, after thorough discussion, expressed itself as being overwhelmingly in favor of a universal rather than a regional basis for an international organization.*

Hull himself became active chairman of the new subcommittee, informally referred to as an Advisory Committee on Postwar Foreign Policy. The Committee included members of Congress and the Senate who were partisans of universalism, and began to explore the possibilities of a more universalist international organization. Furthermore, it maintained close contact with various U. S. government departments and non-governmental agencies, each of which contributed suggestions concerning the nature of a future international organization. In effect Hull's subcommittee launched a universalist campaign.

Hull's major objection to incompatible regionalism focused on his feeling that it would force the universal organization to deal with groups of states rather than with individual nations and that in this situation there would always be the danger of regional groupings uniting in opposition to the universal organization. Moreover, the regional organizations would put small countries at the mercy of the power of neighboring giants, and Hull was not convinced that the big powers would exhibit the same self-restraint which—as he saw it—the United States exercised in the Western Hemisphere.

Hull did not oppose regional organizations per se and other arrangements supplementary to the universal international organization, so long as these did not infringe on the powers that should reside in a worldwide organization. Thus he accepted the idea of compatible regional associations that were effectively subordinate to a world organization, an arrangement which he believed had some advantages in facilitating peaceful settlement and in promoting economic and social cooperation. His objective was to have,

> subordinated to the world organization and within its framework, groups of nations located in a given area [which] might with entire consistency carry forward the policies we had adopted in our structure of Pan American cooperation provided they did not go further than the Pan American system. The American republics had agreed to consider any danger or threatened danger to any American nation from outside the hemisphere as a danger to all of them, and to cooperate in meeting it. Under a continuance of this policy, after the creation of a world organization the American republics would proceed to deal with such danger locally, while simultaneously bringing the matter before the council of the universal organization, and cooperating within the framework of that body. When a house catches fire, the nearest neighbors hasten there with the common objective of putting out or preventing the spread of the fire until the Fire Department, which has been instantly notified, can arrive on the scene.[10]

Roosevelt finally began to accede to Hull's universalism at about the time the U. S. Department of State was preparing a draft of the Four-Nations Declaration for presentation to the Moscow Conference in October, 1943. This was a particularly crucial point at which to influence the United States' position. United States preparatory works and papers were very important because the United States' views were generally the most influential. The United States State Department frequently devoted numerous resources and qualified personnel to a careful study of those matters to be discussed at subsequent international meetings. More often than not, American preparatory drafts were accepted by the other powers with only minor changes. As a result, the conference declaration stated that the views of the four nations—United States, United Kingdom, Russia and China—favored universal rather than regional security systems. Article 5 of the declaration asserted:

> *that for the purpose of maintaining international peace and security pending the re-establishment of law and order and the inauguration of a system of general security they [the big powers] will consult with one another, and as occasion requires, with other members of the United Nations with a view to a joint action on behalf of the community of nations.*

Suprisingly enough, at Moscow, Winston Churchill did not object to Hull's arguments against incompatible regionalism. Nor was it difficult to convince the Soviet Union of the advantages of having a strong Security Council where Soviet participation was duly secured.

In December, 1943, Hull submitted to the president a memorandum calling for a worldwide, rather than regional, basis for the international organization. Soon thereafter, on February 3, 1944, President Roosevelt gave the Secretary of State formal clearance to plan the United Nations Charter on the basis of his universalist views.[11] Hull's December memorandum inspired the work of a State Department group, headed by Leo Pasvolsky, on postwar international organization. This group made extensive studies of the League of Nations and other international agencies but, in general, relied on the broad principles of universalism contained in the Four-Nations Declaration. Pasvolsky's study focused on the primary functions of international organization and was the basis for the United States' universalist proposals presented at the Dumbarton Oaks Conference in October, 1944.

One may wonder what precipitated the transition in Roosevelt's views from his initial sympathy with Welles's regionalist position to a more universalist outlook closer to Hull's opinions. In the first place, it should be pointed out that what is presented here represents the gradual evolution of Roosevelt's views, the slow clarification of what were, at the outset, relatively uniform predilections about postwar international organizations. The president's first discussions with Welles occurred long before the war had ended, when matters of international organization were largely peripheral to the president's main interests. Moreover, it was clear that the president did not want to prejudice future negotiations on international organizations or stir up disagreement among the Allies by committing himself to specific proposals. Thus, discussions at this point were informal and tentative, and the views of most of the participants, including the president, appeared to be in flux.

> The President himself frequently took occasion in private talks to discuss his ideas of the postwar world freely and informally, implicitly or explicitly leaving the impression that they were developing more or less independently of the Department of State. The very informality of his approach indicated that he was less interested in systematically developing a detailed plan of postwar organization than in testing reactions to various ideas and in launching "trial ballots" without committing himself.[1][2]

It was the British position in general, and Churchill's proposals of July, 1943, in particular, that sharpened the debate. Churchill's plan to establish a Commission for Europe, alongside other regionally based councils, represented a specific, official recommendation for an autonomous regional organization. For Secretary Hull, this position implied a long-term United States involvement in European affairs above and beyond that warranted by the United States' peace commitments. As Hull says:

> *We did not think that the people of the United States would support this country's participation in a European council and a Pacific council, in addition to a Western Hemisphere council, and also in a universal organization. We felt that the American people were more ready to take responsibilities in a world organization than in any regional plan except perhaps one embracing this hemisphere.*[13]

It was the prospect of the extension of United States responsibilities to Europe to this extent that appears to have prompted Roosevelt to turn away from an incompatible regionalist perspective toward the universalist approach of the United States' proposals at Dumbarton Oaks.

In essence, the United States' Dumbarton Oaks Proposals set forth the Security Council as the agency responsible for the maintenance of international peace and security. The document stated that the Security Council was to have a monopoly on enforcement action and only rather grudgingly included some provisions for the functioning of compatible regional organizations to maintain peace and security in their own areas. The American proposals were acceptable to Great Britain, the Soviet Union, and China (although China further proposed that there be a Security Council approval of regional arrangements in order to insure their conformity with the purposes of the universal organization).

> *1. Nothing in the Charter shall preclude the existence of regional arrangements or agencies for dealing with such matters relating to the maintenance of peace and security as are appropriate for regional action, provided such arrangements or agencies and their activities are consistent with purposes and principles of the Organi-*

zation. The Security Council should encourage settlement of local disputes through such regional arrangements or by such regional agencies, either on the initiative of the states concerned or by reference from the Security Council.

2. The Security Council should, where appropriate, utilize such arrangements or agencies for enforcement action under its authority, but no enforcement action should be taken under regional arrangements or by regional agencies without the authorization of the Security Council.

3. The Security Council should at all times be kept fully informed of the activities undertaken or in contemplation under regional arrangements or by regional agencies for the maintenance of international peace and security.[14]

While the activities of compatible regional organizations were viewed as legitimate only in security matters affecting their own region (economic, social, or cultural aspects were not dealt with), their competence in these areas was clearly limited. Their charters had to be fully consistent with the purposes and principles of the universal organization. As a result, they were empowered to use all means to maintain peace and security, except enforcement action; in the application of enforcement action they were wholly subordinate to the Security Council.[15] The Security Council, provided here with a strong universalist framework, would thus hold a monopoly of force in the international community.

REASSERTION OF INCOMPATIBLE REGIONALISM

Challenges to the universalist framework established at Dumbarton Oaks characterized the intense diplomatic bargaining of the period immediately after the Dumbarton Oaks Conference and before the San Francisco Conference. Regional forces in several parts of the world joined together to give new strength to the case for incompatible regionalism; the pressure was exerted both by individual countries and by concerted group action. Disagreement with the proposals advanced at Dumbarton Oaks was expressed in the form of proposing numerous amendments to the portion of the document outlining regional arrangements. In their defense of incompatible regionalism, some countries also threatened to walk out of the San Francisco negotiations, while other nations merely demanded the same treatment as the more active or influential regional groups had received. The latter attitude, for example, was adopted by the members of the Arab League in reference to the active role performed by the Latin American delegations before and during the San Francisco Conference. In so doing, the members of the Arab League were also seeking recognition of their newly established regional organization. While the Arab League regional grouping lacked the historical background and experience of the Inter-American System, its members had similar vested interests in the maintenance of their regionalism. It is interesting to note, however, that the organization they had created actually had more compatible features than the inter-American one. After the signing of the pact of the Arab League on March 22, 1945, its members, for which Egypt acted as a spokesman, tried to keep it either associated with, or subordinated to, the United Nations.

Challenge to universalism came from some of the European states as well. Countries such as France, Czechoslovakia, and Poland advanced the cause of incompatible regionalism by seeking safeguards for the continuance of regional security arrangements against renewed German aggression. The position of the Soviet Union, however, was not clear. While Stalin hesitated to put the system of bilateral and multilateral assistance pacts established with Eastern European countries under restrictive universal control, he did foresee the possible use of the United Nations, a Western creation, as a means of protecting Soviet interests. It appeared that he would be willing to join this universal organization only so long as the Soviet Union obtained the right to veto any United Nations action inimical to its interests.[16] The smaller European countries in general were uneasy about the power that was to be granted to the Security Council, and in effect, to the superpowers.

> *Many of the Governments of the smaller nations of Western Europe approached this Government [U.S.] from time to time with respect to postwar problems, and the suggestions of many of them were singularly helpful. The views advanced by the Nederlands and Norwegian governments were in the highest degree useful. It is necessary to say, however, that in most of these cases the views were regional rather than universal.[17]*

The Latin American group in particular, strengthened the case of incompatible regionalism before the San Francisco Conference. Several reasons account for their influence: first, numerical strength as a result of their twenty votes; second, their cohesiveness and unified action: and third, their successful experience with a strongly regionalist organization which they continually stressed. At this time the Inter-American System was one of the most outstanding examples, if not the most outstanding one of successful regional action in both military and nonmilitary matters. The Latin American states were not ready to give up what they already possessed for something not yet within their grasp. They wanted to safeguard the substantial gains their relations with the United States had yielded during the era of the Good Neighbor Policy, and were reluctant to join a universal arrangement which might loosen or interfere with the United States' commitments in the area.[18] Therefore, Latin American governments demanded the maintenance of an effective role in peace and security matters for the Inter-American System.

While their main efforts were in the side of regionalism, Latin American governments hedged their bets by also seeking a stronger role in the universal organization which was being drafted. They tried to gain a stronger voice in the United Nations by arguing for greater powers for the General

Assembly and by vying for a larger Latin American representation in the Security Council. Latin American nations aligned themselves with other small powers to fight against what they regarded as the privileged position of the sponsoring powers. Whatever benefits they received were more the consequence of splits in the big power unity than of their own efforts. And, when all was said and done, Latin America made greater gains, as will be analyzed in the next chapter, in the struggle to preserve an autonomous Inter-American System than in the efforts to democratize the universal organization by strengthening the General Assembly. In general, the Latin American nations can be seen as the principal agents in the framing of the regionalist provisions of the United Nations Charter.

LATIN AMERICAN VERSION OF
INCOMPATIBLE REGIONALISM

As mentioned above, Latin America feared that a universal organization might usurp its regional jurisdiction and loosen American commitments in the Western Hemisphere which had been obtained during the era of the Good Neighbor Policy. During this era, Latin America came to believe that the United States would cooperate with them on a wide range of issues and would consult with them prior to any major commitment of the region. Latin American governments hoped that the United States would view its own interests in the Western Hemisphere community as superior to those emanating from the proposed universal international organization.

The first blow to such Latin American expectations came immediately after the Moscow Conference. On November 1, 1943, Secretary of State Hull, in the course of informing the United States Congress about the Four-Nations Conference, made several references to the regional issue about which Latin America was anxious to hear. Hull foresaw that:

When the provisions of the Declaration were carried into effect there would no longer be need for spheres of influence, for alliances, for balance of power, or any other of the special arrangements through which, in the unhappy past, the nations strove to safeguard their security or to promote their interests.[19]

Hull's statements dismayed the Latin American governments since they believed his words prefaced a grim future for the Inter-American System. A year later, a second blow to Latin American hopes came when the Dumbarton Oaks Proposals were published. These suggested that the regional organizations' scope of action be limited and in effect, that the trend toward increasing their significance be reversed, a trend to which the Inter-American System had contributed during the previous decade. In addition, Latin American statesmen resented the secrecy of the conversations between the United States and the other big powers. While Latin American governments never really expected an invitation to participate at Dumbarton Oaks, they had expected to be apprised of the United States' views and to discuss them before final decisions had been reached. For example, Prime Minister Churchill and Foreign Secretary Eden had discussed the preliminaries of the Dumbarton Oaks meeting with representatives of the Commonwealth.[20] The United States, however, failed to consult with the Latin Americans and appeared inattentive to its neighbor's views and recommendations on regionalism.

Inconsistency, indifference, and lack of tact seemed to characterize State Department attitudes toward Latin America, especially between 1943 and 1944 when these regional issues were being decided. For instance, Secretary of State Hull reports that he met with all the Latin American representatives, except Argentina's, and that all were fully informed before and during the Dumbarton Oaks Conference; he recorded in his files that he called the ambassadors of the Central American republics on June 26, 1944, to give them a comprehensive report on the conference. Hull also asssserted that he sent circular telegrams, dated July 11, 1944, to all United States diplomatic missions in Latin America, except in Argentina, instructing them to inform those governments about the Dumbarton Oaks conversations and to promise an exchange of views as soon as possible. On September 15, he called together the representatives of Brazil, Chile, Colombia, Mexico, Peru, Bolivia, Uruguay, and Venezuela, and on the following day he gathered representatives of Bolivia, Costa Rica, Cuba, the Dominican Republic, Ecuador, Guatemala, Haiti, Honduras, Nicaragua, Panama, and El Salvador, to inform them about the general progress of negotiations with the big powers and to assure them that their views on the Inter-American community were being defended.[21] On the other hand, Laurence Duggan of the Latin American division of the State Department tacitly denied that Hull made serious efforts to consult with Latin Americans and to give consideration to their views. He wrote:

> *The United States sat down with the British, the Russians and the Chinese at Dumbarton Oaks to plan a world security organization without even a gesture toward the Latin American countries ...*
>
> *The United States' cavalier disregard of their opinion at this time probably irritated their [Latin America's] government circles more than any other single factor.*[22]

Similarly, Sumner Welles stated:

> *In the preparation for the Conference [of Dumbarton Oaks] ... this government was responsible for a serious miscalculation, if the wholehearted rather than the nominal cooperation of the lesser powers was to be secured. For it held no prior consultation with the other twenty Latin American republics regarding its views on world organization ... And it would obviously have been of immense advantage to the United States had the rest of the world known that when the United States spoke at Dumbarton Oaks she*

*interpreted the aspirations of 250 million citizens of the 21
nations of the New World. This opportunity was deliberately
spurned. It was rejected because of timidity and because of the
childish petulance of individual officers in the Department who
were disgruntled by the failure of the Latin American governments
to adopt without question the State Department's wishes concerning hemispheric affairs.*[23]

Another example of the lack of genuine consultation with
Latin America occurred on Columbus Day, October 12, 1944,
at a diplomatic reception at Blair House for the chiefs of
Latin American diplomatic missions. Secretary Hull and
Undersecretary of State Edward R. Stettinius, Jr., mentioned
some of the regional questions discussed at Dumbarton Oaks,
in order to assure the Latin American countries that there
would be frequent opportunities to discuss postwar international organizations with the United States. A series of
eight conferences between Latin American diplomats and
Department of State officials followed.[24] During these meetings, United States officials continued giving assurances to the
Latins that their aspirations were being considered by the big
powers at Dumbarton Oaks and that the proposals were
merely recommendations which were to be finally decided
upon at the San Francisco Conference. However, the State
Department gave no definite answers to questions about the
San Francisco Conference itself and about the charter of the
new organization. Since the United States could not begin
genuine consultations with the Latin American states (because
of its commitment to support the four powers' position),
these eight conferences were formally considered "clarifi-
cations" rather than consultations.

But the fears of the Latin American governments were not
overcome after these meetings; rather, they gained the impression that the United States was holding back vital information
and that the conferences were mere formalities. Moreover, the
sessions were conducted, not by the Secretary of State, but

by a low-ranking State Department official and the information shared was more or less that which James Reston reported in *The New York Times*.[25] Latin America felt that "the Big Four had really worked out a cut-and-dried scheme which the small countries would have to swallow whether they like or not."[26] In spite of the fact that the Blair House meetings clarified some points, the overall effect was negligible; the Latin American governments

> were given the opportunity of presenting their proposals for world organization and of commenting upon the agreements reached at Dumbarton Oaks. But it was notorious that neither their proposals nor their suggested amendments were given serious consideration. More than that, a series of seminars upon the subject of world organization, undertaken for the benefit of the Latin American diplomatic representatives in Washington by a minor official in the Department of State, created a considerable measure of antagonism, because of the belief of the Latin American governments that the United States had studiously ignored their views, but was now attempting to dictate the course which it expected them unquestionably to follow.... And the feelings aroused as a result of our attitude were by no means pacified by the pedagogical efforts of some officials of the Department after the Dumbarton Oaks meeting, to disguise as "consultations" the lectures which they delivered to Latin American diplomats upon the meaning of the tentative United Nations Charter.[27]

Early in 1945, a United States diplomatic move again offended several Latin American republics. Six countries (besides Argentina), comprising Chile, Ecuador, Paraguay, Peru, Uruguay, and Venezuela, had not declared war on the Axis powers and several of them inquired from time to time whether or not a declaration of war was required, in addition to their adherence to inter-American pronouncements against the Axis for admission into the United Nations. The United States replied that a complete rupture of relations was sufficient and that a particular country should declare war only for a specific reason. Suddenly, President Roosevelt told the governments of these six countries that unless they became parties to the United Nations Declaration of 1942 by at least declaring a state of belligerence against the Axis they would not be eligible for an invitation to the San Francisco Conference. This was a bombshell, since the very same six countries had without question been invited by the United States to previous pan-American meetings and to bilateral meetings where United Nations matters had been discussed. Eventually all of them managed to find an excuse for declaring war against the nearly defeated Axis powers. But the manner in which the United States had pressed them to take this action embarassed and annoyed the proud governments; they felt that in the eyes of the world they had been forced to obey orders from Washington under penalty of exclusion from the United Nations.[28]

All of these examples briefly illustrate the overall lack of consideration characterizing United States policies—bilateral and multilateral—toward Latin America at this time. Attempts to gain a clear United States commitment on the issue of regionalism failed repeatedly, and the Latin American governments gradually began to loose confidence in United States promises to defend their incompatible regional system at the forthcoming San Francisco meeting. As a result, Latin America started convening purely Latin American meetings and, with only Argentina missing, they formed a unified front to advance their views. The Latin American governments made clear to the big powers that they wanted priority, if not autonomy, in the settlement of hemispheric disputes and would refuse to rubberstamp the Dumbarton Oaks Proposals.

The San Francisco Conference was to convene on April 25, 1945. In the preceding period the United States was reluctant to convoke the Meeting of Consultation that the Latin American governments had urged. Since early 1945 Latin America had tried to convoke this Meeting of Consultation but the United States initially received the suggestion very coolly. Argentina, the long-time rival of the United States in the hemisphere, could not be excluded from participating in such a meeting and the outcome of such consultation was going to create additional problems for the United States in its dealings with the other big powers. Hence, Latin American diplomats, on their own, called a special Inter-American Conference on Problems of War and Peace, which the United States could not avoid attending. Participation was restricted to those American states collaborating in the war effort, which excluded Argentina and thus removed part of the United States' objection to the holding of such a meeting. The conference (also known as the Chapultepec Conference) was held in Mexico City from February 21 to March 13, shortly after the big powers met at Yalta (February 3 to 11) where they agreed on a voting formula for the Security Council and on the participants at the Conference of San Francisco.

At the Chapultepec Conference, the Latin American states insisted on adopting resolutions which noted the specific regional achievements and principles of the Inter-American System. The Latin American representatives sought to guarantee the survival of this system by forcing the United States to endorse the principles of incompatible regionalism, prior to the San Francisco meeting. Another objective of the representatives carried out at Chapultepec was to reduce the number of contradictions, redundant provisions, and the vagueness which had characterized previous inter-American treaties. The reforms stemming from this conference, especially the Act of Chapultepec, did strengthen the bases and elements of the Inter-American System; they did succeed in giving the Latin American position somewhat more leverage at the forthcoming San Francisco Conference, by serving to clarify the legal and political status of regional organizations of this type.

At the conference of Chapultepec, Senators Warren R. Austin and Tom Connally, members of the United States delegation, concentrated their efforts on the political sub-committee in charge of the regional issue. They tried, unsuc-cessfully, to delay discussion of regionalism until the San Francisco Conference; the United States wanted to remain free of prior commitments before facing the Soviet Union and other big powers in San Francisco. "You fellows," said Senator Connally on one occasion, "want the whole universe to come to you." Alberto Lleras Camargo, Colombian foreign minister answered, "In America we have worked out a real international organization which, up to the present, is only theory in the rest of the world."[29]

At Chapultepec, the United States only partially achieved its objectives to remain free of ties with Latin America on these questions. For instance, the United States, while accept-ing the Act of Chapultepec and other documents formally reorganizing the Inter-American System, did not agree to the commitment to hemispheric defense and hence to what was in effect incompatible regionalism. However, one section of the Act of Chapultepec did amount to a pledge by all the Latin Americans and the United States to convoke an inter-American meeting immediately after the San Francisco Conference for the purpose of designing a hemispheric defense system, a system that would thus be consistent with Latin American preferences for an incompatible type of regionalism.

The intra-regional situation was further complicated by the fact that, as the war was ending, the Soviet Union began to hold quite different views from those agreed upon by the big powers. As a result one could envision several instances in which the United States was going to need Latin American voting support to counter new Soviet demands. The greatly strengthened position of the Latin American states was a consequence of this split in the unity of the sponsoring powers. The United States was placed in a very difficult position and ended up by antagonizing both the Soviets—because of its support of Latin American regionalist views—

and the Latin Americans—because of its reluctance to support more fully their incompatible version of regionalism.

The dilemma of the United States—its ties to both Latin America and the big powers—was illustrated in the issue of Argentina's exclusion from the United Nations. At Chapultepec, the Argentine question was raised as a matter of Latin American solidarity: the republics were reluctant to leave one of their strongest members behind. Moreover, they realized that solving the problem of Argentina would strengthen the bargaining position of the Inter-American System by illustrating its ability to solve intra-regional problems democratically.[30]

The difficulties in solving the question of Argentina increased as it became ensnarled with the broader issue of regionalism. Argentina had followed a rather independent foreign policy and had maintained herself neutral while the rest of the continent declared war. Secretary of State Hull had practically closed the door to negotiations with Argentina on her possible alignment with the Inter-American System and her admission to the United Nations. Hull believed that before she would be admitted to the United Nations, Argentina "should make a full apology for having deserted the cause of the American republics." However, Hull also admitted that the general attitude of the United States government was to keep aloof from the Argentine government.[31]

At the Chapultepec Conference, the United States did not consent to discuss the Argentine question until other business matters were finished. Finally, the issue was considered on the last day of the conference. After considerable debate, it was decided (Resolution 59) that should Argentina give evidence that she restricted Axis activities in her country, the American republics would resume relations with her and would support her membership in the United Nations. Argentina subsequently declared war on the Axis powers on March 27, and on April 4 signed the Act of Chapultepec. United States

support of the resolution which dealt with Argentina's fulfillment of the requirements for admission into the United
Nations, however, raised some difficulties for this country
since once again its Latin American policies conflicted with
what had been agreed upon by the big powers at Yalta. At
that meeting President Roosevelt had committed himself to
support no action in favor of the Argentine government.
Moreover, the big powers had agreed that only those governments declaring war against the Axis by March 1, 1945,
would be invited to San Francisco as original members of the
United Nations.[32]

The United States' position at the Chapultepec Conference
was helped by the fact that the results of the Yalta Conference were not known. When they became public in early
March, 1945, shortly before the end of the conference, after
the French and Chinese agreements were finally secured, Latin
America was again shocked, especially over the proposed
Security Council veto formula. Actually, when Secretary of
State Stettinius announced the Yalta voting formula at Chapultepec, there was little time left for discussion of its content and its implications for incompatible regionalism.[33]

At the San Francisco Conference, divisions were widened
among all nations—large and small, rich and poor—especially
where the regional issue and the admission of Argentina were
concerned. Both problems, moreover, were tied up with rather
delicate issues in which the Soviet Union had special interests.
Concerted Latin American action in favor of incompatible
regionalism proved to be too strong a pressure at San Francisco, working at odds with the United States attempting to
avoid a split among the big powers. The United States,
although it unwillingly supported regionalism in the Western
Hemisphere, faced the disturbing possibilities of similar autonomous security systems in other parts of the world. For
instance, such regionalism might provide a pretext for Soviet
expansion and domination of Eastern Europe, and in fact,
Soviet demands for plural membership—the admission of all

the states under its sphere of influence as individual members —seemed to be pointing in this direction. The United States, concerned about Soviet expansionist tendencies in Poland and the Balkans, did not want to open the door through which the Soviet Union could exempt Eastern European countries from the Security Council's jurisdiction by forming a regional organization in Eastern Europe that would clearly be incompatible with the United Nations.

At the same time, in the case of Argentina, the Soviet Union interpreted the combined support of the United States and the Latin American states for Argentina's admission into the United Nations as confirmation that the Latin American states were satellites of the United States despite the fact that the United States had been reluctant to join the effort.[34] Argentina's admission to the United Nations became tied up with the admission of the Ukraine and Byelo-Russia and later with that of Poland. To begin with, at Yalta the United States and the Soviet Union had agreed that the Ukraine and Byelo-Russia be permitted to become members of the United Nations.[35] This concession was unknown to the Latin Americans who, in the meantime, saw the opportunity to base their endorsement of such a concession on the condition that Argentina be admitted simultaneously. But, at a secret meeting attended by representatives of the Big Four and by heads of delegations of Brazil, Chile, and Mexico, Secretary of State Stettinius (Cordell Hull resigned in November, 1944) made efforts to be released from the pledge made at Mexico City in behalf of Argentina, in order to avoid encouraging Soviet demands for multiple membership. At one point the Soviet Union had proposed representation of sixteen Soviet republics in the United Nations, a plan which greatly worried United States officials. But for reasons which need not be discussed here, Molotov reduced his demands and seemed to be offering Soviet support for Argentina's admission in return for the admission of the Lublin Polish government in addition to Byelo-Russia and the Ukraine. Yet while Molotov was in a position to seek the admission of three Soviet states rather than sixteen, it later turned out that he did not have precise instructions from his government on the exchange of these states for Argentina's admission, and was thus unwilling to commit himself when the question of Argentina membership was raised. In view of this uncertain situation, Latin Americans decided, in principle, to refuse to vote for the admission of the Ukraine and Byelo-Russia. They changed their position only after the United States promised that, should they vote for the admission of these two countries, the United States would secure Argentina's admission. But things turned out to be more complicated than just a simple case of exchange.

At the fifth plenary meeting of the San Francisco Conference, after Byelo-Russia and the Ukraine's admissions were accepted, Molotov attempted to continue his opposition to Argentina's admission until such time as the Lublin Polish government was accepted. However, although these efforts were defeated and Argentina's admission was secured by a vote of thirty-two to four, this turned out to be a Pyrrhic victory for the United States and Latin America. Molotov used the opportunity to discredit the United States by making public recent denunciations which top United States government officials had made against the Argentine government. He depicted the United States position as one attempting to force admission of a Fascist state into the United Nations. This offensive tactic distracted attention from important questions of Byelo-Russia and the Ukraine's lack of true sovereignty, the subservient character of the Lublin Polish government which the Soviets backed, and, more important, the Soviet Union's previous agreement to vote for Argentina (despite its belief that it was a Fascist regime) if Poland were admitted as well. Latin America was also left in an embarrassing position when it appeared quite obvious that it had followed United States direction and had voted in favor of Byelo-Russia and the

Ukraine admissions before having secured Soviet endorsement of Argentina's entrance.[36]

The voting on these admissions pointed up the crystalization of two rival blocs, a situation which became a familiar part of the functioning of the United Nations: one composed of the Soviet Union and its satellites, and the other consisting of Western countries and the United States. The bitter debate that ensued at this time thus initiated a host of diplomatic and political struggles between the United States and the Soviet Union; the divisions that appeared over the membership issue constitute one of the principles harbingers of the cold war.[37]

The interaction of these divergent forces was mirrored in the document which emerged from the discussions at San Francisco, the United Nations Charter. The desire to reach agreement on issues about which no consensus existed resulted in a charter that was, at the least, vague, and at the most, contradictory. In the regional sections in particular, the differing intentions of the participants at the conference, the two major conceptions of regional and international organizations vying for support, paved the way for the shifting interpretations and controversies that later ensued. At the same time, as we shall see, out of the conflict between universalist conceptions and incompatible regionalist ones, a document evolved with some characteristics of neither, a charter that in fact possessed a measure of *compatible* regionalism.

3

THE UNITED NATIONS CHARTER:
Regional and Universal Clauses

NAPOLEON'S COUNSEL that "a constitution should be short and ambiguous" seems to have guided the San Francisco negotiations, particularly in the drafting of the charter's provisions on regional organizations. The section of the United Nations Charter dealing with regionalism is very short; only four Articles (51 to 54) specifically discuss the subject of regionalism although there are other references to regionalism in the charter. The regional provisions are also ambiguous; instead of channeling the activities of regional organizations so that they are clearly compatible with the universal principles, contradictions can be found among the provisions in the regional chapter, and in some instances even within the same article. The four articles which deal preeminently with regionalism resulted either from the conflict of the combination of the two major tendencies that were apparent at the San Francisco Conference whenever regional questions were discussed. On the one hand, there was a universalist trend, sponsored mainly by the big powers, which sought to guarantee the control of the Security Council over all issues concerning the maintenance of peace and security. On the other hand, there was a strong incompatible regionalist trend, supported mainly by the Latin American countries seeking autonomy, or at least a formal recognition of the freedom of action of their regional system. In a sense, compatible regionalism was unrepresented at the conference; as will be shown below, this tendency did not constitute an independent force, but rather one which emerged from the struggle between universalist and incompatible regionalist forces.

In general, the charter was to insure the compatibility of regional with universal organizations, to reaffirm United Nations supremacy and to subordinate regional agencies to Security Council authority. Regional organizations were not to detract from the primary responsibility of the United Nations to maintain peace and security, and were to be appraised by the universal organization according to their consistency with the terms, purposes, and principles of the United Nations Charter.

But beyond this general framework, there was very little precise definition of the position of regional organizations vis-a-vis the United Nations. Due to the prevailing tensions at the San Francisco Conference, not only among the big powers but also between big and small countries, it was very difficult to find a specific definition of regionalism with which all, or the majority, of delegations would agree. All attempts to define regionalism based on continental scope, permanency, or geographical proximity, including or excluding alliances of a military character, were unsuccessful. Egypt's delegate made frequents attempts to define regionalism, for example:

> *There shall be considered as regional arrangements organizations of a permanent nature, grouping in a given geographical area several countries which, by reason of their proximity, community of interests or cultural, linguistic, historical or spiritual affinities, make themselves jointly responsible for the peaceful settlement of any disputes which may arise between them and for the maintenance of peace and security in their region, as well as for the safeguarding of their interests and the development of their economic and cultural relations.* [1]

The definition met with insurmountable obstacles in spite of the fact that it left out those military aspects likely to produce incompatibility. It distinguished regional arrangements for the peaceful settlement of disputes from treaties of a military character, whose mention was introduced by the big powers in what became the second paragraph of Article 53 (see below).

With every regional grouping pressing its own unique demands, and with divisions appearing, even among the great powers, over the regional issue, it appeared that any detailed consideration of regionalism would have precipitated lengthy and largely inconclusive debates; in this context no one view would have satisfied all participants nor been sufficiently comprehensive to cover all the circumstances envisioned. As a result, most of the delegates at San Francisco were persuaded that the most agreeable solution would be the establishment of a very general or flexible framework for the functioning of regional organizations. Here, advocates of regionalism, on the one hand, could not be offended by tight, precise definitions, nor could the advocates of universalism oppose a situation in which the guarantors of compatible regionalism would be the major powers on the Security Council; the unity of the big powers in the Security Council would be the basis for assuring the compatibility of regional organizations by forcing their members to comply primarily with the purposes and principles of the United Nations. Therefore, in the course of its normal functioning, the Security Council was seen as defining the nature of the regional organization and, in practice, outlining its role in every possible circumstance.

These flexible arrangements provided some concessions to regional demands; regional organizations, for instance, were granted some initial responsibility in the settlement of local disputes, although the extent of this responsibility was left undefined. At the same time, these arrangements yielded to the Security Council the pragmatic control of any jurisdictional dispute between regional organizations and the United

Nations which might appear; in all respects, the Security Council was clearly intended to be the most powerful organ within the United Nations. In effect, this implied that compatible interpretations of every single clause of the regional provisions in the United Nations depended on the agreement of the big powers. In the long run, we shall see, the flexibility of the relationship outlined in the charter was the source of its ambiguity as well; regionalists could readily find ways to interpret provisions in the United Nations Charter to suit the incompatible purposes of their organizations and facilitate a "downward transfer" process.

The committee that dealt specifically with the question of regionalism at San Francisco was Committee III/4. Since the provisions of the Dumbarton Oaks Proposals viewed the functions of regional organizations only with respect to the maintenance of international peace and security, the work of Committee III/4 centered only on security and political aspects of regionalism. Economic, cultural, or social aspects of regionalism were given little or no attention at all.

The committee held only six meetings, on May 4, 9, 15, 23, and June 8 and 11, 1945, and its discussions took place under the menacing cloud of the veto of the permanent members of the Security Council over the activities of regional organizations. Although the veto power had to be tolerated in other sections of the same charter as a sine qua non, this committee worked to remove the danger of the veto power from the regional section of the charter. Delegates of small countries agreed that the great powers should not be allowed to veto regional action within an area with which they were not virtually concerned. Regional security organizations working parallel to the universal one, but free from its control, were discussed as an alternative way of avoiding the veto.[2]

Amendments to the Dumbarton Oaks Proposals' regional provisions proposed by all the nations participating at San Francisco were so numerous that a subcommittee was created within Committee III/4 to analyze, classify, and amalgamate them. The subcommittee was made up of representatives of Australia, Chile, Czechoslovakia, Egypt, France, Mexico, Norway, the Soviet Union, the United States, and the United Kingdom; the Colombian delegate acted as chairman and China as rapporteur. Four meetings were held on May 10, 11, 14, and 15, 1945. The intense opposition to the Dumbarton Oaks Proposals' universalist emphasis, which especially characterized the attitudes of the Latin American and the Arab countries, were mirrored in the difficulties encountered by this subcommittee. It is likely that the many difficulties this subcommittee had to deal with led the United States delegation to announce that it was already preparing a formula (which eventually became Article 51) to guide the security aspects of the relationship of regional agencies to the world organization, in an effort to pacify the regionalists and to lessen the burden of coordinating all the proposed amendments turned over to this subcommittee.

Practically all of the participating nations at the San Francisco Conference submitted amendments that were in one way or another connected with regionalism. But specific regional amendments were particularly numerous among the Latin American delegations, Belgium, France, the Netherlands, Czechoslovakia, Australia, New Zealand, Turkey, and Egypt.

The amendments had varied objectives. Some, such as those advanced by the Latin Americans, searched for a general definition of the nature and status of regional arrangements. A second group of amendments was directed toward formal recognition—juridical, political, moral, or a combination of these—of regional arrangements by the universal organization. Proponents of recognition were the Latin American and Arab delegations, which anxiously desired an express recognition of the Inter-American System and the Arab League. Another set of amendments outlined the role of regional arrangements in the peaceful settlement of disputes. While some delegates desired complete regional autonomy in settling disputes, others granted independence to regional organizations only in specific circumstances. Finally, several amendments dealt with regional jurisdiction over the adoption of sanctions and enforcement action.[3]

The final report of the subcommittee became the blueprint for the charter provisions on regional organizations. The four main articles of the charter which dealt with regional organizations will be analyzed in detail in the next section and other relevant regional provisions will be briefly mentioned.

ARTICLE 52: COMPATIBILITY AND INCOMPATIBILITY IN THE PEACEFUL SETTLEMENT OF DISPUTES AT THE REGIONAL LEVEL

The incapacity and unwillingness of the participants at San Francisco to precisely define the nature and function of the proposed international system, as described above, was reflected in the ambiguities of Article 52. This article attempted to define the condition under which regional organizations may be compatible with the universal organization, a task which was particularly difficult without a prior consensus in the international community on the relationship of the two. While the article did not contradict itself, it did attempt to reconcile two divergent tendencies which provided the basis for later contradictory interpretations. The first three paragraphs suggest a significant regionalist inclination in that they appear to allow for the strongest degree of regionalism that would be compatible with a universal organization; the last (fourth) paragraph, on the other hand, guaranteed the supremacy of universalist organization. The net effect of the article, stemming in particular from the first three paragraphs, was an infringement upon the United Nations' monopoly over the mechanisms for the maintenance of international peace and security contained in the Dumbarton Oaks Proposals.

Paragraph 1 in Article 52 attempted to define the compatibility of regional arrangements by stating:

Nothing in the present Charter precludes the existence of regional arrangements or agencies for dealing with such matters relating to the maintenance of international peace and security as appropriate for regional action provided that such arrangements or agencies and their activities are consistent with the Purposes and Principles of the United Nations.[4]

This paragraph referred to virtually all regional organizations —those in existence or in process of formation when the charter came into force, as well as those subsequently established. Regional arrangements were awarded international personality, and regional action to maintain peace and security was declared the first recourse of states seeking international mechanisms for the settlement of disputes. At the same time, conditions were outlined for their functioning. First, their authority was limited to cases "appropriate for regional action," and second, their relationship to the universal organization had to be compatible, that is "consistent with the Purposes and Principles of the United Nations." Hans Kelsen has noted that any inconsistency whatsoever might invalidate the existence of regional organizations. He has pointed out that this part of Article 52 is even stronger than provisions in Article 103, which ensure the predominance of the United Nations Charter (see section below on Articles 54 and 103).[5]

The possibility for incompatible interpretations can be seen particularly in paragraphs 2 and 3 of Article 52 in the provisions for the settlement of local disputes.

The Members of the United Nations entering into such arrangements or constituting such agencies shall make every effort to achieve pacific settlement of local disputes through such regional arrangements or by such regional agencies before referring them to the Security Council.

The paragraph strengthens the obligation to settle local disputes at the regional level before referring them to the Security Council; this obligation is further reinforced by a provision in Article 33, paragraph 1, which holds:

The parties to any dispute, the continuance of which is likely to endanger the maintenance of international peace and security, shall, first of all, seek a solution by negotiation, enquiry, mediation, conciliation, arbitration, judicial settlement, resort to regional agencies or arrangements, *or other peaceful means of their own choice. [Emphasis added.]*

However, it should be noted that paragraph 2 of Article 52 is in fact stronger than the provision of Article 33 since the former commits members of regional organizations to exhaust regional pacificatory resources *before* using the Security Council, whereas the latter offers the regional method as one of several options with no particular order of preferences indicated.[6]

The *obligation* to settle local disputes at the regional level effectively paved the way to incompatible regionalism by giving priority to the resort to regional organization. Eventually, the regional option in the solution of local disputes grew more and more imperative for countries belonging to regional organizations, while the importance of the universal alternative concurrently declined. This situation—analogous in sense to a "zero-sum game" between the regional and universal organizations—stemmed from the ambiguous relationship between paragraph 2 of Article 52 and Article 35; it was not clear if the content of paragraph 2 prejudiced the meaning of Article 35, in the sense that its emphasis on the prior recourse to regional mechanisms effectively discouraged referral to the Security Council at the outset as provided for in Article 35:

Any member of the United Nations may bring any dispute, or any situation of the nature referred to in Article 34, to the attention of the Security Council or of the General Assembly.

Supposedly, regional mechanisms would be preferable only in cases of "local disputes," that is, technically, "disputes which exclusively involve states which are parties to such regional arrangements."[7] Moreover, the regional institutions were to predominate only in the case of "disputes" and not in "situations" over which the Security Council has complete jurisdiction (Chapter VII of the UN Charter). Also, in theory, the priority of regional solutions in the peaceful settlement of local disputes mentioned in paragraph 2 of Article 52 was set up only in relation to the actions of the Security Council. The right of the General Assembly to discuss and make recommendations concerning any matter relating to the maintenance of peace and security was not contingent upon action of regional agencies. According to Articles 10 and 11 of the charter, the General Assembly "may discuss any question on matters within the scope of the present Charter" and "may consider the general principles of cooperation in the maintenance of peace and security," as well as "any questions relating to the maintenance of international peace and security brought before it by any Member of the United Nations.[8]

Even while paragraph 2 of Article 52 was being drafted, the situation remained nebulous; it was not at all certain whether recourse to the regional method was optional and whether the Security Council had to respect the provisions of Article 52, paragraph 2, and only remind the parties of their obligation under this paragraph, or whether it could refer the dispute. Some authors have stated that the Security Council cannot transfer its competence.[9] Thus, interpreted with a view to the compatibility of the two institutions, this section of paragraph 2 was merely a procedure through which the universal organization might remind the parties of a dispute of the available terms of settlement, but not a mechanism for the forcible transfer of a case to a regional organization for settlement.

The third paragraph of Article 52 further enhanced the importance of the regional procedure (contained in paragraph 2) through which members of regional organizations could seek pacific settlement for their disputes. Paragraph 3 stated:

> *The Security Council shall encourage the development of pacific settlement of local disputes through such regional arrangements or by such regional agencies either on the initiative of the states concerned or by reference from the Security Council.*

In many ways this paragraph paralleled paragraph 2 of Article 36, which established that:

> *The Security Council should take into consideration any procedures for the settlement of the dispute which have already been adopted by the parties.*

What appeared in the preceding paragraph of Article 52 as seemingly compatible structure, turned out to be a potential source of incompatibility by the third paragraph. Continued compatible application of these provisions depended on the good will of the members, since an incompatible interpretation could be readily justified by the text. Moreover, paragraph 3 effectively committed the Security Council to encourage settlement at the regional level, thus creating a conflict with universal procedures contained in Chapter VI of the charter (Articles 34, 35 [1], and 36 [1]) where the competence of the Security Council was guaranteed.[10]

While paragraphs 2 and 3 of Article 52 just described dangerously strengthened incompatible regionalism, paragraph 4 revealed the universalist preference manifested by some of the charter framers, especially the Soviet Union.[11] This section was, theoretically at least, to counterbalance the potential incompatible features of the first part of the article. Paragraph 4 states:

> *This Article in no way impairs the application of Article 34 and 35.*

Article 34 established that:

> *The Security Council may investigate any dispute, or any situation which might lead to international friction or give rise to a dispute,*

in order to determine whether the continuance of the dispute or situation is likely to endanger the maintenance of international peace and security.

while Article 35, in its relevant part assured that:

Any member of the United Nations may bring any dispute, or any situation, of the nature referred to in Article 34 to the attention of the Security Council or of the General Assembly.

The aim of these three sections of the charter (Article 52, paragraph 4, and Articles 34 and 35) was to secure the primacy of the Security Council in the maintenance of peace and security by defending (1) the duty of the Security Council to investigate disputes or situations and to determine whether they might endanger peace and security, (2) the right of members to bring such cases to the attention of the Security Council or the General Assembly, and (3) the obligation of the Security Council to recommend appropriate measures at any stage of a dispute. (This last duty was more explicitly stated in Article 36.)

The inclusion of the fourth paragraph of Article 52 relieved universalist misgivings while it dismayed incompatible regionalists. The Peruvian delegate expressed fear that this provision might result in one or two rather disturbing possibilities: (1) the simultaneous handling of a dispute by a regional organization and the Security Council, or (2) the usurping by the Security Council of even those cases that may be adequately handled on the regional level. Both these possibilities of double jurisdiction were unacceptable to Peru, as well as to the other Latin American delegates. Albert Lleras Camargo, head of the Colombia delegation and chairman of Committee III/4, argued that there could not be double jurisdiction because the Security Council was bound to limit its action to the investigation of a situation which might threaten the peace and to the encouragement of the regional settlement of the problem; he felt that members of regional systems were obliged to make every effort to reach a peaceful settlement through their own organization before referring the problem to the Security Council.[12]

The inconsistencies of Article 52, the combination of the first three paragraphs with the fourth one, contributed very little to ensuring that regional organizations would be compatible with the United Nations. While this part of the charter allowed champions of universalism to congratulate themselves that the supremacy of the Security Council had not been impaired, it also allowed those who favored incompatible regionalism to assert that they had won a victory for the autonomy of regional organizations.

ARTICLE 53: COMPATIBILITY AND INCOMPATIBILITY IN THE ADOPTION OF "ENFORCEMENT ACTION"

Article 53 of the United Nations Charter embodied the principle that the adoption of enforcement action was to be monopolized exclusively by the universal organs. The power of regional arrangements to take action in the case of threats or breaches of the peace, or acts of aggression, was at the same time greater and less than its authority in the case of peaceful settlement of disputes; it was greater in the sense that the Security Council was directed to utilize regional agencies for carrying out enforcement measures; it was less in the sense that authorization of the Security Council was required before measures which might be considered "enforcement action" were taken by regional agencies.[13]

The initial part of Article 53 established that:

> *The Security Council shall, where appropriate, utilize such regional arrangements or agencies for enforcement action under its authority. But no enforcement action shall be taken under regional arrangements or by regional agencies without the authorization of the Security Council. . . .*

Thus, regional organizations were prevented from adopting enforcement action, unless specifically authorized by the Security Council. Moreover, according to Article 27, paragraph 3, substantive "decisions in the Security Council ... shall be made by an affirmative vote of seven members including the concurring votes of the permanent members." This meant that the Security Council authorization required by Article 53 was subject to the veto; thus a permanent member could veto action of a regional organization of which it was not a member even if the parties of such a regional organization approved.

It should be recalled that the principle prohibiting regional organizations from adopting enforcement action was advanced without qualification in the Dumbarton Oaks Proposals. Yet no clarification of the term "enforcement action" had been attempted since that time. Lack of definition in this part of the charter paralleled the ambiguities of the regional arrangements described in Article 52. At the time the San Francisco Conference convened, the big powers favored a broader interpretation of the meaning of enforcement action so that, besides the use of force, all kinds of political, economic, and social measures would require approval by the Security Council.[14] This interpretation was consistent with Article 2, paragraph 4 of the charter which had placed the monopoly of force in the hands of the Security Council.

All members shall refrain in their international relations from the threat or use of force against the territorial integrity or political independence of any state, or in any matter inconsistent with the Purposes of the United Nations.

However, this was only a political consensus among the big powers and was not specifically translated into charter provisions. As a result it was not clear whether enforcement action referred only to measures involving the use of force or whether it also included other measures—political, economic, diplomatic, etc. But an authoritative source has pointed out "that it is probable that the latter interpretation corresponds to the intention of those who drafted the Charter,"[15] especially to the four major sponsoring powers.

Apparently this reluctance to define the term "enforcement action" stemmed from an attempt to reconcile the initial prohibition of the article with the exception proposed by the big powers, and adopted at the conference itself, in the second part of the first paragraph of Article 53. Such an exception, included as a result of Soviet and French pressure, legalized treaties of mutual assistance,[16] and eliminated the necessity for prior Security Council authorization in the initiation of enforcement action arising from such treaties. The net effect of this, however, was to open the door to a de facto recognition of the right to take enforcement action outside of the machinery of the universal organization. The exception was defended on the ground that mutual assistance treaties were necessary precautions which had to be taken under the political circumstances of the time. The underlying premise here was that international peace and security would be safeguarded if the existing instruments for the permanent and effective demilitarization and control of the enemy states were utilized to their fullest extent.[17]

At San Francisco, the sponsoring powers presented the delegations of small and middle-sized countries with the text of the amendment excluding mutual assistance pacts from the constraint of Article 53.[18] Understandably, Latin America and other groups of smaller countries were less concerned with this provision since it was undoubtedly introduced by the big powers to meet big power demands, most notably the demands of the Soviet Union and France.

The terms of the exception to the general limitation on regional enforcement actions read as follows:

> ... with the exception of measures against any enemy state, as defined in paragraph 2 of this Article, provided for pursuant to

Article 107 or in regional arrangements directed against the re-newal of aggressive policy on the part of such state, until such time as the Organization may, on request of the Governments concerned, be charged with the responsibility for preventing further aggression by such a state.

2. The term enemy state as used in paragraph 1 of this Article applies to any state which during the Second World War has been an enemy of any signatory of the present Charter.

This exception is twofold. The first part refers to measures provided for pursuant to Article 107 which states:

Nothing in the present Charter shall invalidate or preclude action, in relation to any state which during the Second World War has been an enemy of any signatory of the present Charter, taken or authorized as a result of that War by the Governments having responsibility for such action.

The second part focuses on those regional arrangements directed against renewal of aggression from ex-enemy states (treaties of mutual assistance formed during World War II); where the former World War II enemies were concerned, the United Nations could become involved only "on request of the Governments concerned." In both instances, postwar political developments rendered the exception unimportant; with the realignment of world forces in the years following World War II, the designation of "enemy state" derived from the war situation became increasingly meaningless.

United States approval of this provision, which technically excluded United States veto over Soviet actions in a zone of special Soviet concern, namely the states of Eastern Europe with whom the Soviet Union signed mutual assistance pacts, was obtained in the first days of the conference at Molotov's insistence. At that time the United States' delegation, whose members were still mildly opposed to incompatible regional enforcement action, was not alert enough to gain a corresponding exception for the Inter-American System in the

Western Hemisphere (and for some regional treaties in other parts of the world) since in these regions there was no likelihood of a renewed Axis aggression as existed in Western and Eastern Europe. Under the pretext of a continuous German menace, any group of countries could initiate without difficulty regional organizations which would remain unaccountable. But other regions who could not use this pretext would be left under complete control of the Security Council.

This lack of action on the side of the United States to favor the Inter-American System at that early date caused problems with the United States' later position on regionalism, particularly when the Latin American states were concerned. It was after the United States had agreed to Soviet and French demands to include this exception in Article 53 that the United States decided to support Latin American incompatible regionalism in what became Article 51. By then, the American bargaining position, vis-à-vis the other big powers, had diminished considerably and it did not have any grounds on which to fight for its recently acquired regional interest. The pulling and tugging ultimately created an impasse which split the sponsoring governments and embittered United States relations with the Latin American group to the point that Latin American delegates threatened to walk out of the conference if their demands for incompatible regionalism were not met.

ARTICLE 51: COMPATIBLE AND INCOMPATIBLE SELF-DEFENSE

When an exception was introduced to the text of Article 53 excluding incompatible European mutual assistance pacts from Security Council control, Latin America was angered; while Europe would have freedom of action for her incompatible defense regional arrangements, the Inter-American System, as well as other regional pacts, remained dependent upon the Security Council. Senator Vandenberg, American representative to Committee III/4 and the Latin American delegates, engaged in a running debate on this issue in the course of which several formulas were attempted for the purpose of extending to the Western Hemisphere the same exception awarded to Europe in Article 53.

The United States' delegation was already engaged in the study of several alternatives which would satisfy Latin American demands for incompatible regionalism especially where security matters were concerned, and which would, at the same time, satisfy the universalist positions of the big powers, especially the Soviet Union. The first formula suggested by the United States delegation consisted of an addition at the end of the first paragraph of Article 53, immediately after the exception introduced in favor of Europe and the Soviet Union, excepting the "Act of Chapultepec of the Inter-American Conferences on Problems of War and Peace, signed at Mexico City on March 8, 1945, until such time as the Organization may, by consent of the Governing Board of the Pan American Union, be charged with this function."[19]

This formula was welcomed by Latin America but was vehemently opposed by some members of the United States delegation, by the rest of the sponsoring governments, and by the Arab group who took advantage of the opportunity to demand equal mention of the Arab League in Article 53. Some of the United States delegates, Leo Pasvolsky in particular, felt that no more exceptions should be made to the authority of the Security Council, while others, including Arthur H. Vandenberg, John F. Dulles, and Nelson Rockefeller, were inclined to grant Latin America some of the same privileges already extended to the soviet Union and Europe. However, the latter group of officials, although not opposed to the autonomy of the Inter-American System, were as fearful as the rest of the delegates of introducing generalizations which would allow for wider independence of other regional organizations such as the Arab League. Nevertheless, Senator Vandenberg threatened to introduce a Republican reservation in the United States Senate if Latin American regional demands were not at least partially satisfied.[20]

Secretary of State Stettinius was unable to solve these divisions in the American delegation when negotiations over the regional issue were conducted with Latin America, the Soviet Union, and the rest of the sponsoring governments. Indecisiveness characterized the handling of the United States delegation's position on these delicate issues. At one point, Stettinius was even willing to sacrifice the defense of pan-Americanism in order to assuage demands of Soviet universalism. Vandenberg reported, "Stettinius does not have a seasoned grasp of foreign affairs. He rarely contributes to our policy decisions. We improvise as we go along. Stettinius is not really Secretary of State. He is really 'General Manager' of the State Department (which is a totally different thing)."[21]

Difficulties in the United States' delegation over the regional issue reached a critical point and the matter had to be referred to President Truman for decision in a memorandum which analyzed both views. The president instructed the delegation to keep on looking for a formula that would reconcile both views,[22] a formula that would recognize the paramount authority of the universal organization in all enforcement action and yet would permit independent regional action in case of undue delay or ineffectiveness. The delegation came up with several formulas but they were all rejected by the Soviet and the British.

Finally, a compromise was designed, one which inserted into the charter a completely new article. With only minor alterations this formula became Article 51.

> *Nothing in the present Charter shall impair the inherent right of individual or collective self-defense if an armed attack occurs against a member of the United Nations, until the Secretary Council has taken measures necessary to maintain international peace and security. Measures taken by Members in the exercise of this right of self-defense shall be immediately reported to the*

Security Council and shall not in any way affect the authority and responsibility of the Security Council under the present Charter to take at any time such actions as it deems necessary in order to maintain or restore international peace and security.[23]

The formula contained in Article 51 overcame obstacles which had stymied previous United States' efforts. Reference to the Act of Chapultepec was omitted so that the Arabs could not demand equal mention of the Arab League; the language was general enough to please both universalists and regionalists. The American delegation could then approve the resolution and interpret it in ways that would minimize the Senate's objections.[24] Everybody could give the formula the most convenient interpretation.

Soviet agreement had to be obtained as soon as possible because Molotov was returning to Moscow, and Gromyko, his alternate, was believed to be less flexible. Consultation with Soviet and British officials followed on March 12, but only British acceptance was secured at that date.

When the time came to present the formula to the small nations, Vandenberg remarked that it was about time "to get them out of the doghouse and into the penthouse."[25] Stettinius convoked an urgent meeting on May 15 with the Latin American delegations to announce the United States' formula, sponsored on their behalf. Stettinius explained that this formula was to be interpreted as an exception to Article 53 operating in much the same way as the other exceptions were to operate. The Latin American states were not completely satisfied with the United States' formula, since it was hard for them to believe that two words, "collective self-defense," could solve such a big problem. Since they were not sure that such a formula would really satisfy their demands, they preferred an explicit reference to the Inter-American System.[26] But, in spite of the initial opposition, Latin America finally acceded when Stettinius, after consulting with President Truman, promised to convoke a new inter-American conference, immediately after San Francisco, to implement the Act of Chapultepec defense treaty. Senators Conally and Vandenberg pledged the honor of the United States to the completion of such a treaty.[27]

Molotov left for Moscow on May 9 and Gromyko refused to agree to the formula unless he was so instructed by Moscow. He was equally opposed to allowing the United States' delegation to present the formula as an American plan. The United States found it necessary to take somewhat drastic measures to gain the acceptance of the formula. With Latin American and British agreement secured, a press statement was issued, on May 15, publicly committing the United States to the equivalent of Article 51, as a means of forcing Soviet acceptance at that late stage of the San Francisco Conference. The plan worked; Gromyko received his instruction on May 18 and only minor changes were suggested by the Soviet government to this formula.[28]

But once the article was agreed upon, conflicts arose as to the section of the charter in which it would be placed. The decision was referred to the Coordination Committee, which was a regular committee of the conference, in charge of the organization and harmonization of the work of the different commissions and committees of the conference. The United States' delegation favored inclusion of this formula in Chapter VIII of the Dumbarton Oaks Proposals (which actually remained as Chapter VIII, in the United Nations Charter, on regional arrangements). The Soviet delegation maintained that the previous section (Chapter VIII), dealing with the powers and duties of the Security Council and United Nations members with respect to threats to the peace, was the appropriate place for the new formula. Since Committee III/4 was more inclined to favor the United States view, this issue was sent to the Coordination Committee by a majority decision (twenty-nine to nine) with the recommendation that the article be placed in Chapter VIII.[29]

But despite the recommendation, the Coordination Committee and the Advisory Committee of Jurists, which also analyzed the content of the new article, favored the Soviet views and recommended that Article 51 be the final article of Chapter VII. The Committee of Jurists declined to accept the suggestion of Committee III/4, since limiting the right of self-defense to regional arrangements would put a state which was not a party to such arrangements at considerable disadvantage.

The location of Article 51 in Chapter VII turned out to be very significant in that it implied that the use of armed force in collective self-defense was an activity quite distinct from the measures taken as "enforcement action" under regional arrangements (Article 53). This placement showed that Article 51 was intended as exception to the monopoly of "enforcement action" entrusted to the Security Council in Chapter VII. It also had the effect of diverting attention from the requirement of Article 54 concerning the duty to inform the United Nations of the activities of regional organizations (see below).

As a consequence of all the pressures that had been involved in the drafting of the article, the final product was not very precise and, in fact, invited contradictory interpretations. Only in this way was Article 51 able to satisfy the demands of both universalists and incompatible regionalists. The United States delegation interpreted the inclusion of the article as a definite gain for universalism, since it deemed to reconcile opposing international procedures, while preserving the ultimate responsibility of the Security Council. Latin America, on the other hand, sided with the Colombian delegate, Alberto Lleras Camargo, who viewed the formula in a somewhat incompatible way.

The Latin American countries understood, as Senator Vandenberg has said, that the origin of the term "collective self-defense" is identified with the necessity of preserving regional systems like the

> *inter-American one. The Charter in general terms, is a constitution and legitimizes the right of collective self-defense to be carried in accord with the regional pacts so long as they are not opposed to the Purposes and Principles of the organization as expressed in the Charter. If a group of countries with regional ties declares their solidarity for their mutual defense, as in the case of the American states, they will undertake such defense jointly if and when one of them is attacked. And the right of defense is not limited to the country which is the direct victim of the aggression but extends to those countries which have established solidarity through regional arrangements, with the country directly attacked. This is the typical case of the American system. The Act of Chapultepec provides for the collective defense of the hemisphere and establishes that if an American nation is attacked all the rest consider themselves attacked. Consequently such action as they may take to repel aggression, authorized by the article which was discussed in the subcommittee yesterday, is legitimate for all of them. Such action would be in accord with the Charter, by the approval of the article; and a regional arrangement may take action, provided it does not have improper purposes as, for example, joint aggression against other states. From this, it may be deduced that the approval of this article implies that the Act of Chapultepec is not in contravention of the Charter.*[30]

Egypt claimed parallel application for the Arab League. But, while Egypt declared itself to be against the specific inclusion of alliances and mutual assistance pacts, France interpreted the article as extending in general to all cases of mutual assistance against aggression, a clearly incompatible view.

Czechoslovakia believed that the text reconciled the right of self-defense with the maintenance of a central authority capable of dealing with the problems of security. New Zealand's delegate (like Australia's) also adopted a universalist stand when it attached primary importance to the supremacy of the Security Council and expressed apprehension lest regional arrangements tend to produce conflict between regional groups.[31]

In addition, a measure of confusion arose as to the intrinsic meaning of the term self-defense and the individual and collective connotations given to it in Article 51. Self-defense per se is the right of the individual state attacked and of no other state. The charter's provisions for individual self-defense, which referred to the ability of the members of the United Nations to use force in order to defend themselves against an armed attack, was consistent with this right. But the issue became clouded when Article 51 extended the right to use force to other states allying themselves with the victim of an armed attack, an action that, strictly speaking, cannot be termed self-defense. Here, the question arises as to whether only those cases in which defensive measures are carried out by nations united prior to the aggression by an international treaty can be categorized as "collective self-defense" or whether the term applies as well to an ad hoc response of several nations in the face of an unexpected attack.[32]

It should especially be noted that the right of self-defense, individual or collective, was restricted to an armed attack, a much narrower concept than aggression per se; therefore, an act of aggression which did not have the character of an armed attack did not justify recourse to force as an exercise of the right of self-defense. Definition of armed attack was left to be decided by the state attacked and the other states willing to assist it in its defense. Of course, this involved the danger of preventive wars and of states considering such things as state interference in the civil war of another state as an armed attack. Moreover, a vicious circle might ensue since the state against which self-defense was exercised would have the same competence to interpret Article 51 in its favor and deny that it was guilty of launching an armed attack (especially if it interpreted the term differently from its opponent); it might even consider itself entitled to exercise self-defense on its own.

The fact that self-defense measures were admitted only until the United States machinery of collective security was put into action suggests that technically the application of Article 51 was intended by the charter as only a temporary measure, not as a substitute for the United Nations collective security system. In case of a paralysis in the Security Council (for instance, as a consequence of a veto), the right of self-defense could be indefinitely continued by both parties of an armed conflict until the Security Council could fulfill its function. The right of self-defense would stop when the Security Council took measures necessary to restore international peace. Yet, confusion could arise since the charter did not determine who (the Security Council, or the victim of an armed attack, or the countries assisting it) was competent to decide whether the Security Council had taken the measures necessary to maintain or restore international peace and security.

In addition to all these ambiguities, there was the problem concerning the information which the states exercising self-defense should report to the Security Council. This information was a posteriori because in the exercise of the right of self-defense, the state or states concerned were not obliged to wait until the Security Council determined the existence of an armed attack. The action which, technically, the Security Council could adopt followed the action already adopted in self-defense individually or collectively by the state or states concerned.[33]

Thus, while Article 51 in some senses did limit the competence of regional organizations to redress hostile conduct, the vague language of the provision and its frequently contradictory connotations raised the possibility of incompatible behavior as well. On the one hand, it did attempt to preclude regional organizations from forcefully counteracting threatening conduct short of armed aggression; instances not involving armed attack remained clearly under the tutelage of the universal organization. On the other hand, the ambiguous meaning of "collective self-defense" and the largely reactive, and hence, subordinate role of the Security Council, meant that in these instances there would be no universal mechanism to guarantee that regional responses were limited and proportional, that regional organizations remained compatible with the universal one.

ARTICLES 54 AND 103: UNIVERSALIST OBLIGATION TO INFORM AND GUARANTEE OF REGIONAL COMPATIBILITY

These two articles included almost intact the universalist approach of the Dumbarton Oaks Proposals. One guaranteed the effective control of regional organizations by the Security Council through the duty to inform the Security Council of regional activities; the other established a hierarchical relationship which promoted regional compatibility. Article 54 provides that:

> *The Security Council shall at all times be kept fully informed of activities undertaken or in contemplation under regional arrangements and by regional agencies for the maintenance of international peace and security.*

It thus imposed upon the members of regional organizations the obligation to provide the Security Council with information about their activities in advance when the matter concerned the maintenance of peace.

This provision, although paralleling one in Article 51, in fact went further than the Dumbarton Oaks article since it referred not only to measures organized by regional associations in the exercise of collective and individual self-defense but also to other measures (not in response to an armed attack) taken by regional organizations for the maintenance of peace and security.

Yet, while Article 54 had been subject in the following years to some incompatible interpretations that have diminished its initial universalist strength, Article 103 has remained unchallenged and unweakened. Article 103 stated:

> *In the event of a conflict between the obligations of the Members of the United Nations under the present Charter and their obligations under any other international agreement, their obligations under the present Charter shall prevail.*

In the case of Article 54, in spite of its general applicability, it became customary to report to the Security Council a posteriori of measures adopted by regional organization. For example, mutual aid for the development of the capacity to resist an armed attack, or sanction measures contemplated by regional organizations against one of its members, were not usually reported to the Security Council. Article 103, which provided the basic hierarchical framework to promote compatibility of regional treaties with the United Nations Charter has been invoked and used less frequently than Article 54.

COMPATIBILITY AND INCOMPATIBILITY IN THE UNITED NATIONS CHARTER: A GENERAL APPRAISAL

The work at the San Francisco Conference was essentially more political than juridical. The charter provided the United Nations with a pyramidal structure whose main foundation was a political one: agreement among the permanent members of the Security Council. The guarantee that whatever action undertaken by the United Nations would be supported by the states which controlled the bulk of the world's economic, military, and political power was the sine qua non for the effective functioning of the United Nations. The legal initiation of the use of force was monopolized in the Security Council, where the power of the United States, the Soviet Union, Great Britain, France, and China was duly recognized.

Upon the recognition of the power of a group of states, and upon their agreement, depended the continuation of the balance between universal and compatible regional organizations and the ability of the former to keep the latter kind of organizations within compatible limits if not in a process of "upward transfer." But despite the basic decision that the United Nations was going to be a universalist unity of individual states and not an association of regional organizations or groups, the charter was permeated with ambiguous provisions that eventually permitted the concentration of regional strength in several parts of the world.

The United Nations Charter added to the basic universalist provisions of the Dumbarton Oaks Proposals a series of regional provisions which easily led to incompatibility. The use of vague and general language paved the way for the undermining of universalism by incompatible regionalists who began to interpret United Nations provisions in ways suitable to their views and interests. While the regional provisions that were introduced into the charter were claimed not to detract from the primary responsibility of the United Nations, it is precisely these parts that have been the most troublesome since 1945.

The forces of incompatible regionalism can credit themselves with two achievements in the charter. First, in the field of peaceful settlement of disputes, no explicit definition of regional organizations—their functions and jurisdiction in the settlement of local disputes—was provided. This resulted from ambiguities in Article 52, especially paragraphs 2 and 3. The second gain was in allowing for the initiation of enforcement action by regional organizations without prior Security Council authorization, a situation resulting from the combined effects of Article 53 and 51 (see table).

The small degree of compatibility which can be derived from the United Nations Charter was a result of a struggle between universalists and incompatible regionalists. In spite of the efforts of many delegates, especially Australia and New Zealand, compatible regionalism did not become a significant independent force at San Francisco, but was more the result of the struggle between two different and opposing trends, in addition to the nominal strength that universalism still commanded. The fact that the regional provisions of the United

SETTLEMENT OF LOCAL DISPUTES

ARTICLE 52.   1. Nothing in the present Charter precludes the existence of regional arrangements or agencies for dealing with such matters relating to the maintenance of international peace and security as are appropriate for regional action,

provided that such arrangements or agencies and their activities are consistent with the Purposes and Principles of the United Nations.
[Note relationship with Article 103.]

2. The Members of the United Nations entering into such arrangements or constituting such agencies shall make every effort to achieve pacific settlement of local disputes through such regional agencies before referring them to the Security Council.
[Note relationship with Article 33, paragraph 1.]

3. The Security Council shall encourage the development of pacific settlement of local disputes through such regional arrangements or by such regional agencies either on the initiative of the states concerned or by reference from the Security Council.
[Note relationship with Article 36, paragraph 2.]

4. This Article in no way impairs the application of Article 34 and 35.

ARTICLE 34. The Security Council may investigate any dispute, or any situation which may lead to international friction or give rise to a dispute in order to determine whether the continuation of the dispute or situation is likely to endanger the maintenance of international peace and security.

ARTICLE 35. 1. Any Member of the United Nations may bring any dispute, or any situation of the nature referred to in Article 34, to the attention of the Security Council or of the General Assembly.

2. A State which is not a Member of the United Nations may bring to the attention of the Security Council or of the General Assembly any dispute to which it is a party if it accepts in advance, for the purposes of the dispute, the obligations of pacific settlement provided in the present Charter.

3. The proceedings of the General Assembly in respect of matter brought to its attention under this Article will be subject to the provisions of Article 11 and 12.

ENFORCEMENT ACTION

ARTICLE 53.   1. The Security Council shall, where appropriate, utilize such regional arrangements or agencies for enforcement action under its authority. But no enforcement action shall be taken under regional arrangements or by regional agencies without the authorization of the Security Council,

EXCEPTIONS:

I. Upon the state against which action is taken.

[a] with the exception of measures against any enemy state as defined in paragraph 2 of this Article, provided for pursuant to Article 107

[b] or in regional arrangements directed against renewal of aggressive policy on the part of any such state, until such time as the Organization may, on request of the Governments concerned, be charged with the responsibility for preventing further aggression by such a state.

II. Upon the nature of the action taken.

Nothing in the present Charter shall impair the inherent right of individual

ARTICLE 51.

| UNIVERSAL COMPATIBLE REGIONAL | INCOMPATIBLE REGIONAL |

or collective self-defense if an armed attack occurs against a Member of the United Nations, until the Security Council has taken measures necessary to maintain international peace and security.

Measures taken by Members in the exercise of this right shall be immediately reported to the Security Council and shall not in any way affect the authority and responsibility of the Security Council under the present Charter to take at any time such action as it deems necessary in order to maintain or restore international peace and security.

INFORMATION

ARTICLE 54. The Security Council shall at all times be kept fully informed of activities undertaken or in contemplation under regional arrangements or by regional agencies for the maintenance of international peace and security.

COMPATIBILITY

ARTICLE 103. In the event of a conflict between the obligations of the Members of the United Nations under the present Charter and their obligations under any other international agreement, their obligations under the present Charter shall prevail.

Nations Charter had to be couched in vague terms testifies to the lack of strength of a truly compatible force and to a postwar political reality unfavorable to the development of such an approach for international organizations. Lack of trust among the big powers, and among the big powers and the small and middle-sized ones, as well as rivalries among the big ones and the small ones, characterized the political context within which the United Nations Charter was drafted. Demands of each one of these countries (individually or in groups) had to be satisfied, especially those of the big powers. The only way to accomplish this was by stating general principles which could be given diverse interpretations to suit contradictory interests.

It seems that the work of these forces in the background explains the ambiguities of the formulas governing the relationship between universal and regional organizations in the United Nations Charter. The only logical expectation at the time of the drafting of the charter was that all kinds of international organizations were going to coexist and that political developments rather than juridical circumstances would play a greater role in shaping their relationship. A clear definition of the scope and extent of compatible regional organizations was left to be worked out under future circumstances; only in the application of these formulas to specific situations would their precise limitations and implications become clear.

In spite of this general optimistic belief after the conference, that both viewpoints, universalist and incompatible regionalist, had been reconciled into a degree of compatible regionalism that preserved the ultimate responsibility of the Security Council, there were some pessimistic interpreters who feared that regional organizations could readily be emancipated from Security Council control in critical cases. They were overshadowed by the enthusiasm over the immediately successful diplomatic outcome of the conference. As later developments will show, they were perhaps the most realistic of all analysts.

4

THE COLD WAR AND THE RISE OF INCOMPATIBLE REGIONALISM: Tendencies after San Francisco

SUBSEQUENT EVENTS revealed that many of the political expectations of the participants at San Francisco, such as the anticipated primacy of universal organs, were utopian. It was illusory to expect that a concert of the major powers, the victors in the war, would police the world in the name of the United Nations. It was unrealistic to base all hopes for the restoration of a stable world on the continuation of the major powers' wartime cooperation.[1] Big-power consensus, regarded during and immediately after the war as the guarantee of peace, began to crumble almost immediately after the San Francisco Conference, at the Meeting of Foreign Ministers of the great powers at London in October, 1945. Conflicts regarding the settlement of some war-ravaged areas in Central Europe, the Balkans, and the Middle East led to a rapid deterioration of relations between the United States and the Soviet Union. This was accompanied by a steady disintegration of universalist hopes after 1945 and a concurrent rise of incompatible regionalist tendencies.

Largely in response to the materially changed international situation, namely, the global confrontation of rival political and ideological systems, incompatible regionalism evolved first in the security field. Even associations that antedated the cold war conflict revamped their security provisions to deal with the new circumstances, aligning themselves either with the United States or the Soviet Union.[2] In this political context, the ambiguities and inconsistencies of the regional sections of the United Nations Charter were exploited to the advantage of incompatible regionalists. Most notably, the incompatibility of inter-American regionalism grew as the world struggle became more intense. The United States and Latin America, at this point, had a common interest in interpreting these sections of the charter, especially Articles 51 and 52, in less compatible ways. Thus, inter-American activities since 1947 focused on the possibilities for strengthening the status of Article 51 and for emphasizing those parts of Article 52 favorable to the exclusive jurisdiction of regional organizations in the field of collective security and the peaceful settlement of disputes. Essential to their efforts was the actual existence of a strong regional organization serving to discourage Security Council consideration of inter-American disputes and helping to prevent Security Council regulation of inter-American security measures.

Inside the United Nations, the paralysis of the Security Council stemming from continuing disagreements among the permanent members created a situation in which efforts on behalf of peace and security were frequently directed elsewhere; in several cases, some of the Security Council's political and security functions were transferred to the General Assembly, where unanimity was not required and the effective functioning of the body could continue despite dissension. Outside the United Nations, the effects of the cold war were manifested by the establishment of new regional collective security arrangements. These arrangements provided a second mode of insuring national security and brought about a decentralization of the United Nations' security function which the framers had not foreseen.[3]

Western countries, with the United States taking the lead, began to shift their emphasis from Chapter VII (Executive power of the Security Council) of the charter to Chapter VIII and particularly to Article 51, which provided for decentralized but collective action. As a result, the importance of regional arrangements, as provided for in Article 51, was enhanced; a number of treaties were signed, based on the right of collective self-defense, such as the Rio Treaty of 1947 (see below) and the North Atlantic Treaty of 1949. While, in practice, the distinction has often been blurred, in theory, regional organizations deriving from Chapter II and arrangements based on Article 51 differed substantially, as has already been shown (see Chapter III above). For example, states organized for self-defense may exercise their right of collective self-defense without the prior authorization of the Security Council (Article 51) whereas regional organizations may take enforcement action only with that authorization (Article 53). Moreover, under Article 51, countries are bound to report to the Security Council only those measures exercising the right of self-defense, whereas regional organizations, under Article 54, must keep the Security Council fully informed of all activities, whether already undertaken or only contemplated.

The failure to clearly define the general nature of regional arrangements, added to the vague provisions defining the role of collective security agents, led in several instances to a confusion of the two. Often, regional arrangements simultaneously functioned as collective self-defense mechanisms, while associations ostensibly organized on the basis of collective self-defense claimed regional organization status. For instance, in the case of the Organization of American States, a basis of collective self-defense, the 1947 Rio Treaty, was established before its constitutional foundation as a regional organization. Others, like NATO or the Warsaw Pact, have a legal stand only as collective self-defense arrangements. It has been contended that the latter kind are actually regional organizations, but this is open to question because of the express terms of their treaties and the extent to which they reflect the nature and purposes of military alliances.

Furthermore, within the new international context, changes within regional organizations and within universal organizations had very important implications for the relationship of the two kinds of organizations, particularly in terms of power. The United States, an ardent advocate of universalism in 1945 and, at Latin American insistence, of incompatible regionalism at San Francisco, soon became disappointed with universalist formulas. Its disillusionment led to a systematic effort to avoid the Security Council and to strengthen the Inter-American System and other regional systems: it sought at once to bypass the Soviet veto, which often paralyzed the Security Council, and to avoid Soviet intrusion into the affairs of non-Communist-dominated regions.

While this was the reason for United States preference for regionalism, the raison d'être for regionalism in Latin America lay in a desire to secure a counterweight against the United States through a firm network of Latin American-inspired obligations and institutional safeguards. This attitude is not suprising, since an analysis of the expectations entertained by Latin America with respect to the development of the Inter-American System reveals a latent anti-United States pattern: a fear of the return to interventionist policies on the part of the United States. These fears were only partially overcome by the period of the Good Neighbor Policy and seem to have been reinforced by the United States' refusal to sponsor Latin American views at San Francisco. In addition, the economic factor played an important role: the United States became increasingly concerned with the reconstruction of Europe and looked with growing indifference upon its neighbors' postwar economic needs.

Latin American inclinations toward incompatible regionalism turned out to be particularly important in upsetting the universalist-regionalist balance of the United Nations Charter. Latin America had traditionally preferred involvement in those international organizations where its relative political and military inferiority was less evident. So, when the cold war dimmed universalist hopes, the way was paved for Latin Americans to favor a regional organization, where theoretically there were no privileges for the big powers. They began to interpret ambiguities of the dual jurisdiction in the United Nations Charter's regional provisions to the effect that the Security Council (1) should leave initial efforts in settling disputes to regional agencies, and (2) could not " intrude" in the regional settlement of disputes until the latter had failed.

This chapter documents the trends in Latin America's and the United States' thinking since 1945 and the kinds of institutions that subsequently evolved. However, before the analysis can proceed chronologically, a flashback is necessary in order to better illuminate the forces which came into play after 1945. These forces were not innocent ones; they had faced each other before in the arenas of both international organization (the League of Nations) and regional organization (various bilateral United States-Latin American relations). As these forces rearranged themselves for repeated confrontations and compromises often carried out in the polite language of constitutional interpretation, especially involving the United Nations Charter, they bore the legacy of past encounters. The next two sections, describing the League of Nations and the development of the Inter-American System are devoted to an examination of this historical legacy. We shall then return to the postwar arena, with an examination of the Rio Treaty and charter of the OAS.

THE LEAGUE OF NATIONS: ANTI-UNITED STATES UNIVERSALISM AND MONROE'S INCOMPATIBLE REGIONAL DOCTRINE

Prior to World War I, Latin America, isolated and weak, remained on the periphery of international relations. During the first half of the nineteenth century, most diplomatic relations of the Latin American states were limited to countries within the area, and several attempts were made to establish a regional federation. The infrequent contacts with non-Latin American countries, particularly the United States and Europe, generally consisted of intervention by the larger countries to recover or gain territories, to force the payment of international debts, or otherwise to interfere in the international affairs of the countries and the region. The Hispanic American regionalism which had grown from Bolivar's dreams of a Hispanic American federation was weak. The failure of this movement to prevent external intervention and to solve inter-Latin American disputes, especially those which ocurred during the second half of the century (the War of the Pacific, 1897-1883, between Peru, Chile, and Bolivia, and the Paraguayan War, 1864-1870, between Argentina, Uruguay, Brazil, and Paraguay) discouraged Latin American regional experiments.

It was World War I that ended Latin American isolationism and triggered a chain of transformations. Traditional political and social systems that had dominated Latin America for almost a century began to change, becoming relatively more democratic due to the emergence of new political groups and social forces. Latin America gained a new economic role as a source of raw material for the more rapidly industrializing societies of the United States and Europe. In her international relations, Latin America became aware of the advisability of using legal concepts such as sovereignty, juridical equality of states, nonintervention, self-determination, peaceful settlement of disputes, and arbitration to offset her military weakness.

A predilection towards universalism had previously been acquired by the Latin American states when they were invited to participate in some European international meetings, the most significant of which were the Hague Conferences of 1889 and 1907. In spite of their minor role, the Latin American countries' involvement in these events enhanced their national pride, their sense of sovereignty, and their respect for universalist formulas. The Latin American states joined the League of Nations after Versailles with little hesitation, notwithstanding that their participation in World War I was far from active.[4] It was apparent at the time that Latin American statesmen feared interventions from Europe and the United States; their optimism for a universal organization was equalled only by their disillusionment with any kind of continental regionalism.

Concurrent with Latin American attempts at regional federations and other forms of organizations, the United States sponsored a hemispheric regional movement that turned out as unsuccessfully as the Hispanic American movement had. The United States initiated the pan-American movement in 1889-1890 with the convening of the First International Conference of American States at Washington. Yet the work of the pan-American movement during its first decades failed to convince Latin America of the utility of such an attempt as a basis for regional action. The four inter-American conferences that were held from the time of its inception until World War I accomplished little in the way of establishing a machinery for dealing with inter-American disputes or, above all, for serving as a means of restraining United States activities in Latin America; rather, the movement became more generally identified with United States intervention and attempts to control the area than with genuine aspirations of cooperation. Thus, Latin America welcomed the League's universalist orientation, for the League could provide it with some counterweight to United States hemispheric influence. Latin American statesmen expected League protection from the United States intervention, especially as a consequence of the insertion of Article 10 into the covenant, a provision which guaranteed territorial integrity and political independence for the members of the League.[5]

At the same time, during the framing of the league's covenant, Latin American hopes for the universal protection of the League were dashed when Article 21 was adopted, the article which specifically mentioned the Monroe Doctrine as an example of regional pacts.[6] This kind of regionalism was intolerable for Latin America since it preserved and even encouraged United States predominance and control. In fact, in Latin America the Monroe Doctrine was traditionally considered the symbol of United States intervention; a unilateral political declaration which the United States refused to "multilateralize," thus denying Latin America's sovereign rights. Moreover, it had been used to justify the highly arbitrary interventionist policies of the United States throughout Latin America. Therefore, most of the Latin Americans participating in the League refused to recognize the doctrine and made reservations when they ratified the treaty.[7]

Inclusion of Article 21 in the covenant was surprising since the international atmosphere at the end of World War I was rather hostile to regionalism. For instance, the first draft of the covenant advocated a very strong universalism, and one of its major contributors, President Wilson, was particularly apprehensive of regional pacts. The explanation for the acceptance of an article that implied a reservation to the universalist provisions of Article 10 lay in the domestic political situation in the United States, the need to accommodate United States opposition, particularly from Republicans headed by Henry Cabot Lodge,[8]

The United States, Wilson's effort notwithstanding, was able to steer clear of all attempts to circumscribe its freedom of action in Latin America. France and Great Britain, hoping that the United States would join the League, did not antagonize the United States by courting Latin American sympathies. By remaining aloof from the League, the United States was free from universal commitments and thus free to block any attempt by the league to intervene in such inter-American disputes as the Peruvian and Bolivian claims United States was free from universal commitments and thus free to block any attempt by the League to intervene in such inter-American disputes as the Peruvian and Bolivian claims against Chile in the Tacna-Arica disputes over the Ancón Treaty of 1904, the Costa Rica-Panama dispute of 1920, the

Chaco War (1928-1935), and especially the cases of United States intervention in Cuba (1922), Honduras (1924-1925) and Nicaragua (1926-1927).

Furthermore, the League became more concerned with European affairs and grew indifferent to problems in the Western Hemisphere. There were only two exceptions: the conflict between Peru and Colombia over Leticia in 1933, during which a League committee verified the reoccupation of the area by the Colombian government; and during the Chaco War, when the League imposed an arms embargo on Bolivia and Paraguay. But in these two instances the league's role was either not mentioned, as in Leticia, or was inadequate, as in the case of the embargo during the Chaco Wars.[9]

RISE AND DECLINE OF HEMISPHERIC INCOMPATIBLE REGIONALISM

Their involvement in both regional and universal agencies had proved to be discouraging experiences for the Latin American states. They were unable to offset the power of the United States in the immediate post-World War I years, through either the pan-American movement or through the universalist League. However, the Latin American states did use one tool to retaliate against United States intervention: they refused to invest the Pan-American Union, a body dominated by the United States since its inception in 1910, with political functions. Latin American statesmen did not consider the pan-American movement particularly important during its first years, since United States interests at this point were concentrated merely in its commercial and financial aspects. In time, however, the United States attempted to use the pan-American framework as a tool for exercising more political control over its neighbors. Latin America adopted a legalistic attitude and refused to recognize any political or military authority in the periodic inter-American conferences or in the Pan-American Union that subsequently emerged. The impo-

tence of the union in the face of United States power had
been pointed out quite clearly when it proved incapable of
coping with United States interventions in Central America
and the Caribbean during the first decades of the twentieth
century.

But change was in the wind. Although after the war the
United States' power continued to be unchallenged in the
Western Hemisphere, indigenous Latin American movements
were developing—movements demanding fundamental changes
in both political institutions and societal structures. While
some movements led to revolution, as in the case of Mexico,
in other instances changes were brought about, without the
intervention of armed forces, through a widened franchise, or
the coming to power of more broadly based groups. The need
for a fundamental reappraisal of policies became urgent in the
United States. Through trial and error, and repeated discussions, serious doubt arose as to the adequacy of the United
States' interventionist practices. Eventually, the efficacy of a
noninterventionist policy for the United States was recognized.

The virtual reversal of the old policies began with Presi-
dents Coolidge and Hoover and reached a climax during the
Roosevelt administration. The Nicaraguan intervention of
1926-1927 in particular, had proved the bankruptcy of the
United States interventionist policies. The stationing of American marine units in Nicaragua for the purpose of stabilizing
the country's finances and thereby forestalling intervention by
other powers proved to be ineffective; after years of United
States military tutelage, Nicaragua's situation did not improve.
Moreover, the antagonism and expense the United States'
actions had generated, both within Nicaragua and throughout
Latin America, were clearly not worth the effort. The impact
of experiences of this sort on United States policy-makers was
evident in the reduction of the use of force and instances of
intervention. The withdrawal of United States troops from the
Caribbean and Central America (including the withdrawal of

marines from Haiti in 1933-1934), and the abolition of financial controls in the Dominican Republic in 1940.

At the same time, new treaties more favorable to Latin American countries were promulgated. These included: a new canal treaty with Panama in 1936 ending the right of intervention hitherto enjoyed by the United States; a new treaty with Mexico in 1937 surrendering the right to protect the isthmus of Tehuantepec; a 1941 treaty settling the Mexican oil expropriation claims and, in the same year, an oil treaty with Venezuela; all amounting to the abandonment of a policy of indiscriminate protection for American investments in Latin America. For the economic point of view in particular, Latin American statesmen were relieved when the unpopular Smoot-Hawley Tariff Act of 1930 was substituted for the policy of the trade agreement acts, and when the Export-Import Bank was established in 1934. It was apparent at the time that, while many means of financial and diplomatic pressure were maintained by the United States—as in the case of Mexico, Bolivia, and Argentina—there had been an overall improvement in relations with Latin America.[10]

Extracontinental developments also had a bearing on the transformation of United States-Latin American relations. Dangerous affinities with German and Italian nationalistic policies began to appear among influential political groups in Latin America, essentially in Argentina and Chile. The United States at this point was particularly sensitive to the anti-United States feeling prevalent in Latin America. It is likely that the United States advanced the new policy of nonintervention in an effort to counterbalance extracontinental influences and to gain Latin American diplomatic alignment and economic support in the event of another war. While friendly relations were being fostered in Latin America, the situation in the rest of the world was rapidly deteriorating. The power of the Nazis had aggrandized in Germany. Italy had invaded Ethiopia, and the Japanese had attacked China. The theme of extracontinental intervention entered United States-Latin

American relations at this early date (1938-1939) and contributed to the substantial changes that later ensued in inter-American relationships during the period of the Good Neighbor Policy and after World War II.

Continental regionalism was enhanced when inter-American relationships were "multilateralized" and given collective responsibility in the task of preventing extracontinental influences through a series of inter-American resolutions adopted since 1938. Hemispheric solidarity was appealed to, especially by the United States, in view of the hostilities in Europe, and became a major concern of the area. Regional links which set the countries of the Western Hemisphere apart from the rest of the world were emphasized by both the United States and Latin America in what has been called the "hemispheric projection of the natural policy of isolation."[11]

Latin America's first reaction to United States extracontinental fears was one of reluctance. For example, at the 1936 Buenos Aires Conference, called primarily to strengthen Latin American legal cooperation in the face of deteriorating conditions in Europe, tendencies toward a strong and even incompatible type of regionalism were not particularly marked. Argentina, reflecting the universalist views of many other Latin American countries, made clear that she would unconditionally oppose any regional distinctions or separations of continents.[12] But United States efforts on behalf of isolated hemispheric security, and hence incompatible regionalism, slowly gained acceptance, as the Latin American states began to receive the benefits of the Good Neighbor Policy. The controversy which, in effect, centered around the issue of universalism or regionalism, was settled inside the Pan-American Union in favor of the regional conception. As will be shown below, from the time of the Lima Conference in 1938, when the necessity for regional distinctions appeared to be a foregone conclusion, incompatible regionalism gradually evolved in the Western Hemisphere.[13]

Inter-American cooperation was channeled through a new international political and economic system: the consultation method, through Meetings of Ministers of Foreign Affairs, which would guide and control the attitudes of Latin American vis-à-vis developments in Europe and Asia. The consultation system originated in 1936 at Buenos Aires was perfected in 1938 at the Lima Conference, and was later applied to align Latin America with United States positions during the war—first neutrality, and later belligerence. The system, which consisted of Meetings of the Ministers of Foreign Relations of the Latin American countries and the Unites States Secretary of State, proved to be the most impressive outcome of the Good Neighbor Policy. Gradually, through these Meetings of Consultation, the confidence that United States policies began to instill in Latin America was reciprocated by the latter's endorsement of resolutions sponsored by the United States.

The First Meeting of Consultation, held in Panama 1939, organized a common front of neutrality in the European war. The strong desire to preserve the continent as a "hemisphere of peace" militated against involvement in the European conflict.[14] The Declaration of Panama favored a safety belt around the continent in order to free it of belligerent activity. More importantly, this action supplied a significant legal precedent for Latin American regionalism: it was the first collective action of the twenty-one American republics bearing upon the rights and interests of third powers outside the Western Hemisphere, since it concerned maritime zones technically within the "open" seas, where all countries of the world had established rights.[15] Moreover, the declaration of neutrality was an effective blow against the current universal organization, the League of Nations; many Latin American states were still members of the League and were under an obligation to participate in some of the belligerent activities undertaken by the organization, such as the sanctions against Italy for her attack on Ethiopia.[16] In addition, as the economic counterpart to the position of political neutrality, the

Panama Meeting of Consultation considered and initiated steps toward the solution of economic difficulties that would arise as a result of the war, and it established a body in charge of fostering inter-American economic cooperation.

However, the policies of neutrality had to be abandoned for the actual defense of the hemisphere. When Belgium, the Netherlands, Luxembourg, and France were invaded, the question of the fate of the European colonies in the hemisphere was raised. The Second Meeting of Consultation, held in Havana a year later, took up this question and, in effect, continentalized the principle of nonrecognition of the transfer of territory from one to another non-American power, a tenet until then supported solely by the unilateral declaration of the Monroe Doctrine. In order to cope with the problem of attempts to transfer territory, a system of provisional administration of European colonies and possessions in the Americas was established. Since the United States was the only country in the Western Hemisphere with enough military strength to deal with Axis intervention, this system of administration was equivalent to granting to the United States the authority to occupy any European possession considered a hemisphere danger spot.[17] Understandably, the Latin American statesmen were initially reluctant to accept this resolution and the system which it established. Many representatives felt that it threatened their neutrality in the war and further, that it was a hollow gesture; they felt that if any move was to be made along these lines, it should aim at eliminating all vestiges of colonialism in the Western Hemisphere rather than a few of its manifestations.[18] Their reluctance was overcome, however, when it became clear that all of the continent would be endangered if those European colonies became centers for Axis espionage and military activities.

In addition, the Havana meeting agreed on security and reciprocal economic assistance through the principle of "all for one and one for all." Economic and financial cooperation were expanded, and the capital and lending power of the

Export-Import Bank was increased to assist in the stabilizing of the economies and the orderly marketing of products of the Western Hemisphere. All this was substantiated by the United States' promise of unlimited help to relieve the economic distresses caused to Latin America as a consequence of the war. Equally welcome to Latin America was the establishment of a committee (which later became the Inter-American Peace Committee) for the peaceful settlement of inter-American disputes.

In some other aspects the United States was not so successful in getting Latin American support, such as instituting precautionary measures against foreign, i.e. Axis, subversive activities. The reluctance was due to the still prevalent Latin American fears of United States interference with their domestic affairs. However, Latin Americans, Argentina expected, finally cooperated with the United States in this regard when the danger of Axis activities did appear imminent. Moreover, the initial hesitance of Latin America to cooperate in the construction of military bases (which proved so effective during the war in combating the submarine menace and carrying out the African campaigns) was replaced by growing willingness to participate, after the United States proclaimed that the agreements would not entail actual transfer of sovereignty over the areas concerned.

These changes represent early attempts to transform the Western Hemisphere into a separate entity acting, to a degree, through corporate agencies of its own. The record of pan-Americanism during these years confirms the slow but continuously growing force of an incompatible regionalist conception, a conception which was conspicuously absent in the early history of the pan-American movement.[19] It was reflected, for instance, in the growth of mechanisms for inter-American consultation on many issues, provisions for economic assistance, and institutions for the peaceful settlement of inter-American disputes. Extracontinental developments, in particular, hastened these trends by repeatedly pointing up the deficiencies of the League and the necessity for regionally based security measures. It is clear that Latin American regionalism grew more incompatible to the extent that it represented an effort to compensate for the weaknesses—military, economic, or political—of the universal organization. It was precisely the development and strengthening of this regionalist conception that prepared the hemisphere for its prompt reaction to the Pearl Harbor attack.

The Third Meeting of Consultation, held in Rio in 1942, led to an almost unanimous rupture with the Axis by severence of diplomatic and commercial relations or through actual declarations of war.[20] Militarily, the United States bore the main burden of hemispheric defense, but it was aided by strategically located Latin American countries through the adoption of definite measures such as military agreements with Panama and Brazil. Politically, the control of governments in power was strengthened as a consequence of United States diplomatic and economic policies in order to diminish the likelihood of Axis-inspired revolutionary movements in Latin America. For instance, the lend-lease aid and loans to Latin American republics by the Export-Import Bank continued to be expanded. This policy of cooperation, which involved close United States alignment with Latin American elites, ensured the supply of strategic raw materials, strengthened Latin American economies in the interest of the war efforts, and diminished Axis appeal in the hemisphere. At the same time, it laid the United States open to the criticism of supporting military dictatorships in Latin America.

The Pearl Harbor attack, and the ensuing participation of some countries of the hemisphere in the war, had unexpected consequences for the regionalist views of officials of the United States and Latin America: for reasons and in ways we saw in Chapter II, as the United States became more and more involved in the war, its incompatible regionalist views, especially in matters of hemispheric security, gradually gave way to an ever growing universalism, while Latin American incom-

patible regionalism became more firmly entrenched. Developments in the two years that elapsed between the Rio Meeting
of Consultation in 1942 and the Dumbarton Oaks Conference
in 1944 strengthened the tendencies of United States adherence to universalism and Latin American support for incompatible regionalism. When the United States assumed a role of
world power, universalism supplanted its hemispheric focus.
Moreover, the United States was disappointed with changes,
since 1930, in some Latin American societies, which had
relapsed into more or less stable dictatorships or rapid succes-
sions of coups, Argentina being the most dramatic example.
Faith in the development of stable and liberal governments
gave way to skepticism and a policy of support for strong and
stable military dictatorships.

While support for incompatible regionalism rapidly declined
in the United States, it increased in Latin America, which
produced a more substantial diplomatic, economic, and political defense of it than would have been expected in 1939.
Diplomatically, the war made Latin America conscious of her
international status and encouraged a sense of regional distinc-
tiveness among a majority of the Latin countries. While their
prestige had been enhanced by the fact that almost half of
the Latin Americans were original signatories of the Declaration of the United Nations, January 1, 1942, this declaration
was not enough to persuade Latin America of the blessings of
universalism—particularly a universalism which at this stage
was weak and vague. In addition, the Latin American states
realized that in the postwar world they would urgently need
financial and other assistance which only the United States
could provide on a large scale and for which the Pan American Union framework might constitute a preliminary commitment. Politically, Latin American governments were sus-
picious of the Soviet Union and feared that it would use its
role in a universal organization to hamper pan-American
regional security measures.[21]

As the end of the war approached, it became more difficult
to harmonize United States hemispheric interests with its

global economic and political interests. United States involvement in other regions, coupled with Latin American remoteness from the world's main political and military struggles of the war, turned Latin America into a low-priority area, especially in economic and diplomatic matters. European problems began to attract United States attention almost exclusively. At the same time, Latin America hoped for the continuity of the pan-American wartime cooperation and for American aid in economic peacetime readjustment. Latin America considered the United States' assumption of this burden as its obligation, as well as a proof of its sincerity in the Good Neighbor Policy. By giving high priority to European considerations, the United States evoked Latin American criticism and suspicion. Latin American statesmen felt that "the Rio Grande was allowed to become wider than the Atlantic Ocean."[22] They were convinced that during the war the United States had taken more from Latin America than it had given in return during the same period.[23] that it had taken advantage of Latin American military dependence to acquire raw and strategic material at very low prices and that, with the war ending, it was slowly returning to its traditional attitude of neglect. Hence, Latin America's efforts to tie the United States down in a strong regional body, and its objection to a universal organization increased.

Plans to develop inter-American regionalism were made before the San Francisco Conference by Latin America. The Mexico City Conference of 1945 prepared the Latin American countries to face jointly what they considered the universalist menace of San Francisco. At that time, definite plans were drawn for (1) a collective security treaty,[24] (2) an organic pact encompassing the overall regional system, and (3) an instrument consolidating existing machinery for peaceful settlement of disputes at the regional level.

The first Latin American regionalist attempts in the months immediately after San Francisco met with failure. The United States was not ready to support such a move. Hemispheric solidarity weakened during the postwar period to the point that the fulfillment of the Mexico City recommendations was threatened. Initially, the tension between the United States and Argentina (see above, Chapter II) had been responsible for delaying the execution of the Mexico City resolutions. In subsequent years, the whole postwar situation—for example, the growing disparity in power between the United States and the Latin American states, the United States' new universalist orientation—seemed to militate against a continuation of the wartime solidarity. In 1945, the Rio Conference at which part of the Latin American aspirations were to be incorporated into a treaty, was postponed at the request of the United States. The scheduled Rio Conference had been especially important to the Latin American states; since Latin Americans viewed the United Nations as a barrier to the development of the Inter-American System, they sought a written charter or constitution to guarantee its survival and sustain the United States' positive commitments in the region.

All this changed with the advent of the cold war and United States disappointment over the United Nations universalism. Those developments paved the way for a "downward tranfer" and brought about some of the changes which Latin American governments had favored in the earlier period. United States fear of developing regional instruments for collective security was overcome with the gradual deterioration of American-Soviet relations. Ways were sought to reconcile incompatible regionalist, collective security arrangements with the United Nations' universalism; declarations of loyalty to the purposes and principles of the United Nations were added to the charters of regional organizations in order to present these groupings as constructive programs for strengthening the United Nations.

The Western Hemisphere became a sort of testing ground for this kind of international organization relationship. The pre-World War II theme of protection from extracontinental aggression reappeared, although Communism supplated Nazism as the major focus. Latin American regionalist views, primarily concerned with economic measures, proved useful because they could be applied to security fields. The Inter-American Treaty of Reciprocal Assistance, or the Rio Treaty as it is commonly known, was the first of the cold war regionalist pacts and in many ways the forerunner for NATO and other incompatible regional treaties.

SAN FRANCISCO AFTERMATH: THE RIO TREATY AND INITIAL INTER-AMERICAN DOWNWARD TRANSFER

Latin and North American efforts to weaken the United Nations' rule over regional operations proceeded, after San Francisco, in the same general direction as before but using somewhat different weapons. With the existence of a United Nations Charter of which the provisions were vague and often inconsistent, controversy at this point often centered around legal concepts or competing interpretations of constitutional clauses. Latin American policies aimed at a "broadening" interpretation of the first part of Article 52 (especially paragraphs 2 and 3) and a "constricting" interpretation of Article 53. Broadening interpretations of paragraphs 2 and 3 of Article 52 tended to emphasize the competence which regional organizations should be granted in the settlement of local disputes, and the duty of the Security Council to encourage such settlements within the exclusive framework of regional organizations. Constricting interpretation of Article 52 tended to minimize the Security Council's control of regional organizations when such agencies applied enforcement action. This was accomplished by emphasizing that only those measures involving the use of force actually required the authorization of the Security Council; in all other cases (that is in measures of an economic, political, or diplomatic nature short of military force) regional organizations were free to adopt any action which suited their interests. In thus interpreting the charter, Latin America hoped to return to the

Good Neighbor Policy and to force upon the United States a form of regional collaboration similar to the one that had existed during the war, especially in the field of economic assistance and peaceful settlement of disputes.

On the other hand, United States policies were oriented toward a "broadening" interpretation of Article 51, which would permit the development of regional agencies for collective self-defense. Since it hoped for a unified Western Hemisphere front against Communist intervention, a broadening interpretation of Article 51 tended to emphasize the rights of collective self-defense not only in cases of armed attack, but also when an armed attack was imminent. Also it tended to stress the aspects of enforcement action which regional organizations were permitted to adopt without prior authorization by the Security Council.

Such differing objectives on the part of the major participants can partially explain the dual character of the Inter-American system—as a collective security arrangement under the authority of Article 51 and as a regional organization under the authority of Chapter VIII. While the United States wanted to use the Inter-American System as a weapon to combat Communism, Latin America viewed it as an aid in tackling her economic and social problems, as a means of sustaining United States involvement and hence, commitment to the area.

The Latin American states, hoping to clarify the position of regional organizations while the universal organization was being set up, were thus particularly anxious to hold the Inter-American Conference provided for in the Chapultepec documents and scheduled for October 20, 1945. The repeated postponements of the conference, largely as a result of United States pressure, served to antagonize the Latin republics. It appeared to prove that the extracontinental responsibilities of the United States were again affecting its views on the inter-American System, forcing it to adopt a highly restrained regionalist position. Although no specific explanation for this postponement was given, there were several obvious reasons. Difficulties at the Conference of Foreign Ministers in London (September 11 to October 2, 1945, ending three days before the United States requested postponements), especially with the Soviet Union, made the United States reluctant to enter, at that early date, any contractual security commitment with Latin America.[25] In addition, conflicts between the United States and Argentina contributed to the delay. The United States accused Argentina of repudiating her international obligations and was unwilling to enter into any security pact in which Argentina, whose regime was viewed as Fascist and uncooperative, was likely to become a member. The United States also feared that Latin America would not support its position vis-à-vis Argentina, especially after the United States' open intervention in the internal affairs of Argentina during the Blue Book-Braden affair.[26]

The conference was again postponed by the United States, after it had been scheduled for March, 1946, for more or less the same reasons, as before. In fact, it was only after the United States-Soviet Union split had sharpened, that the United States began to favor incompatible regional security arrangements erected as a counterweight to Soviet ideological and territorial expansion. The Conference for the Maintenance of Peace and Security finally met in Rio at Quintandha, near Petropolis, from August 15 to September 2, 1947. Negotiation of a treaty of reciprocal assistance and continental solidarity in the face of aggression was the only item on the agenda. Although some economic questions were formally raised by Latin America, the work of the conference was concentrated on drafting the Rio Treaty.[27]

A compromise on collective defense of the Western Hemisphere was reached in the Inter-American Treaty of Reciprocal Assistance (Rio Treaty) signed on September 2, 1947. Although observers have frequently emphasized those aspects of the Rio Treaty relating to Article 51, the provisions of the treaty that involved Chapter VIII of the United Nations

Charter were also notable. In fact, it was the combination, and often, the confusion, of these two parts of the United Nations Charter in the body of the Rio Treaty that contributed to distorted interpretations of the original United Nations provisions.

The Rio Treaty transformed the optional right of self-defense under Article 51 into an explicit duty of the signatories. The original mechanisms provided in Article 51 for collective self-defense were optional, they might or might not be adopted by members of regional organizations inclined to pursue collective security activities. If the duty to assist the victim of an armed attack were to be made obligatory, it was necessary to surround it in a contractual arrangement binding upon all the members of the regional organization. In other words, it was in the regionalist interest to institutionalize collective self-defense by a treaty signed prior to such collective action. This view broadened Article 51, since this United Nations provision did not suggest the need for a previous contractual commitment among the members of the international community, or even among the members of parts of it, but referred to a voluntary and spontaneous international reaction to repel an armed attack. The interpretation of Article 51 expressed in the Rio Treaty was especially important since this was the first treaty for collective security signed after the establishment of the United Nations.

The Rio Treaty basically distinguished (1) the quality or type of aggression and established different processes for facing "armed attack" or "aggressions which are not an armed attack"; and (2) the origin of the aggression or the character of the aggressor, setting apart the American from the non-American aggressor and introducing a special stage of "pacifying consultation" in case of conflicts between two or more American states. The consultation method, initiated in 1939 and practiced very successfully during the war, was incorporated as the functional support of the whole inter-American collective security system and as the foundation of inter-

American solidarity. The geographical limits of the security zone, defined in Article 4, were similar to the safety belt boundaries noted at the Panama Meeting of 1939.[28]

The process used to face armed attacks was outlined in Article 3.

> 1. *The High Contracting Parties agree that an* armed attack *by any State against an American State shall be considered as an attack against all the American States and, consequently, each one of the said Contracting Parties undertakes to assist in meeting the attack in the exercise of the inherent right of individual or collective self-defense recognized by Article 51 of the Charter of the United Nations.*

> 2. *On the request of the State or States directly attacked and until the decision of the Organ of Consultation of the Inter-American System, each one of the Contracting Parties may determine the immediate measures which it may individually take in fulfillment of the obligation contained in the preceding paragraph and in accordance with the principle of continental solidarity. The Organ of Consultation shall meet without delay for the purpose of examining those measures and agreeing upon the measures of a collective character that should be taken. . . .*

> 4. *Measures of self-defense provided for under this Article may be taken until the Security Council of the United Nations has taken the measures necessary to maintain international peace and security. [Emphasis added.]*

The actions to be taken against the attacker were also detailed by the treaty. Before the Organ of Consultation would meet,[29] the parties to the treaty could adopt measures individually to assist the victim of the aggression if they were requested to do so by the victim. Support for the state under attack became juridically binding only after the Organ of Consultation had met and decided on collective measures by a two-thirds majority; the only exception to this was the provision that no state was required to use force without its consent (Article 20). The Rio Treaty equipped the Organ of

Consultation with discretional capacity to adopt measures of collective character "until the Security Council of the United Nations had taken the measures necessary to maintain international peace and security." However, the treaty did not explicitly state who was to decide—the Security Council or the members of the Inter-American System—when the "necessary action" had been taken. Still, it seems clear that the signatories of the Rio Treaty, eager to increase regional autonomy, tacitly assumed that it was up to them to make that decision. Moreover, if the Security Council were paralyzed by the use of the veto, the Organ of Consultation would remain the only arbiter of the situation and would decide whether to apply the measures mentioned in Article 8 or continue their use.[30]

In the case of inter-American response to an aggression which is not an armed attack, Article 6 of the Rio Treaty applies.

> If the inviolability or the integrity of the territory or the sovereignty or political independence of any American State should be affected by an aggression which is not an armed attack or by an extracontinental or intracontinental conflict, or by any other fact or situation that might endanger the peace of America, the Organ of Consultation shall meet immediately in order to agree on the measures which must be taken in case of aggression to assist the victim of the aggression or, in any case, the measures which should be taken for the common defense and for the maintenance of the peace and security of the continent. [Emphasis added.]

In this case the Organ of Consultation would not be acting as an agent of collective self-defense under Article 51 (which deals exclusively with armed attacks) but as a regional arrangement under Chapter VIII of the United Nations Charter subject to the limitations on enforcement actions of Article 53. Technically, under the United Nations Charter the Organ of Consultation would not be able to apply any of the measures of Article 8 (of the Rio Treaty), especially the use of armed force, without a previous authorization of the Security Council. If the Security Council were paralyzed, the Organ of Consultation could not use its discretion as it could if Article 51 were applicable. The incompatibility of this specific part of the Rio Treaty is particularly evident; it makes no effort to reconcile its mechanisms with those of the universal organization and in fact contains no references to the United Nations or the Security Council.

Article 7 of the Rio Treaty set up the procedure to be followed when the aggressor was one of the American states, a procedure that was to operate without prejudice to the latest right of self-defense under Article 51 of the United Nations Charter. A special kind of consultation, a pacifying consultation, would be imposed upon the American states involved in a dispute, to persuade them to suspend hostilities and to restore the *status quo ante bellum.* If these pacifying mediations were rejected, the American aggressor would not be given any special consideration and would be treated in the same way as a non-American aggressor by the Organ of Consultation.[31]

With the provisions set up for handling inter-American disputes, American regionalists scored a point in their efforts to gain greater regional autonomy. Article 2 of the Rio Treaty effectively reinforced paragraphs 2 and 3 of Article 52 of the United Nations Charter since it contained an agreement to "submit every controversy which might arise between them [the American nations] to methods of pacific settlement and to endeavor to settle any such controversy among themselves by means of the procedures in force in the Inter-American System before referring them to the General Assembly or the Security Council of the United Nations." This article, which could thus be interpreted as a contractual commitment to use the mechanisms of the Inter-American System before those of the United Nations, initiated the process of "downward transfer." It represented one of the first attempts to interpret ambiguities in the United Nations' regional provisions in favor of an incompatible type of regionalism.

In recognizing its relationship with a universal organization, reference was made in Articles 1 and 10 of the alleged compatibility of the Rio Treaty with the United Nations.

> *Article 1. The High Contracting Parties formally condemn war and undertake in their international relations not to resort to the threat or the use of force in any manner inconsistent with the provisions of the Charter of the United Nations or of this Treaty.*
>
> *Article 10. None of the provisions of this Treaty shall be construed as impairing the rights and obligations of the High Contracting Parties under the Charter of the United Nations.*

Yet other parts of the treaty disregarded compatibility and went beyond the provisions of the United Nations, envisaging a major political role for the pact signatories in action which did not require prior authorization by the Security Council. In the long run, provisions to repel forms of aggression not constituting armed attack proved more important and raised more difficulties in the relationship between the United Nations and the Inter-American System than did the broadening interpretations of Article 51.

In its relationship to Article 51, the Rio Treaty provided an example of a regional security system which effectively circumvented the veto of the United Nations Security Council. A few months after the signing of the Rio Treaty, Senator Vandenberg guided through the Senate a resolution bearing his name which advised the President to pursue a general policy of support for the development of regional and other collective security arrangements in several parts of the world; these arrangements would allegedly operate within the United Nations framework but would not be subject to Security Council veto, especially by the Soviet.[32]

Less than a month later, the United States began preliminary discussions with Canada, France, Belgium, the Netherlands, Luxembourg, Portugal, Denmark, Norway, and Iceland that eventually led to the establishment of the North Atlantic

Treaty Organization on April 4, 1949. This treaty provided the necessary strength, in the face of United Nations universal weakness, to meet the threat of Soviet expansionism. The advantages of NATO offered a mutual assistance in maintaining security and were later applied to other regions through the South East Asia Treaty Organization of 1954 and the Baghdad Pact of 1955. Paralleling the development of collective self-defense arrangements among non-Communist countries was the signing of the Treaty of Friendship, Cooperation and Mutual Assistance by members of the Soviet bloc at Warsaw in May, 1955.

The Rio Treaty provided a political precedent for NATO and other Western alliances, without substantially altering the legal situation at the time it was drafted. It was technically assumed since 1945, during the San Francisco Conference, that such a treaty between the countries of the Western Hemisphere would be compatible with the United Nations; the availability of the United States in the defense of the Western Hemisphere had been traditionally taken for granted.[33] In comparison, what was novel and dangerous, was the precedent set up by the Rio Treaty for the establishment of collective security military arrangements which detracted from the power and control of the Security Council.

In spite of Latin American support for these incompatible regionalist developments, Latin Americans feared that the United States would use the Rio Conference exclusively to strengthen its political position in the struggle against the Soviet Union. Rather, they hoped to balance their involvement in the cold war—their entrance into a military alliance with the United States—by gaining United States economic cooperation as well. The economic negotiations, however, failed. The conference was given wide attention in the United States as a political event initiating an important sequence of military alliances among Western nations against Soviet policies. President Truman made a special trip to Rio for the closing session. But the United States would not add economic help to the military cooperation it offered.[34] In a dramatic moment of the conference, Secretary of State George C. Marshall told the delegates to stick to the job of writing a continental defense treaty and postpone discussions of inter-American economic questions.[35] Latin American efforts were defeated despite their insistence that promises of military and political cooperation were of little value if economic cooperation was not established to alleviate their underdeveloped situation.

Latin American dissatisfaction with United States' economic policy was brought into the open, during the interval between the Rio (1947) and the Bogotá Conferences (1948), by the establishment of the United Nations Economic Commission for Latin America (ECLA) in 1948, despite United States opposition.[36] The United States contended that there would be a duplication of efforts by the Inter-American Economic and Social Council, which had been functioning since the Mexico City Conference of 1945, and the proposed Economic Commission for Latin America. The United States also tried to sidetrack the question by attempting to refer it to the Ninth Inter-American Conference, scheduled to meet in Bogotá in March, 1948. It was a rare occasion when Latin Americans were able to vote as a bloc and to gather sufficient backing from other voting groups in the United Nations General Assembly for the establishment of ECLA.

Unlike what had happened in the security and political realms, where the Latin American attitude has been incompatible with the universal organization, Latin American preference, for what amounts to an economic regionalism compatible with United Nations efforts, has not changed since February, 1948.[37] when ECLA was established, and has in fact been strengthened since that time. In the work of ECLA, the Latin American countries were in constant opposition to the United States on economic matters. For years, the United States favored the OAS Inter-American Economic and Social Council, and regarded the efforts of the competitor ECLA with political disapproval as well as a deep distrust. ECLA's projects were viewed as a continuous incitement to Latin American countries to "gang up" against the United States in order to force economic and other concessions through the United Nations.[38]

Yet the most serious studies of Latin America's economic situation, the impetus toward economic integration, as well as government planning and land reform projects, came from ECLA and not from the OAS. This accounts for the Latin American preference for United Nations-sponsored regional activities, such as the Latin American Free Trade Association and the Central American Common Market, which worked within a compatible regional framework and avoided United States hegemony.[39] Only during the most successful months of the short-lived Alliance for Progress was there a United States acceptance of ECLA and a coordination of the work of ECLA with the OAS Inter-American economic and Social Council.

THE CHARTER OF THE OAS AND INSTITUTIONALIZATION OF THE INTER-AMERICAN SYSTEM

What had begun as a tendency toward incompatible regionalism on the part of the Latin American states and the United States, emerged in 1948 in the form of a regional organization whose aims and orientation were fundamentally incompatible with the universal organization; in a sense, the trends that had manifested themselves after the San Francisco Conference of 1945 culminated in the establishment of the Organization of American States, which embodied incompatible inter-American regionalism. The Ninth International Conference of American States, held in Bogotá from March 30 to May 2, 1948, drafted and adopted the charter of the OAS and thus gave an overall institutional framework to the previously loosely organized principles and agencies of the Inter-American System. The new pact also included the economic, social, and cultural aspects of the Inter-American System, which had not been considered at the Rio Conference. The adoption of the charter of the Organization of American States was the most significant achievement of this Bogotá meeting. The substitution of coordination and integration for the extreme flexibility and multiplicity of resolutions that had characterized Pan-American relationships in the past was a sine qua non for the survival of the Inter-American System in areas other than collective security.

Latin American expectations for this conference exceeded those of the United States. Lack of United States support was a reflection of the general declining interest of the United States government in Latin America. For instance, the number of State Department advisors who knew Latin America well had notably decreased during the last few years. Some, such as Sumner Welles and Nelson Rockefeller, had resigned and the Office of the Coordinator of Inter-American Affairs, with its fifteen hundred employees, was absorbed into other governmental agencies.

The United States' delegation to the Bogotá meeting, consisting of ninety-three members, was headed by top government officials who were mainly interested and trained in European economic matters. The delegation did not include representatives of the cultural, labor, or social fields, nor did the delegates have substantial knowledge of the Latin American economic situation. General Marshall, head of the delegation, ". . . was never cut to be a diplomat. Impatient with ceremony and the tidbits of society, he never liked 'sitting around' looking for a formula."[40] Interested in restoring war-devastated areas of Europe, the two inter-American conferences with the backward Latin American nations may well have seemed a loss of time to him. He was successful as a diplomat and tactitian when he dealt with the military protection of the hemisphere at the Rio Conference, but at Bogotá, he and his leading delegates "seemed to be wanderers in the dark. The delegation might have been excellent in a European conference, but it was completely lost in what was for them the psychological, diplomatic, and economic fog of inter-American problems."[4][1]

To make matters worse at the Bogotá Conference, a violent political eruption, the notorious *bogotazo,* which disrupted the work of the conference for several days, attracted much more attention than the diplomatic work. The violence, triggered by the assassination of the chief of the liberal party, J. Eliecer Gaitan, on April 10, was also indirectly provoked when the conference elected, as president, the Colombian Minister of Foreign Affairs, Laureano Gomez, one of the most reactionary elements in the Colombia Conservative party. This election made the conference very unpopular, and its meeting site became a center of the violence which swept the city.

But despite this turmoil and the lack of United States expertise among their delegates, the United States and Latin American delegates achieved partial fulfillment of their aims. The United States gained one of its main political objectives: the focus of Latin American interest on the anti-Communist fight and the drafting and signing of the first inter-American anti-Communist pronouncement. On the other hand, Latin America succeeded in designing the OAS as an instrument which could theoretically restrain the United States in the exercise of its power. The charter condemned wars of aggression, and recognized a series of rights and duties of states such as: the jurisdiction of states within the limits of their national territories (exercised over both nationals and aliens), and the guarantee of nonintervention (including collective intervention and coercive political and economic measures).

The chapters of the OAS Charter which dealt with peaceful settlement of disputes and collective security were short, since two separate documents already covered them: the Pact of Bogotá (signed also in the ninth conference in 1948) and the Rio Treaty (signed in 1947). The OAS Charter referred to the Rio Treaty and incorporated it as supporting document in the Inter-American System. The Organ of Consultation, whose functions were outlined in the Rio Treaty (the Meeting of Foreign Ministers of the OAS Council,[42] acting as the Provisional Organ of Consultation), was kept as the principal regional body for dealing with security questions.

In the field of peaceful settlement of disputes, the charter restated some of the Rio Treaty's "incompatible" provisions. Article 20 of the OAS Charter stated:

> *All international disputes that may arise between American States shall be submitted to the peaceful procedures set forth in this Charter, before being referred to the Security Council of the United Nations.*[43]

It should be noted that Article II of the Pact of Bogotá included a similar provision, although in the pact, the settlement of disputes was dealt with exclusively from the juridical point of view, without mentioning political negotiations (which the OAS Charter and the Rio Treaty include). While the Pact of Bogotá provided for procedures of good offices and mediation, investigation, conciliation, judicial procedures, and arbitration to settle disputes, reservations to its text (made by several countries, including the United States) rendered practically inoperative its major provision, namely the principle of compulsory arbitration and jurisdiction of the International Court of Justice.[44]

Article 102 of the OAS Charter attempted to provide for the compatibility of the OAS with the United Nations by stating:

> *None of the provisions of this Charter shall be constructed as impairing the rights and obligations of the Member States under the Charter of the United Nations.*

However, the combination of this article with Article 20 of the same OAS Charter led to a contradiction similar to the one contained within Article 52 (paragraphs 2 and 4) of the

United Nations Charter. In either place was it made clear which one of the two organizations would prevail, particularly when intraregional disputes were involved. At the same time, the purpose of the conference—the strengthening of the Inter-American System—made it apparent that, in practice regional rather than universal commitments were to be stressed.

Articles 1 and 4 of the OAS Charter made other references to the universal system, underlining the separate identity of the OAS and the fact that its relationship with the United Nations was only one aspect of its nature.[45] Both of these articles carefully circumscribed this relationship, considering it relevant only to the extent that OAS activities came within the United Nations framework—as a regional agency with regional obligations. In the peaceful settlement of disputes and in the area of collective security, the OAS Charter and the Rio Treaty studiously avoided United Nations control.

The relationship of the OAS with the United Nations in other areas was defined in several ways. The duty to report to the United Nations every OAS action in the field of peace and security was established through Article 61 of the OAS Charter and Article 54 of the United Nations Charter. Inter-American treaties were to be registered with the Secretariat of the United Nations, and a standing invitation was issued to the United Nations to send a representative to every inter-American conference (resolution 34 of the final act of the conference).[46]

The OAS Charter was, from an incompatible regionalist view, a necessary step in the institutionalization and strengthening of a regional organization vis-a-vis the universal United Nations, temporarily satisfying the incompatible regionalist views of the United States and Latin America. Coupled with the Rio Treaty, its primary focus lay in the greater responsibility it placed on the part of all the American states in the field of collective security and peaceful settlement of disputes.

To a large extent, important provisions of the United Nations Charter were revised in a period of only three years.

To survive, the delicate balance between universalism and compatible regionalism created in 1945 required, not only the good faith of the United Nations members participating in regional pacts, but also a constant upward transfer and a continuous compatible interpretation of the United Nations' regional provisions. Being so subtle a balance, any weight added to the side of regionalism was likely to distort the initial structure of the universal organization and to bend it towards an incompatible regionalism. With the signing of the Rio Treaty and the OAS Charter, Latin America and the United States incompatible regionalists achieved a long-sought objective: to interpose the OAS as a barrier to Security Council control. Bases were laid so that in all practical circumstances regional, rather than universal, provisions would prevail. The way had been paved for the development of an incompatible regional instrument, and neither the United States nor the Latin American countries had any hesitation in encouraging this trend.

5

INCOMPATIBILITY IN THE PEACE-
FUL SETTLEMENT OF DISPUTES
AT THE REGIONAL LEVEL

DURING THE TWENTY years following the establishment of
the United Nations and the OAS, the United States found it
increasingly difficult to identify its political goals with the
advancement of universal organs, especially the United
Nations.[1] While the United States was devoted to the ideals
of the United Nations, it found it necessary to engage in a
policy which encouraged incompatible regionalism in response
to the new international problems it faced. The tendency
toward incompatible regionalism was manifest in the interpretations and applications given to articles in the United Nations
Charter by the United States as well as the Latin American
governments. For instance, interpretation of Article 51, which
recognized the inherent right of self-defense in the event of an
armed attack, was expanded, in view of the conditions of
nuclear warfare, to legitimate preventive action taken against
an imminent, but not yet initiated, armed attack. Clearly, in
nuclear warfare, enormous strategic advantages would accrue
to the aggressor, hence, the crucial time for defensive action,
and, above all, for preparation, would be before an attack.
However, provisions to repel nonarmed aggressions proved
most important and raised more difficult issues about the
relationship between the United Nations and the Organization

of American States in the years after the Bogotá Conference. The United States and Latin America attempted to broaden the interpretation of paragraphs 2 and 3 of Article 52 to permit a decentralized procedure for the peaceful settlement of disputes, a procedure that would allow for the settlement of intraregional disputes in a forum in which the Soviet Union and its satellites had no influence (see table).

While "broadening" interpretations were employed to expand regional freedom from universal control in the case of Article 51 and 52 (2 and 3), a "constricting" interpretation was applied to Article 53 in order to limit the requirement of prior authorization by the Security Council for all enforcement action adopted by regional organizations. This interpretation restricted the number of instances to which the article applied by maintaining that the term "enforcement action" included only measures involving the use of armed force. The net effects of a constricting interpretation of Article 53 and a broadening interpretation of Article 51 and 52 (2 and 3) were the same: the enhancement of regional incompatibility.

The growing incompatibility of regional organizations was reflected in the historical experience of the OAS after 1948; in the pursuit of concrete political goals, member states sought to rely on incompatible procedures and interpretations, and in so doing initiated downward transfers of functions onto the regional level. This development is particularly evident in two fields of regional activity: the peaceful settlement of disputes and the adoption of enforcement action. The first issue, the settlement of disputes through regional agencies, is considered in this chapter, while the next chapter deals with the development of regional activities in the field of enforcement action.

Each instance in which the issues of the peaceful settlement of disputes and enforcement action were debated had certain characteristic political features. In the first place, each was related to the fear—whether real or imagined—of extracontinental intervention. With the possibility of Communist intervention in the Western Hemisphere, the United States assumed a more active leadership position, repeatedly emphasizing the threats to peace and security arising from indirect aggression or subversion. Any attempt of extracontinental powers, especially the Soviet Union, to materially assist or even support Latin American governments or factions in any way promoted the United States to start the inter-American machinery against aggression; in many instances when indigenous revolutionary movements were involved, this seemed to be merely "crying wolf." Nevertheless, under the influence of the United States, the OAS was used to further American interests by taking a hostile and quite active stand against governments or movements suspected to be sympathetic with Communism.

United States policy of containment of Communism had begun to focus on the Western Hemisphere in the mid-1950s when there appeared to be the possibility of establishing a Communist bridgehead in this hemisphere in Guatemala. Later, the emergence of Fidel Castro, directly challenging the power of the United States, promoted the full-scale adoption of this policy. At this point, the political and ideological fight against international Communism received greater emphasis in the Inter-American System than military cooperation to meet possible armed attacks. Furthermore, the threat of Communism revitalized the former dominant role of the United States in the Western Hemisphere, but under circumstances in which its influence was unfortunately channeled into actions that led to greater regional incompatibility.

The position of the OAS vis-à-vis the United Nations evolved in the context of changing United States-Latin American relationships; the growth of the OAS incompatibility was particularly evident in the course of disputes pitting the United States against a Latin American government—classic examples of the difficult role played by regional organizations in the struggles of powerful and weak states. In order to meet the threat of a Communist penetration in the Western Hemisphere, the United States favored a stronger incompatible

Article 52: Expanding Interpretation

1945

Paragraph 2. Members of regional organizations shall make efforts to achieve peaceful settlement of local disputes through such organizations before referring them to the UN.

Paragraph 3. The Security Council shall encourage such regional solution.

Paragraph 4. The Security Council has competence to investigate any situation [Articles 34, 35].

UNIVERSALISM COMPATIBLE REGIONALISM

PRAGMATIC PROCESS

1961

Setback to United Nations primary jurisdiction.

Yielding of jurisdictional ground to the OAS demands for exclusive competence.

Pragmatic referral of cases [through the Security Council] to the OAS.

Careful avoidance of Paragraph 4, Article 52.

Emphasis of Paragraph 3.

INCOMPATIBLE REGIONALISM

regionalist position, supporting the OAS as the sole arbiter of the regional questions. The United States preferred to deal with these cases in a forum which it could more easily dominate than the United Nations. While Latin American support for the United States' preferences varied according to the different occasions, the differences in their attitudes are better explained by the stability and popular backing of the governments in power than by the type of situation involved. For the most part, however, the Latin American countries which found themselves confronted directly or indirectly with the United States feared United States predominance and influence in the OAS and generally preferred to discuss disputes before the United Nations. The examples of disputes of this kind referred to here are the Guatemalan and Cuban complaints of 1954, 1960, and 1961. These issues were discussed both at the regional level and in the broader forum of the United Nations. In the course of the conflicts, the exclusive jurisdiction of the OAS in the peaceful settlement of disputes of its members was contested by Guatemala and Cuba, who were unwilling to submit themselves to an organization actually dominated by the United States.

While there were verbal assurances of conformity and subordination of the inter-American procedures to the United Nations, in practice, the opposite was the case. The net effect of the regional activity in the Inter-American System was a downward transfer, reducing reliance on the United Nations and deemphasizing the need for coordinating regional action with the United Nations. Without resorting to juridical modifications of the United Nations' provisions, clauses in the United Nations Charter were molded and bent, if not actually broken, without much protest. In each case, when the compatibility or incompatibility of regional mechanisms for the peaceful settlement of disputes was at issue in the OAS or the United Nations, the regional organization came out the victor.

It was clear that regional agencies acquired more autonomy in the maintenance of peace and security than had been envisaged in San Francisco; the links that had been set up between regional arrangements and the world organization in effect ended up by existing at the practical pleasure of the former.[2] Whereas in 1945, regional organizations were seen as "backstops" for the universal organization, providing a secondary line of defense in the event of a United Nations failure, after two and a half decades, the universal organization became the backstop for regional organizations, a line of defense especially for small countries unwilling to rely on regional organizations dominated by the large powers. The major part of this chapter is devoted to the problem faced by international organizations in the handling of these large nation-small nation disputes.

Nevertheless, despite the fact that this chapter concentrates on cases which were discussed but not settled by the OAS, it should not be inferred that all peaceful attempts to resolve disputes within the Inter-American System were failures. A brief analysis of the relative successes and failures of the system in the solution of specifically *intra-Latin American* disputes follows in order to provide a basis for comparison with the handling of *United States-Latin American* disputes in the same regional forum, which will be analyzed next.

THE OAS AND INTRA-LATIN AMERICAN DISPUTES

The Inter-American System served to relieve the United Nations of the burden of settling delicate *intra*-Latin American disputes. The Organization of American States intervened in almost all the disputes which occurred among Latin American states after 1948.[3] Although it was not successful in every instance and the parties were often dissatisfied with its procedures of conflict-resolution, the record of OAS performance has provided incompatible regionalists with a strong arguing point.

Latin American enthusiasm for a regional process in the peaceful settlement of disputes derived from a desire to avoid publicizing the unpleasant facts of conflicts among themselves because of a sense of brotherhood. For instance, interventions of Latin American governments in the domestic affairs of their neighbors were frequent, but were minimized by other Latin American states and condoned as insignificant pecadilloes. On the other hand, Latin Americans met cases of United States intervention with a relentless campaign to make the doctrine of nonintervention an absolute rule of law. As a matter of fact, the problem of intervention has been viewed by Latin Americans almost exclusively as a struggle in which Latin Americans were defending themselves against intervention by the United States.[4]

The causes of the repeated interventions, armed conflicts, disputes, and tensions among Latin American republics were varied. Disagreements over boundaries have existed since colonial times and have been a constant source of controversy in the region. The Spanish colonial authorities were very lax in the establishment of clearly delineated administrative borders and the resultant recourse to *uti possidetis* or de facto control over territories disputed since colonial periods has been of little help. Other types of conflicts have arisen from the efforts to prevent or promote more democratic governments in neighboring countries. The subversive activities of political exiles seeking other countries' aid to overthrow the governments from which they had fled or were expelled has been a constant problem. For instance, Costa Rica became a center where refugees from oppressive dictatorships found protection and support, while dictatorial Nicaragua, Haiti, and the Dominican Republic encouraged conservative or military plots to overthrow the governments of Costa Rica, Guatemala, or the Dominican Republic when these countries were under democratic governments. Racial antagonisms (especially between Haiti and the Dominican Republic), clandestine traffic in war surplus arms and the use of illegally obtained American military supplies, training, and missions also increased the frequency of disputes between these countries.

The conflicts were exacerbated by strong animosities between heads of states, for instance between José Figueres and Anastasio Somoza, Rafael Trujillo and Rómulo Betancourt, Juan Bosch and François Duvalier.

Nevertheless, the OAS operated most effectively in these intra-Latin American disputes, since here there was a clear commitment by the United States, as well as by the Latin American governments, to utilize the OAS machinery to the fullest extent. Other factors which have contributed to the success of the OAS in its intra-Latin American mediatory activities include its respect for the sovereignty and domestic jurisdiction of the disputing parties, and its high regard for protocol. On some occasions, where the OAS has been capable of working out only "face saving" devices, this kind of prudent involvement was, in fact, a sound approach because of sensitive political circumstances. The OAS has also made use of flexible procedures, as in the appointment of ad hoc investigating committees in every case, and the manner in which these committees carried out their tasks.[5] Finally, wide opportunity for the exercise of personal influence has been given to mediators assigned to each controversy.

The OAS used various means of dealing with these conflicts. If the situation were an emergency, cases were channeled to the Organ of Consultation, while less serious conflicts were handled by the Inter-American Peace Committee.[6] As soon as a dispute was brought to the OAS, the Organ of Consultation quickly organized the committees for observation or investigation, usually including the United States, Mexico, Argentina, and Brazil, because of the potential power and political influence the representatives of these countries brought to the committees' recommendations and negotiations.[7] In addition, inclusion of United States representatives in these committees was useful for the material support that the United States government usually contributed, such as access to some remote areas via military aircraft.

The purposes of the ad hoc committees appointed by the Organ of Consultation or the OAS Council have been fact finding, as in the case of Costa Rica-Nicaragua dispute (1948-1949), or mediation, as in the 1949 conflict between Haiti and the Dominican Republic. Competent and respected diplomats have been appointed to these committees.[8] In general, it may be said that the OAS presence had a calming effect in troubled areas.

The solutions the OAS has arrived at for Latin American disputes have been equally manifold.[9] They have ranged from the simple reinforcement of principles of peace, solidarity, nonintervention, and existing treaties (for instance in 1949-1950 when there were several attempts to overthrow the government of the Dominican Republic) to the achievement of ceasefire agreements (as in the case of Honduras and Nicaragua in 1957). In other instances, the OAS established new special committees to investigate and mediate specific controversies when the Organ of Consultation had stopped considering the case.[10] The OAS also established a collective naval patrol under its direction during the Panamanian dispute of 1959. In other instance the OAS sought long-term solutions and, hence, recommended referral of a serious controversy to universal organs. However, this happened only in 1957, when the OAS recommended that the Honduran and Nicaraguan territorial dispute be referred to the International Court of Justice. The OAS also, on a rare occasion, assumed the technical job of boundary fixing and the supervision of population transfers. (Such a role was assumed by the Inter-American Peace Committee in 1960 and 1961 to carry out the arbitral decision of the International Court of Justice which put an end to the 1957 territorial dispute between Honduras and Nicaragua.)

But there have also been several negative aspects of OAS performance during the past twenty-five years. For instance, in some cases, OAS interventions, by essentially leaving a situation unchanged, have only exacerbated the conflict. The recurrent outbursts of tensions between certain countries, for instance Costa Rica and Nicaragua, Haiti and the Dominican Republic, have provided evidence that the OAS has focused on the superficial aspects of these conflicts, leaving the central issues unsolved. In other cases, reluctance to impinge upon the domestic jurisdiction of the states involved has, in effect, channeled action toward the reestablishment of the status quo.

The OAS has also been hesitant to name a particular country or countries delinquent when they have been found guilty of intervention or aggression. With the exception of the case of the Dominican Republic in 1961, which will be analyzed later, and recent Cuban condemnations, in the majority of instances, the OAS has not gone beyond verbal admonitions in politely worded resolutions (as, for instance, in the case of the Dominican Republic in 1950, when Haiti, Cuba, and Guatemala were found guilty of conspiring against the Dominican Republic). Another OAS failure has been its inability to solve disputes like the Peru-Ecuador 1942 border dispute, which probably stems from a fear of encouraging other treaty revisions. Since 1942, when the Protocol seeking to end this dispute was signed in Rio and later ratified by both countries, Ecuador has been contesting the treaty's content, arguing mainly that it was imposed by military occupation. The OAS has been unwilling to give any support to Ecuador's claims, since this might initiate a series of similar claims among many Latin American countries who are not very satisfied with the treaties that have delineated their borders. Similarly, the OAS has been unable to implement peace solutions in the Lauca River dispute between Chile and Bolivia. The OAS Council has not accepted Bolivian claims that Chile had committed aggression by diverting waters of the Lauca River for Chilean irrigation projects. Offended by what it considered lack of OAS interest, Bolivia withdrew from the OAS and returned only in January, 1965, when a

new government gained power. The new regime has not pressed this issue as much as the previous Bolivian government
had.

The parties to all these disputes did not appeal to the
United Nations for assistance,[11] and members of the OAS or
the United Nations never questioned the adequacy or legitimacy of the OAS in the handling of these disputes. The
Secretary General of the United Nations was informed of the
OAS's activities in compliance with Article 54 of the United
Nations Charter. In most cases, however, such communication
with the United Nations was ex post facto, since documents
describing OAS action were sent to the United Nations several
days after such action had been initiated.

In its efforts to devise workable methods for the peaceful
settlement of disputes between Latin American countries, the
OAS has gained undue strength and an exaggerated prestige
that has been used as a general argument to oppose the
intervention of the United Nations in the course of other
conflicts. In fact, on the basis of OAS success in handling
intra-Latin American conflicts, incompatible regionalists also
justify OAS involvement in the settlement of disputes between the United States and other Latin American states.

The precedent of relying on regional solutions to Latin
American conflicts has helped to cut off Latin American
recourse to the United Nations whenever a dispute involved
the United States as well. Clearly it has been in the United
States' interest to laud the efficiency of the OAS in intra-
Latin American disputes, in order to justify its exclusive
involvement in cases of United States-Latin American controversy. Yet, in these instances, the disproportionate distribution of power among the parties has made the OAS incapable
of using the same flexible diplomatic techniques it has developed in dealing with strictly Latin American disputes. The
following section focuses on several disputes between the
United States and the Latin American republics in which the

latter have seriously contested the OAS's exclusive competence to deal with the conflict and the former has vigorously
supported it.

GUATEMALA (1954)

In the Guatemalan case of 1954, the question of Communist extracontinental intervention was first raised in the Inter-
American System. The United States believed that the regime
of Jacobo Arbenz Guzmán, in power since 1950, was dominated by Communists. The United States was led to this belief
because, among other things, the government of Guatemala
had adopted policies of agrarian reform and nationalization
which had taken property away from several foreign interests.[12] Since United States foreign policy had, under the
influence of Secretary of State John Foster Dulles, returned
to a policy of indiscriminate protection of United States
private investments abroad, it obviously supported the exaggerated claims made by the American companies whose interests were affected by Guatemalan expropriatory policies. In
addition, a new political alignment of leftist forces siding with
Arbenz emerged, whose example threatened the security of
neighboring dictatorial regimes in Nicaragua, Honduras, and El
Salvador. It was clearly disturbing for United States foreign
policy, premised on the fear of Communist intervention
throughout the world, to tolerate the existence in the Western
Hemisphere of a government coalition of strong leftist forces,
supposedly endorsed by the Communists within and outside
of Guatemala, even though such a government had been duly
elected through constitutional means.

As a counterweight to what seemed an unfavorable political
and military situation,[13] the United States did not hesitate to
give political, economic, and military support to the Guatemalan exiles who used Honduras and Nicaragua as spring-
boards for regaining political control in Guatemala. When the
conflict began to sharpen as preparation for an invasion of

Guatemala from Nicaragua and Honduras was under way, Nicaragua broke off diplomatic relations with Guatemala, and Honduras rejected a Guatemalan proposal to conclude a non-aggression treaty; at the same time the United States concluded agreements for military assistance with Honduras and began to provide both Honduras and Nicaragua with arms and training.

As early as April 23, 1953, Guatemala complained to the Security Council about Honduras's and Nicaragua's open hostility. On this occasion, however, the complaint was not discussed since no specific accusation had been filed and no demand had been made for a specific consideration of the case in the Security Council. It had only been brought to the Council's attention.[14] On June 17, 1954, insurgent forces, composed mainly of Guatemalan exiles but with some Nicaraguans and Hondurans, began to cross the frontier from Honduras into Guatemala, under the command of Colonel Carlos Castillo Armas, an obscure military leader who headed the Guatemalan exile group. Two days later, as the situation became more dangerous and greater numbers of people were killed in the attacks of towns along the border, Guatemala attempted to gain a reconsideration of the matter in the Security Council, and immediate action against what it considered an armed attack.[15]

At the same time, Guatemala initiated proceedings in the OAS, demanding the intervention of the Inter-American Peace Committee. Up until that time, Guatemala had abstained from calling upon the OAS for several reasons. (1) It had not ratified the constitutional documents of the OAS—the Rio Treaty and the OAS Charter—and thus they were not binding on her. (2) It feared that the United States might use the OAS as a forum in which to accuse Guatemala of being Communist, thus promoting the overthrow of the Arbenz regime. (3) A majority of the dictatorships and military regimes in Latin America were fearful of the examples of revolutionary change set in Guatemala, such as the land reform measures, and thus Guatemala feared these regimes would automatically oppose it. (4) The OAS expressed hostility to Guatemala shortly before this time; at the Tenth Inter-American Conference, in Caracas, March, 1954, the United States expressed its concern over diplomatic and commercial links between Guatemala and Communist-bloc countries. The United States rallied Latin America against what it saw as the challenge of international Communism, leading to the famous Caracas resolution.

> *The domination or control of the political institutions of any American State by the international Communist movement, extending to this Hemisphere the political system of an extracontinental power, would constitute a threat to the sovereignty and political independence of the American States, endangering the peace of America, and would call for a Meeting of Consultation to consider the adoption of appropriate action in accordance with existing treaties.*

At the Security Council meeting scheduled immediately thereafter on Sunday, March 20, Guatemala's main argument rested on Articles 33, 35, and 39 and the right to present a complaint to the United Nations. The Guatemalan representatives interpreted the case as an act of aggression rather than an internal dispute and called upon the Security Council to halt Honduras's and Nicaragua's illegal action in support of Guatemalan mercenaries. They also requested the Security Council to send an observation committee to investigate the charges.

The United States, Honduras, Nicaragua, Colombia, and Brazil (the last two were the Latin American representatives in the Security Council), defined the disturbance as civil strife, a revolt of Guatemalans against Guatemalans, and proposed that the OAS deal with the matter since, in their view, the principles laid down in paragraphs 2 and 3 of Article 52, which allowed for a regional treatment of the complaint, could not be renounced by Guatemala.[16] Brazil and Colombia submitted a resolution which stated:

The Security Council . . . , Noting that the Government of Guatemala has dispatched a similar communication to the Inter-American Peace Committee, an agency of the Organization of American States; . . . [and] Conscious of the availability of Inter-American machinery which can deal effectively with problems concerning the maintenance of peace and security in the Americas; . . . Refers the complaint of the Government of Guatemala to the Organization of American States for urgent consideration; . . . [17]

France added a paragraph which called upon United Nations members to abstain from rendering assistance to any action likely to cause bloodshed.

Soviet Ambassador Tsarapkin was the only Security Council member who defended the Guatemalan arguments. He tried to alter the resolution presented by Brazil and Colombia in order to prevent giving priority to the OAS over the Security Council in the handling of this matter. Such an action, he felt, would clearly contradict Article 36 of the charter. In turn, the Soviet delegate suggested a resolution, the terms of which were rather similar to the French addition to the Brazilian-Colombian draft.

The rest of the permanent members of the Security Council, as well as nonpermanent members, Denmark, Lebanon, New Zealand, and Turkey, backed the draft resolution sponsored by Colombia and Brazil. However, it failed to be adopted because of the Soviet Union's veto which effectively blocked the trend toward regional incompatibility at this time. Later, France's proposal, reintroduced as a separate resolution, was unanimously accepted.

Except for some furtive legal arguments concerning paragraphs 2 and 3 of Article 52, made especially by the United States, Colombia, and Brazil, the Security Council essentially avoided directly confronting the issue of regional incompatibility in the peaceful settlement of local disputes by using practical, nonlegal arguments to justify the transfer of jurisdiction of the case to the OAS.[18] In spite of the Soviet veto, incompatible regionalism had scored a substantial pragmatic victory; the OAS was left with de facto freedom to carry on its regional efforts to solve the dispute even in the face of Guatemala's rejection of its exclusive competence. Moreover, all the claims of victory by the universalist, who maintained the Security Council had asserted its jurisdiction over the matter in passing the French resolution, appeared to be rather weak in the light of the effective independence the regionalists had gained. The arguments that had been used to defend the OAS's jurisdiction in this instance—the allegedly strong regional tradition, the availability and efficacy of the Inter-American System—had been used frequently by the United States and the Latin American countries in several contexts and were, for the most part, supported by other Security Council members.

United States Ambassador Henry Cabot Lodge went even further than simply acknowledging the net effect the Security Council's action would have in practice; his interpretation of the Council's move in effect rejected the universal or compatible regional assumptions which several of the Council members had taken for granted when voting. (1) He accused the Soviet Union of having designs in the Western Hemisphere and of intervening in the affairs of the continent by endorsing the Guatemalan complaint. He even warned the Soviet Union "to stay out of this Hemisphere and do not try to start your plans and your conspiracies over here." (2) He questioned the good faith of the Guatemalan request for Security Council jurisdiction, suggesting that it was basically improper for that country to bring the case to the United Nations. (3) He interpreted the part of the resolution vetoed in the Security Council as being in effect a recognition of OAS jurisdiction, which all the Council members, except the Soviet Union, had acknowledged. These views were introduced later when the Security Council discussed the Guatemalan complaint for the second time.

Guatemala felt that the Security Council action had left things rather vague, especially concerning Guatemala's preference for United Nations jurisdiction over the case. Despite the Soviet veto and the overall nature of the discussion in the Security Council, Guatemala felt that in actuality the influence of incompatible regionalists was such that the Security Council would probably not deal with the complaint again until the OAS had first submitted a report. In an effort to forestall this delay, Guatemala withdrew the case from the OAS on June 21, 1954, and declined to allow the Inter-American Peace Committee to concern itself with the situation, in order that the involvement of this OAS committee not be taken as a pretext for Security Council inaction. In so doing, it hoped to stimulate general international political pressure in favor of the view that the incident presented a case of "aggression" (which only the Security Council could handle under Article 33) and to induce Security Council action. This maneuver was not successful, however, because as soon as Guatemala withdrew the case from the OAS, Nicaragua and Honduras, who up to this point had not demanded any OAS action, requested the Inter-American Peace Committee to continue its investigation.[19] As a result of these efforts to cancel OAS action, and the reintroduction of the case into the OAS by Nicaragua and Honduras, the arrival of the OAS Inter-American Peace Committee in Guatemala was dangerously delayed.

As hostilities intensified, Guatemala, once having removed the case from OAS jurisdiction, thought its commitment to follow OAS procedures had been terminated. The Guatemalan delegate, with fresh evidence of aggression, insisted on new Security Council action, declaring that the Security Council resolution of June 19 had not been observed and requesting that the Security Council exert its authority in order to halt the hostile actions of Honduras and Nicaragua. The Guatemalan petition also reiterated its opposition to referral of the question to the OAS, using the legal support of paragraph 4 of Article 52, Article 103, as well as Articles 34, 35, and 39. Guatemala expected that its urgent insistence upon another Security Council meeting would call attention to the ineffectiveness of the June 20 resolution and would gain support for the adoption of adequate measures.

Ambassador Henry Cabot Lodge, then acting president of the Security Council (and thus the only one empowered to convoke it), was not eager to respond to Guatemala's latest request. Indeed, he did not convoke the Security Council until June 24, after four days of urgent Guatemalan appeals and after the Soviet delegate demanded it.[20] The Security Council finally met on June 25. In spite of the fact that the whole matter was formally dealt with only in the stage preliminary to its being placed on the agenda, the Council became fully engaged in discussion of the case. Heated debate took place between Ambassadors Lodge and Tsarapkin, the latter accusing the former of delaying tactics to prevent the Security Council from discussing the question. Because the agenda had not been approved, the Guatemalan delegate could not participate in the discussion, and its point of view was therefore tacitly conveyed in the Soviet's defense of its arguments.

At this meeting, only the United States used the legal argument that paragraph 2 of Article 52 justified the primary jurisdiction of the OAS and the duty of OAS members to use OAS resources. Lodge even termed Guatemala's request for United Nations jurisdiction an effort to create international anarchy rather than international order. He considered this case the first real test of the formula of Articles 51 and 52, and additionally invoked Article 20 of the OAS Charter (favoring regional discussions of a case before referring it to the United Nations) to oppose consideration by the Security Council of the Guatemalan case. He harshly stated, "Either Guatemala is a member of the Organization of American States and therefore bound by Article 52, paragraph 2 or else it is guilty of duplicity to such an extent that it cannot come before the Security Council with clean hands."[21]

Denmark, Lebanon, and New Zealand joined the Soviet Union in voting to place the Guatemalan complaint on the agenda, while Brazil, Colombia, China, Turkey, and the United States opposed it. (Britain and France abstained.) The motion thus failed. With this failure, the Soviet Union warned that a dangerous campaign on the part of regionalists to undermine United Nations jurisdiction in the maintenance of peace and security had begun. He added, "It is obvious that if the United Nations is to be dealt such serious blows and if entire continents are to be withdrawn from its jurisdiction, the Organization will be reduced to nothing."[22]

But, despite the success of the action endorsed by the United States preventing the adoption of the agenda, the other Security Council members did not share the United States' interpretation of those events. Many continued to favor some degree of Security Council universal jurisdiction. Some observers even claimed that the initial decision itself, to place the matter on the agenda of the Security Council on June 20, implied the jurisdiction of this body over the matter.[23]

Another issue left equally vague in the two occasions during which the Security Council dealt with the Guatemalan requests was the debate between the United States, Brazil, and Colombia, who invoked articles in Chapter VII to support their position and the Soviet Union, who found legal justification in Chapters VI and VII.[24] Although the Security Council made no effort to clearly assert the primary responsibility of the United Nations in the maintenance of peace and security, by passing a resolution vaguely supporting universal priority, the OAS was still not in a position to assert, even by default, a legally exclusive jurisdiction over intraregional disputes, or to question the right of countries in the Western Hemisphere to present their complaints in the United Nations. However, it was in the interest of the United States and several other

Latin American states to interpret the support given to the Brazil-Colombia draft resolution by all the Security Council members as effectively signifying that the OAS had exclusive jurisdiction. Moreover, these countries felt that even the vetoing of the resolution did not inhibit OAS exclusive concern with the case.[25] This interpretation was very dangerous, not only because it belittled the importance of the Soviet veto, but also because it overlooked the fact that an act of aggression had, in fact, been committed with which, according to the United Nations Charter, the Security Council alone could deal.

Meanwhile the OAS continued to work on the matter. On June 26, in an obvious attempt to emphasize OAS jurisdiction over the case even more clearly, the United States and nine Latin American countries—Brazil, Cuba, Costa Rica, the Dominican Republic, Haiti, Honduras, Panama, and Peru—asked for a Meeting of Consultation to consider the charge that Guatemalan Communism constituted a threat to hemispheric peace. The request was accepted by the OAS Council and the meeting was scheduled for July 7 at Rio. Obviously the goals for which this meeting was convoked were completely divorced from any effort to settle the particular controversy at hand. Such a meeting sought more to condemn Guatemala for its ties with the Communist bloc than to give assistance to it or to condemn the invasion. However, it is interesting to note that there were some Latin American states, especially Mexico and Argentina, who were unwilling to join this demonstration of OAS anti-Communist solidarity at such a critical moment.

The unfavorable response of the OAS to Guatemalan claims occurred at the very time when Guatemala in effect had no other recourse for the solution of the dispute than a regional mechanism. After the Security Council's failure to include the Guatemalan complaint on its agenda, Guatemala, trying to make the best of this diplomatic disaster at the United Nations, reported to the OAS that it did accept the visit of the Inter-American Peace Committee. However, before this committee arrived in Guatemala, on June 29, the Arbenz government fell and the next day the Meeting of Consultation was canceled.

It is interesting to speculate what the outcome of the OAS action would have been had Guatemala not withdrawn its case from the OAS on June 21 and had the Inter-American Peace Committee been sent earlier. It is likely that the imminent arrival of OAS observers in Guatemala, after they had finally been granted permission on June 26, might have hastened the attack of Castillo Armas and the downfall of the Arbenz government. That there was a great deal of foreign activity was supported by the subsequent refusal by the military junta which assumed control of Guatemala to give sufficient guarantees of personal safety to the observers of the Inter-American Peace Committee, which by that time had reached Mexico City, to continue their trip to Guatemala.[26]

From the time the Security Council failed to assume a universal stand on June 20, in accordance with the United Nations Charter, to the actual downfall of Arbenz, on June 29, the OAS remained the sole arbiter of the affair; the lack of Security Council action had effectively created a vacuum into which the OAS could step. Soon, other Latin American governments, in addition to Mexico and Argentina, began to recognize the dangers of exclusive OAS jurisdiction. This in fact had been the lesson of the Guatemalan affair: the Latin American states would be forced to present all complaints they may have with the United States to the OAS rather than to the United Nations. Behind the legal arguments the United States used to prevent discussion of the Guatemalan case in the United Nations was the clear assertion that a potential threat, international Communism, existed in the Hemisphere. But in maintaining this position the United States lost considerable prestige in the eyes of many Latin American countries who felt that, despite the general desirability of a regional authority, the actual situation suggested a considerable degree of United States intervention always an unpleasant subject. Some Latin Americans even voiced serious criticisms during the following session of the General Assembly. For example, the delegate of Ecuador stated in the General Assembly on October 1, 1954:

> We are members and staunch supporters of the Organization of American States, but we cannot by any means agree that it has exclusive jurisdiction in a dispute such as the one I have just mentioned. . . . We hope that there will be no more such negative decisions by the Council, lest the prestige of the Organization suffer and one of the fundamental objects of the Charter—protection against attack—become illusory or come too late.[27]

Similarly, the delegate of Uruguay stated on September 29, 1954 that his government considered that:

> The principles of the regional system and the safeguards which it offers cannot be invoked in order to prevent States from having direct and immediate access to the jurisdiction of the United Nations or to deprive them, no matter how temporarily, of the protection of the agencies of the world community. The legal protection afforded by both systems should be combined, never substituted for one another. . . . The delegation of Uruguay considers that any protest to the United Nations against aggression is entitled at least to a hearing.[28]

The representative of Argentina, also, stated in the General Assembly, on October 4, 1954:

> The existence of regional agreements does not mean that they or the agencies created under them take precedence over the United Nations, or that the United Nations should refrain from discussing or endeavoring to settle problems submitted to it by a government representing a Member State. . . . To hold that the regional organization has exclusive jurisdiction would in our view lead to the absurd position that a Member State of the United Nations which was a party to a regional agreement would be at a disadvantage as compared to other states which for some reasons were not members of regional agencies. We cannot accept a legal argument that

would involve a discriminatory situation in regard to the United Nations Charter, and which would make the security of a country depend on the special political characteristics and circumstances of a regional arrangement. The Argentine Republic cannot accept a view that might deprive it of the right, as a Member of the United Nations, to request the United Nations to consider or settle any international problem affecting it.[29]

While the Secretary General of the United Nations was realistic enough to recognize he could not stem the tide toward collective defense pacts, he saw the need to strike the proper balance between universal and regional organizations and he tried to remind members where their primary loyalties should lie. In his *Annual Report* he stated:

The importance of regional arrangements in the maintenance of peace is fully recognized in the Charter and the appropriate use of such arrangements is encouraged. But in those cases where resort to such arrangements is chosen in the first instance, that choice should not be permitted to cast any doubt on the ultimate responsibility of the United Nations. Similarly, a policy giving full scope to the proper role of regional agencies can and should at the same time fully preserve the right of a Member nation to a hearing under the Charter.[30]

CUBA I (1960)

Six years later a situation similar to the Guatemalan one began to develop in Cuba. After the fall of the dictator Fulgencio Batista, and the inauguration of Fidel Castro's regime in 1959, relations between Cuba and the United States rapidly deteriorated. On July 6, 1960, the United States reduced the Cuban sugar quota and the Cuban government retaliated with a series of expropriations and nationalizations, a substantial proportion of which involved properties owned by United States companies and individuals. Trial and executions of Cuban war criminals had aroused widespread protests, especially in the United States. Castro began to rule by decree since January, 1959, and had postponed elections. The Eisenhower administration accused Cuba of transforming itself into an instrument of Communist intervention in the Western Hemisphere while Cuba accused the United States of aggression by allowing incursions into Cuban airspace from United States territory.

On July 11, 1960, Cuba complained to the Security Council about what it considered United States intervention in Cuban domestic affairs; it denounced the United States as being responsible for threats and such aggressive acts as protecting war criminals and counterrevolutionary elements. Cuba, in order to prevent the transferral of the complaint to the OAS, invoked, primarily, paragraph 4 of Article 52 and Article 103 of the United Nations Charter, when requesting the Security Council meeting.[31]

The United States denied Cuban charges of intervention in a letter sent to the Security Council president on July 15, and argued that the Inter-American Peace Committee had been investigating Caribbean tensions for the past year. The committee's task to explore the problem of dictatorships and democracies in the Caribbean had been outlined at the Fifth Meeting of Consultation, held in Santiago, Chile, in August, 1959. It is likely that this reference to the activities of the Inter-American Peace Committee was introduced in order to give evidence of the important role the OAS was already playing; it was an attempt on the part of the United States to counteract Cuban efforts to restrict discussion of the complaint to the United Nations and completely ignore the OAS. The United States' contention, however, that the matter was in the process of being considered by this committee, was somehow irrelevant to the main Cuban argument; the task of the Inter-American Peace Committee—to investigate tension in the Caribbean due to the activities of political exiles continually inciting uprisings against the local dictators—had, in fact, little to do with Cuba's charge of United States intervention.

That this was the case, was later shown by the actions of some OAS members who moved quickly to initiate a regional action that would be directly related to the charges Cuba had brought before the Security Council. Two days after Cuba sent the letter requesting consideration of its case to the Security Council (July 13), Peru asked for a new Meeting of Consultation, one that would effectively affirm OAS jurisdiction over the matter, in order to consider "continental solidarity and the defense of the regional system and American democratic principles against possible threats. "Indeed, developments in the United Nations seemed to have triggered OAS action. On the same day (July 18) that the Security Council began to discuss the Cuban complaint, the OAS Council approved the Peruvian resolution and scheduled the date of its meeting on Cuba for August 22.[32]

From a political point of view, the calling of this Meeting of Consultation was urgently required by the United States in order to maintain its position in the OAS and in the United Nations. On the one hand, the United States needed OAS support against Castro to prevent the establishment of a Communist regime in the Western Hemisphere; the Soviet Prime Minister had even gone so far as to offer military support to the Cuban government if the island was invaded. At the same time, the United States also needed strong OAS backing to block consideration of the Cuban complaint by the Security Council.

At the meetings of the Security Council on July 18 and 19, Cuba declared that she did not wish to initiate any action in the OAS, fearing United States maneuverings as in the Guatemalan case. Furthermore, Cuba considered the first parts of Article 52 of the United Nations Charter optional and thus, did not feel compelled to approach the OAS. On the other hand, the United States relied heavily on the Guatemalan case to assert OAS jurisdiction and requested that the Security Council drop the matter. United States views were echoed by Argentina and Ecuador, who sponsored a resolution containing essentially pragmatic arguments in favor of OAS competence. This document asked the Security Council to state its concern for the situation, but to note as well the fact that the OAS was already investigating the matter. It requested that the Council thus suspend consideration of the case until a report from the OAS could be submitted. In addition, it invited OAS members to promote the peaceful settlement of the case and admonished United Nations members to avoid increasing tensions between Cuba and the United States.[33]

The Argentina-Ecuador resolution was adopted by the Security Council with Poland and the Soviet Union abstaining. It is probable that the Soviet Union did not veto this resolution, as it had in the case of Guatemala, because it felt that the danger to the Cuban government was not as imminent as had been the threat to Guatemala in 1954. Furthermore, in the course of the debates at the Security Council it was clear that only Britain, France, and the United States adopted the incompatible regionalist position and asserted Cuba's legal obligation to use OAS procedures first. The other Security Council members who supported the draft resolution based their actions on an essentially universal interpretation, claiming that the resolution did not preclude the OAS members' right to access to the United Nations if they were dissatisfied with the regional treatment. Even Argentina and Ecuador, drafters of the resolution, acknowledged such interpretation. The votes of the remaining Council members, Italy, Ceylon, Tunisia, and China, were, in varying degrees, based on the practical consideration that since the OAS was already discussing the case, the regional process should be allowed to continue without interference from the United Nations.[34]

The Soviet Union was unsuccessful in passing any of the amendments to the resolution which would have replaced all references to the OAS with references to the UN. The Soviet Union rejected both British, French, and United States legal views as well as the strictly pragmatic views of the rest of the Security Council members. Soviet representative Sobolev insisted that the resolution was a political evasion of the responsibility of the Security Council to handle Cuban charges. Moreover, he complained that the Cuban complaint was sent to the OAS, whose members were generally unfavorably disposed to Cuba and were more likely to condemn it at the outset than to hear its charges against the United States.

The Guatemalan case was in effect repeated. While those Security Council members who advocated a universalist stand felt that the United Nations' primary jurisdiction and the right of members to have recourse to the United Nations had not been impaired, it was clear, as in the Guatemalan case, that in actual practice, the Cuban complaint was being handled exclusively by the OAS, in keeping with the demands of incompatible regionalists. But it was not clear what position the Council as a whole had taken on the general right of the United Nations' members to have any recourse to the United Nations. While the United States, Great Britain, and, to some extent, the Latin American representatives, claimed that the resolution implied the legal commitment of members of regional organizations to exhaust regional channels before bringing their cases to the United Nations' organs, the rest of the Security Council members failed to endorse this: the remaining members did not accept a measure that would enhance regional incompatibility by precluding Security Council discussion of a complaint before regional steps had been taken. This time, however, incompatible regionalists gained substantially more than in the Guatemalan affair; here the Security Council had actually passed a resolution referring the case to the OAS. In 1954 incompatible regionalists had interpreted a draft resolution vetoed by the Soviet Union as a practical gain because of the support given to it by the rest of the Security Council members. In 1960 incompatible regionalists had before them a concrete statement of the Security Council asserting that the OAS was to deal with the complaint.

At the Seventh Meeting of Consultation, which was designed to continue the activities of the Security Council in the Cuban case after the latter adjourned, the OAS actually set aside the Cuban charges. The Seventh Meeting's agenda included none of the following Cuban complaints against the United States: reduction of the sugar quota, political and military support to Cuban exiles, clandestine flights originating in United States territory, and propaganda campaigns against Cuba. The agenda only included a Peruvian request to consider "continental solidarity and the defense of the regional system and American democratic principles against possible threats." The Declaration of San Jose, issued at this meeting, indirectly condemned Cuba's acceptance of extra-continental military assistance, despite the fact that the United States and a minority of Latin Americans desired a stronger condemnation.

To some observers, the mild results of this meeting, contrary to the United States expectations of a harsher condemnation of Castro's Communist affiliations by all the OAS members, contained an element of retributive justice referring back to something that had occurred in 1954. At Caracas, during the Tenth Inter-American Conference, a majority of Latin Americans went along with the United States in accepting an anti-Communist resolution, expecting to get additional economic aid in return, only to be let down when economic problems were discussed later. At San Jose, Costa Rica, in 1960, the United States committed itself first to a program of economic assistance for the development of the area which included 600 million dollars, only to find that a resolution indirectly condemning Cuba was the best it could obtain.[35]

Cuba resented both having been treated in the OAS as a defendent and the subtle condemnation which it received. At the fifteenth General Assembly session, Fidel Castro emphasized that Cuba's pessimistic expectations of the OAS had been confirmed.[36] When the OAS Council later sent a copy of the final act of the Seventh Meeting of Consultation to the

Security Council, Cuba also complained that inaction on the part of the Security Council had led to these disappointing results on the part of the OAS.[37]

CUBA II (1961)

Cuba was dissatisfied with the treatment received at the OAS's Seventh Meeting of Consultation. Since relations between Cuba and the United States continued to deteriorate, motives for insisting on a renewed consideration of its problems by the United Nations were not difficult to find. (Cuban charges of economic aggression and United States counter-charges of confiscation of property culminated on October 19, 1960, in a United States ban on exports to Cuba. Five days later, as a reaction to the embargo, Cuba nationalized all the important remaining American-owned properties. Meanwhile, Cuba had entered into a series of trade and diplomatic agreements with the Soviet Union and other Communist countries.) Finally, when Cuba appealed again to the United Nations in October, 1960, it followed another strategy by taking its complaints to the General Assembly instead of the Security Council. Cuba reiterated its earlier accusation of OAS ineffectiveness, its right to decide where to submit its complaints, and, in addition, charged that the United States planned to promote the invasion of the island.

Although it was not difficult to introduce the complaint in the agenda, Cuba suffered its first setback when the case was referred to the First Committee of the General Assembly. Referring the case to the First Committee (which Cuba opposed and fought against to no avail) rather than to the Plenary Assembly was significant because: (1) in the First Committee it would be treated routinely whereas in the Plenary Assembly it would have been considered immediately as matter deserving urgent consideration; (2) the agenda of the First Committee was overburdened with other important matters and the Cuban complaint was placed at the bottom of the list having to wait several months to be considered (until April 15, 1961);[38] (3) while imminence of the invasion preparations revealed in the United States and Guatemala required immediate measures by the United Nations, any decision of the First Committee would still have to be approved by the Plenary Assembly in order to be valid.

Since the door of the General Assembly was temporarily closed, Cuba decided to try her luck in the Security Council. Cuba invoked Articles 24 (1), 31, 32, 34, 35 (1), 52 (4), and 103 of the United Nations Charter as well as Article 102 of the OAS Charter in trying to get its complaint included in the agenda of the Security Council. On December 31, 1960, and again on January 3, 1961, Cuba insisted that this was an international dispute and implored the Security Council not to evade its responsibilities as it had done in July of the previous year.[39] The Council finally agreed to discuss the Cuban complaint on January 4, 1961.

Once again an essentially incompatible regionalist position was defended by some of the Security Council members. The United States, for instance, reaffirmed its previous stand, asserting OAS jurisdiction and insisted that Cuba work through the OAS Ad Hoc Committee of Good Offices which had been established at the Seventh Meeting of Consultation.[40] Liberia, Turkey, and the United Arab Republic declared the Cuban charges unfounded, and neither Britain nor France supported Cuba in her second appeal to the Security Council. The British delegate sided with the United States' claim that Cuba had no right to call upon the Council before it had sought a regional solution to its problems.

Most unusual was the posture of Chile and Ecuador, the Latin American representatives to the Security Council, who abandoned the traditional incompatible regionalist line which had been defended by their Latin American colleagues on previous occasions, such as when Guatemalan and Cuban charges were brought before the Security Council. In a draft resolution, Chile and Ecuador endorsed the principle of nonintervention and urged peaceful settlement of the conflict, without mentioning the OAS. Instead, their resolution contained a fervent appeal to the governments of the United States and Cuba to seek a solution through the peaceful means provided by the United Nations, and called upon all governments to refrain from actions which would aggravate existing tensions. However, a lack of support forced Chile and Ecuador to withdraw the resolution. The Security Council then ended its consideration of the matter and Cuba's complaints were left hinging solely on the pending action of the General Assembly's First Committee.

By the time the First Committee considered the Cuban complaint on April 15, the political environment had changed drastically. The committee was compelled to consider not only the Cuban charges of October, 1960, concerning a planned invasion, but the actual Bay of Pigs invasion, which was taking place that very day. After Cuba reported the details of the invasion, the United States Ambassador, Adlai E. Stevenson, denied the charges and subsequently became the center of Soviet attacks. It is now well known that until the disaster unfolded he knew nothing of the invasion plans, but as a result of his public misstatement of the facts, both he and his government were greatly humiliated.[41]

Intense debate in the First Committee was accompanied by the presentation of a number of resolutions which differed substantially in content and support. The Soviet Union and Rumania separately proposed two draft resolutions strongly condemning the United States and demanding cessation of all aggressive activities. In reality, however, the debate centered around two resolutions, one submitted by Mexico and the other by Argentina, Chile, Colombia, Panama, Uruguay, and Venezuela, also endorsed by the United States. Mexico's resolution was similar to the Russian and Romanian resolutions in its condemnation of the United States, but it was drafted in milder terms. Mexico stresssed the principle of nonintervention, the obligation of United Nations members to refrain from promoting civil strife in other states, and appealed to all states to insure that their territories and resources were not used to promote civil war in Cuba.[42] But most important, Mexico made no reference to the OAS.

This omission was regarded as unacceptable by the United States and the other Latin American champions of the OAS, who in turn drew up a fourth draft resolution which praised recourse to the Inter-American System in the peaceful settlement of disputes. The Latin American-United States resolution characterized the situation as a typical American dispute, and declared the OAS the proper organization to solve the problem. It also cited the July 19, 1960, resolution of the Security Council (which had referred the first Cuban complaint to the OAS) in order to strengthen its incompatible regionalist arguments; invoking such a precedent was useful because it added a legal argument for OAS exclusive jurisdiction. In addition, practical arguments about the preferability of using OAS organs were widely cited. Later, Sudanese and Nigerian amendments deleted some parts of this draft, which somewhat weakened the emphasis on the OAS, without materially altering the general thrust of the resolution. These deletions were possible at this particular time because the United States "was too much in the defensive to lead the battle" as it had in the past.[43] Even the most enthusiastic champions of the OAS among the Latin American delegates dared not question the right of Cuba to appeal directly to the Security Council or the General Assembly.

As a result, the outcome of the work of the First Committee was ambiguous. The Soviet Union and Romania withdrew their drafts to support the Mexican one. The draft resolution cosponsored by seven Latin American countries and endorsed by the United States, as amended by Nigeria and Sudan, was dealt with first and adopted, along with the Mexican resolution, in separate votings which required only simple majorities. Despite the fact that both draft resolutions were adopted, the voting of these two documents split traditional

Latin American alignments and indicated that at least some among the Latin Americans began to depart from their uniformly incompatible posture. For instance, Mexico, Cuba, and the Soviet Union bloc voted against the Latin American-sponsored resolution, while Ecuador and the Dominican Republic abstained. The Mexican draft resolution gained the votes of Bolivia, Brazil, Chile, Cuba, and Ecuador. The Dominican Republic abstained and Haiti did not take part in the voting. At the plenary session of the General Assembly only the resolution sponsored by seven Latin Americans received the necessary two-thirds endorsement, with Cuba and Mexico voting against it. However, after the Nigerian and Sudanese amendments, this resolution did little more than exhort all members to take peaceful action to remove existing tensions and did not specifically grant any special jurisdictional right to the OAS. The text of the resolution adopted in the plenary session reads:

> *The General Assembly, ... Having read the statement made by the Minister of Foreign Affairs of Cuba, the Representative of the United States of America and other representatives, ... Deeply concerned over the situation disclosed therein which is disturbing world public opinion and the continuation of which could endanger world peace, ... Recalling the last two paragraphs of the Resolution adopted by the Security Council on 19 July 1960 and the peaceful means of settlement established at the Seventh Meeting of Consultation of Foreign Ministers of the American Republics, ... Considering that the State members of the United Nations are under an obligation to settle their disputes by negotiation and other peaceful means in such manner that international peace and security, and justice, are not endangered,*
>
> *(1) Exhorts all member States to lend their assistance with a view to achieving a settlement by peaceful means in accordance with the Purposes and Principles of the United Nations Charter and to report to the United Nations General Assembly at its Sixteenth Session the measures that they have taken to achieve settlement by peaceful means.*

(2) Exhorts all member states to abstain from any action which may aggravate existing tensions.

No further action was taken at this time by the United Nations or the OAS, due to the failure of the United States-sponsored invasion and United States unwillingness to encourage a new one. The United States began to adopt a policy of self-restraint, and political and budgetary controls were tightly exercised over CIA activities in connection with the Cuban invasion and activities of a similar nature in other parts of the hemisphere.[44]

Cuba again complained to the General Assembly in July, August, and October of 1961 about hostile and aggressive activities of the United States, as well as plans for another invasion,[45] but no United Nations action followed. In November of that same year, when the United States dispatched naval vessels and marines to cruise in the vicinity of the Dominican Republic coast to prevent the Trujillo family from regaining their lost power, Cuba accused the United States of intervention in the Dominican Republic at the Security Council and the OAS but without success.[46] Cuban charges were probably motivated both by the lack of serious criticism which the incident aroused in Latin America, and by the belief that the firm line the United States was taking in the Caribbean could be applied to Cuba as well.

CONCLUSIONS

The tendency, both at the OAS and at the United Nations, to take advantage of the ambiguities of the United Nations Charter in order to emancipate regional organizations from any assertion of controlling authority by the Security Council is unmistakable. In the three cases analyzed above, the basic issues revolved around the right of members to insist on United Nations action and the basis upon which the United Nations can refer cases to regional organizations; in each instance, the issues were solved on the basis of practical considerations whose net effect was to encourage regional incompatibility.

Despite all this legal pulling and tugging, the formal relationship between the United Nations and regional organizations, which had been set up as compatible in the United Nations Charter, remained relatively unchanged since no alterations were introduced in the text. In actual practice, however, the United Nations yielded substantial jurisdictional ground to OAS demands of exclusive competence. To all intents and purposes, the referral of cases to the regional forum, which Inis L. Claude dubbed the "try OAS first" issue, had been generally acknowledged.

In the presentation of the cases in this chapter, arguments used to justify pragmatic solutions which left the OAS the sole arbiter of the Guatemalan and Cuban complaints were cited. Some of these arguments derived from past constructive and efficient activities of the OAS, the advisability of using existing regional machinery that had already proved itself adequate in most cases, and the availability of the OAS processes. Other arguments favoring OAS jurisdiction held that the OAS was better fitted than the United Nations to find the facts and to apply solutions because it was comprised of countries which had many traditional links, a common understanding of their problems, and a good knowledge of the legal instruments and traditions which all of them respected. In addition, it was argued that when the OAS was already discussing a case, subsequent United Nations action would impair OAS prestige. These positions, and the actions to which they led, established a precedent of regional incompatibility which could be used by other regional systems to justify preventing the United Nations from examining a threatening situation until a fait accompli had been effected by the dominant member of the regional system.

To the extent that the United Nations Charter became the background for the debate, the issue was often one of emphasis—the selection of the article or even paragraph that would best serve one's political interest; the inconsistencies of the charter in effect provided something for everyone. While paragraphs 2 and 3 of Article 52 were often invoked by incompatible regionalists, paragraph 4—regarding Security Council primary responsibility in the peaceful settlement of disputes—of the same article was seldom referred to. The superficial way in which this paragraph was treated prevented the United Nations from dealing with matters technically under its jurisdiction. The United Nations were arbitrarily prevented from dealing with serious matters which urgently cried for peaceful settlement in a universal forum. On the organizational level, this meant that the universality of the United Nations was weakened, and in terms of a power analysis, the nature of the United States-Latin American relationship was substantially changed.

The cases here show how two small Latin American countries, confronted with the overwhelming power of the United States, sought relief for their grievances through several organizational channels. Their appeals to two international organizations and the legal arguments they advaned did little to strengthen or clarify the role of compatible regional organizations in the peaceful settlement of disputes. Guatemala used only the Security Council, while Cuba turned to both the Security Council and the General Assembly. Guatemala appealed to both the United Nations and the OAS, while Cuba restricted itself to the United Nations. Guatemala relied on Article 33 to defend its stand in the Security Council while Cuba used mainly Article 52 (4) and 103. From the point of view of the two countries, these efforts were to no avail.

No matter how much some United Nations members defended the right of OAS members to immediate appeal to the universal body, in practice, the complaints sent to the United Nations by OAS members would invariably be referred to the OAS directly, as on July 19, 1960, or indirectly, after United Nations inaction, as in the Security Council on June

25, 1954. While in some instances complaints placed in the agenda that were discussed but not acted upon were then dispatched to the OAS, in other cases they were summarily dismissed without a hearing. This created an unfortunate impression, especially among the small countries. Thus, the referral of these cases to the OAS deprived Guatemala and Cuba of a main source of support in their struggles against the United States: the nonaligned countries and the members of the Soviet bloc. The arguments of some optimistic universalists that the Security Council affirmed its authority by passing the resolutions of June 20, 1954, and July 19, 1960, turned out to be rather untenable in view of the net effects of such documents; these very resolutions gave the OAS the practical grounds upon which to take action and the legal precedent for claiming exclusive jurisdiction.

In the OAS, Guatemala and Cuba found little support for their demands. In each case, the OAS was more inclined to treat them as defendants than as plaintiffs. There were, however, some distinctions between the treatment given to Guatemala and Cuba in the OAS. In the end Guatemala got some degree of institutional support while Cuba did not. In 1954, the Inter-American Peace Committee, headed by energetic Mexican Ambassador Luis Quintanilla seemed quite willing to help Guatemala by having the affair thoroughly investigated.[47] However, another body, the OAS Council, met Guatemala with a hostile attitude, considering it a threat to the hemisphere and calling for a Meeting of Consultation to condemn Guatemala. On the other hand, since 1960 there has been no evidence of a conciliatory attitude toward Cuba in the several instances in which its complaints were brought to the OAS attention. Support given by some Latin American states to Cuban causes at different times has been primarily expressed in individual reactions, through dissenting votes or abstentions when resolutions condemning Cuba have been considered. For instance, in the Seventh Meeting of Consultation, in 1960, there were dissenting votes of Mexico, Venezuela, Bolivia, and Honduras to important parts of the Declaration of San Jose, and Venezuelan and Peruvian ministers refused to sign the final act of the conference on personal grounds, expressing protests over some of the conference decisions. In recent Meetings of Consultation, Mexico, Brazil, Argentina, Ecuador, Chile, and sometimes Colombia have abstained from voting or have voted against some OAS motions against Cuba.

The presence of the United States clearly made these situations qualitatively different from cases of inter-American disputes; it gave a new interpretation to the conflicts and introduced political considerations and diplomatic factors whose implications went far beyond the hemisphere. In each case the fear of extracontinental invasion, particularly the Communist threat, was advanced to support the choice of a regional arena. However, while the United States had many supporters in this concern, there was a strong feeling that the actual Soviet danger was insufficient to justify the injury inflicted on the United Nations universalist principles. The position adopted by United States delegates, for instance, Henry Cabot Lodge, and supported by other Security Council members, in arguing that these cases should be removed from United Nations control and turned over to the OAS, effectively challenged the legitimacy of the universalist position and weakened the case of the parties seeking United Nations action. A similar position on the part of the Soviet Union, denying United Nations authority, and advocating that a Communist-dominated regional organization alone handle a case of intraregional dispute, would certainly arouse strong United States disapproval and charges that the Soviet Union was undermining the world organization.[48]

The Soviet veto in the 1954 Guatemalan case was not intended to paralyze Security Council action, but, on the contrary, to enable the Security Council to handle the case in place of the OAS. The Soviets' action seems to have been based on the assumption that the Security Council alone could discuss and make recommendations about the Guatemalan complaint. In spite of the fact that the resolution adopted later, on June 20, 1954, was very similar to a Soviet proposal, Soviet attempts to block OAS exclusive consideration of the matter and to give the Security Council jurisdiction over the case failed completely.

The United States, whether or not confronted with the Soviet veto, obtained its objectives by effectively channeling consideration of the situations toward regional organs. In the Guatemalan case it interpreted the vetoing of the Brazil-Colombia resolution as not actually precluding OAS action. Then, the resolution passed in the Security Council on July 19, 1960, gave positive juridical ground to the pragmatic claims of the United States that the OAS and not the United Nations should handle this type of problem. The second Cuban resolution, adopted by the General Assembly on April 21, 1961, continued the same trend even though the document was deprived of clear OAS references by the Nigerian and Sudanese amendments.

Moreover, the United States involvement in each of these conflicts was unquestionable, whether it was a case of veiled intervention in Guatemala or an open action in Cuba. It was clear that the United States had at least made the coup against Arbenz possible and had supplied the arms and provided training for the ill-fated Cuban expedition. But, while the CIA had been successful in its immediate objectives in Guatemala, the Bay of Pigs invasion was a disaster which caused considerable damage to United States prestige in Latin America and in the rest of the world.[49] While the alleged threat of Communism had the worthwhile effect of encouraging the United States to assume a dynamic leadership in the continent after the apathy of the postwar period, its influence was not exercised in a judicious manner and more often than not it was channeled into nonlegal courses of action. In so doing, the damage done to relations with Latin America may be said to have outweighed any immediate gain for the cause of incompatible regionalism; most statesmen in Latin America grew cynical as to the genuineness of United States assurances of nonintervention.

In addition to the effect on United States-Latin American relations, the net result of the United States' efforts in terms of the predominance of the OAS in all regional disputes was equally unfortunate; it became evident that neither the OAS, nor any other regional organization, was equipped to handle disputes of this kind—regional disputes which at the same time involved a great, world-wide power and a smaller nation. When the majority in a regional organization is strongly biased against one of the parties of a conflict, and in particular when the bias is shared or encouraged by a great power who wields hegemonic influence over the organization, the efforts of pacific settlement may not be entirely sincere. In some cases such efforts may amount to no more than a screen to prevent United Nations interference, while a disguised armed attack is carried out and completed to the satisfaction of the majority of the organization.[50]

While the United States has tended to shape its policy toward Latin America to meet cold war imperatives, the issues that engage the feelings and convictions of Latin America are not issues of Communism versus capitalism, but of economic and social development. The OAS has extended its role from policeman and mediator to political censor, for, as shown in these cases, it has brushed aside the customary limits of activities of international organizations, and has carried out actions that seek to oversee the internal political order of a country. This, together with a United States-inspired preference for rightist governments, has made the OAS more ready to deal with threats to democracy from the left than from the right. However, it is obvious that, under present circumstances, by far the most formidable threats to democracy in Latin America come from the right.

While Latin Americans depend on the United States' power to shield them from extracontinental attacks, at the same time they depend on United States self-restraint to secure their sovereignty. Although the first danger has diminished considerably, the second one has increased in the last years. But while Latin American statesmen are aware that any international action authorized by OAS will be in effect an action by the United States, they have tried to channel such action through the accepted patterns of the Inter-American System. They know, however, that, in the last resort, the United States will act unilaterally if it feels that its vital interests are threatened. The Bay of Pigs invasion and the Dominican affair of 1965 are dramatic examples of such situations.

A few Latin American countries, in particular Mexico, which had supported regionalism at San Francisco, began to question its value in view of the new political circumstances and developments. Yet, this feeling has not become prevalent among Latin Americans. Rivalries and suspicions emanating mainly from differences in the political systems of their governments and from domestic political weaknesses have made it very difficult to recruit loyal and strong allies among Latin American states to pursue a dynamic policy which could counterbalance United States influence in the OAS. Lack of leadership among Latin Americans is particularly conspicuous despite the prestige and influence of some countries, such as Mexico. In response to Latin American apathy to make the OAS more compatible with the United Nations, Mexico has not assumed the dynamic leadership position it could assume.

Inasmuch as an alternative to the problems of downward transfers and growing regional incompatibility cannot presently be found in a political realignment of OAS forces, hope that a workable solution may be reached lies in the legal enforcement of regional compatibility by the majority of its adherents among members of the United Nations.[51] The problem of jurisdiction of regional organizations in the peaceful settlement of disputes could be solved by allowing the plaintiff choice of the organ to which to appeal.[52] Examples of plaintiffs choosing the international organization for their appeal have occurred twice: (1) in May, 1963, Haiti agreed in the Security Council to have her complaint against the Dominican Republic referred to the OAS; (2) in January, 1964, Panama accepted having her complaint against the United States settled in the OAS. In both instances the Security Council provided for a hearing, the cases remained in the agenda of the Security Council, and in both cases the Council continued to have jurisdiction. Although it can be argued that considerable pressure was exerted on the countries initiating United Nations processes to redress their complaints to the regional forum, the plaintiffs seemed to have been willing in these instances to follow the regional course.

In addition, whenever there are conflicting views among disputing parties as to the organ to which their dispute should be presented, the United Nations could exercise its primary jurisdiction. In support of this suggestion a broadening interpretation can be given to Article 103 of the United Nations Charter that would justify the fundamental responsibility of the United Nations. It is inconsistent to assert that countries belonging to regional organizations should be at a disadvantage as compared to others who have no regional affiliations, whose direct access to the United Nations is guaranteed, and whose right to have their complaints aired in United Nations bodies is not impaired.

In spite of the emotion injected into the defense of the OAS role in the peaceful settlement of disputes by many Latin Americans and the United States, most of the pragmatic arguments that have been used to justify the incompatible path fade away in view of the striking imbalance of power which characterizes the OAS. The restraint, respect of sovereignty, and self-determination that have characterized the OAS's conduct in dealing with disputes between Latin American countries have disappeared when the United States is a party to a dispute. In spite of the fact that the OAS is formally an association of equals, the United States has enjoyed a privileged position. Although the United States cannot exert a paralyzing power in the OAS comparable to the veto in the United Nations, it has traditionally been able to marshall the necessary majority for the policies it supports. Since it contributes approximately two-thirds of the OAS's budget, lack of American support renders ineffectual the adoption of a resolution in almost every field, especially the economic one. In effect, in each case it is the great-power interests to which the interests of the small countries within its sphere of influence must be subordinated.

The inadequacy of this regional forum in dealing with great-power-small-power-conflicts can be contrasted with the record of the universal organization. The effectiveness of universal organs has been proven not only economically, as in the United Nations Economic Commission for Latin America, but also politically, in the peaceful settlement of disputes. For instance, relative to the OAS's handling of the situation, there have been more serious attempts in the United Nations than in the regional organization to reach an agreement of a new canal treaty between the United States and Panama.[53]

It is in this sense that the compatibility or incompatibility of the two organizations is affected by the choice of organization in particular cases. The two organizations, as described above (Chapter I), are compatible only insofar as the divisions of functions and jurisdiction between the two, and the power relations they imply, are harmonious. In this chapter we have seen that when *intra*-Latin American disputes were concerned, the independent functioning of the OAS in the peaceful settlement of disputes was compatible with the functioning of the United Nations. However, when a large world power, such as the United States, and a small power, such as Cuba or Guatemala, were involved, other considerations became relevant and the regional treatment appeared inadequate. The disproportionate distribution of power within the hemisphere worked especially to the disadvantage of the smaller nation when a regional forum was selected. In addition, while these disputes may have been regional in geographical terms, the interest of the United States and the Soviet Union (whether or not the latter's threat was real or imagined) made them extra-continental in implication. While some felt that regional channels must be completely exhausted before universal channels were tried, compatible regionalism would demand choice of organizational levels at the outset.

6

INCOMPATIBILITY IN THE ADOPTION OF ENFORCEMENT ACTION AT THE REGIONAL LEVEL

ONE OF THE MAIN reasons for the establishment of the United Nations was to locate a monopoly of force in a responsible universal body. Only reluctantly did the United Nations' founders accept the idea of individual and regional self-defense in the event of an armed attack. At the San Francisco Conference, however, it was made clear that control of the means of international coercion must depend on the agreement of the great powers; therefore, the United Nations Charter required unanimity among the big powers for Security Council decisions, especially when the use of force was concerned.

The adoption of enforcement measures by regional organizations, even those falling short of military action, were required to have prior Security Council authorization (Article 53). This requirement became more binding than had been expected in 1945 since such Security Council authorization became more and more uncertain—a result of the widening dissension among the members and the continued threat of a permanent member's veto. Therefore, the only escape for a regional organization from Security Council supervision (a path adopted by incompatible regional organizations) was *to contend that the contemplated course of action was not enforcement action.*

In resorting to this mode of escape, incompatible regionalists explained that their position could be derived from the limitations of the Security Council itself. Given the uncertainty of the Council's operation in the postwar world, it could be argued that the requirement of Security Council approval might go beyond simply restricting regional organizations and could effectively squelch helpful regional activities. The power of regional organizations was said to result, by default, from the failure of the members of the Security Council to reach decisions, from the inadequacies of the unanimity rule, which posed a major difficulty in obtaining needed authorization. The OAS has undoubtedly been the regional organization that has been most active in the search for a course of action independent of Security Council control and, as in the field of peaceful settlement of disputes, it has set precedents followed by other regional organizations such as the Arab League or the Organization of African Unity.

The period during which the OAS began to adopt measures that in effect amounted to enforcement action began in 1960. The crucial issue during this period was the legal classification of the sanctions and coercive measures the organization had adopted. This was significant, since the United Nations Charter attempts to distinguish enforcement action, which requires prior Security Council authorization, from collective self-defense, which does not. In more general terms, the activities of the OAS and the issues it raised mirrored the broad problem of the control of coercion in international society.

The question of the OAS's right to impose sanctions and use force independently of Security Council supervision pertains primarily to Article 53 and 54. Efforts on the part of those in favor of an incompatible regionalism were directed at deriving, through the actual work of the UN and the OAS, a constricting interpretation of Article 53. Such an interpretation would, in actual practice, give regional organizations effective autonomy and independence from Security Council control with regard to all kinds of enforcement action—including diplomatic, economic, and political sanctions—which, strictly speaking, the OAS was forbidden to take without Security Council authorization. Incompatible regionalists followed two techniques to obtain results more suitable to their interests whenever the OAS engaged in action which could be viewed as enforcement action. (1) They made use of a constricting interpretation of Article 53 to substantially diminish the limitations on OAS activities. They argued, during the course of UN and OAS consideration of the cases described in this chapter, that enforcement action referred to only those measures where the actual use of military force was involved. (2) They began to apply a broadening interpretation of Article 54 and to assume that pro forma and a posteriori reporting under this article of the United Nations Charter was the only OAS obligation toward the United Nations (see table).

It seems clear that incompatibility in the peaceful settlement of disputes paved the way for incompatibility in the adoption of enforcement action. The results of efforts conducted by incompatible regionalists in the field of peaceful settlement of disputes encouraged them to direct their energies to the field of enforcement action, where a universalist perspective was prevalent and still limited regional activities. The factors which actually made possible the incompatible regional trend evolving around enforcement action are the result of the pragmatic success which had been achieved by regional organizations in the course of the struggle for OAS autonomy in the peaceful settlement of disputes. Where enforcement action was concerned, changes leading to incompatibility began in 1960, with the Dominican Republic case, continued in subsequent developments of the Cuban situation and in the Cuban missile crisis of 1962, and reached a climax in 1965 with the Dominican Republic affair.

DOMINICAN REPUBLIC I (1960)

On June 24, 1960, agents of the Dominican government, headed by tyrant Rafael Leonidas Trujillo (in power since 1930), unsuccessfully attempted to assassinate Rómulo Betancourt, Venezuela's president and Trujillo's life-long political enemy and critic. This was not the first time that the Trujillo government had undertaken such an act in the Western Hemisphere. The most widely known incident occurred with the disappearance of Professor Jesús Galíndez, kidnapped and probably killed by Trujillo's orders as a consequence of the publication of a book depicting Trujillo's atrocities in the Dominican Republic. Other incidents have taken the form of attempts to assassinate political exiles from the Dominican Republic who were outspoken in their criticisms of Trujillo, and influential democratic leaders who were giving support or protection to such Dominican exiles. However, in previous instances of Trujillo's intervention, there was a general unwillingness among Latin American governments to punish the Dominican dictator, either because they feared that this would endanger the principles of nonintervention by bringing about his downfall, or because the charges against Trujillo were not sufficiently substantiated. But, 1960 happened to be a propitious year for effectively punishing Trujillo since Venezuela had gathered convincing proof of the Dominican government's interventions on several occasions and there seemed to exist a general hostility to dictatorships. At the time, the majority of the Latin American governments were democratically oriented and several dictatorships which were likely to defend Trujillo had been recently overthrown, such as Gustavo Rojas Pinilla from Colombia, Marcos Pérez Jiménez from Venezuela, and Fulgencio Batista from Cuba. The remaining ones, Anastasio Somoza of Nicaragua and Alfredo Stroessner of Paraguay, afraid of being included in the same category as Trujillo at the moment when the downfall of

ENFORCEMENT ACTION

Article 53: Constricting Interpretation

1945

No enforcement action shall be taken by regional arrangements without the prior authorization of the Security Council.

Tacitly agreed also that enforcement action involved not only the use of force [Article 42] but also measures not involving the use of force (partial interruption of economic relations and of rail, sea, air, postal, telegraphic, radio, and other means of communication, and the severance of diplomatic relations) [Article 41].

UNIVERSALISM COMPATIBLE REGIONALISM

PRAGMATIC PROCESS

1965

(1) Regional organization should get Security Council authorization only for applying measures involving the use of force.

(2) Regional organizations can impose freely economic, diplomatic and political sanctions without Security Council authorization.

(3) Information of action taken [Article 54] only duty to the UN.

(4) Establishment of independent peace-keeping operations at the regional level without Security Council approval.

INCOMPATIBLE REGIONALISM

dictators was seemingly in fashion, kept quiet and went along with the majority of Latin American governments.

Venezuela filed a complaint against the Trujillo government for the assassination attempt at the OAS Council meeting on July 4, 1960, along with other complaints about Dominican intervention in Venezuelan internal affairs, such as the assistance given by the Dominican Republic government to some Venezuelan generals to organize a coup in April of that same year. In response to this action, the OAS Council unanimously decided (Venezuela and the Dominican Republic not voting) to hold the Sixth Meeting of Consultation on August 20, 1960, in San Jose, Costa Rica. This was the first of the Meetings of Consultation convoked under provisions of the Rio Treaty. Previous Meetings of Consultation had been held in accordance with provisions of the Declaration of Lima of 1938 (which had practically instituted the consultation method, see above) or the OAS Charter. Very shortly thereafter, the Seventh Meeting of Consultation was convoked by Peru, through the OAS Charter, indirectly to condemn Cuban policies (see above, Chapter V).

Based on sections of Article 8 of the Rio Treaty (which lists the sanctions which can be adopted by the Organ of Consultation), the foreign ministers at San Jose imposed a series of diplomatic and economic sanctions, including suspension of arms trade to the Dominican Republic. This condemnation of the Trujillo dictatorship brought to the surface deep anti-United States feelings and resentment of the United States' political, economic, and diplomatic support which had actually maintained Trujillo in power for three decades. Many political groups and newspapers all over Latin American expressed this criticism but, at the meeting, only the Cuban delegate dared to state them openly.

Secretary of State Christian Herter was placed in a difficult situation, since it was frequently implied, in the course of the meeting, that the United States had been responsible for Trujillo's continuance in power. In addition, the United States chose a course of action which would indeed protect the Dominican government from any OAS attack. Secretary of State Herter defended the principle of nonintervention when he initially opposed strong Latin American demands for OAS measures which were aimed at bringing about the downfall of Trujillo, engendering fundamental political changes inside the Dominican Republic. Trying to sidetrack, and hopefully to postpone indefinitely, sanctions against Trujillo, the United States favored only the sending of an OAS committee for supervising elections in the Dominican Republic. The application of sanctions was to be contemplated by the United States' delegate only if the Dominican government refused to follow OAS political supervision. Mexico, among other Latin American states such as Colombia, Argentina, Cuba, Chile, and Brazil, rejected the United States' proposal, since such OAS action would clearly involve an intervention in the domestic affairs of the Dominican Republic and because it was the condemnation of an interventionist action of the Dominican government against Venezuela, and not the holding of elections in the Dominican Republic, that was the object of the meeting. However, despite the official result of the meeting, subsequent developments in the Dominican Republic corresponded with the preferences initially stated by the United States. Thus, elections were held in December, 1962, with OAS supervision, in spite of the traditional Latin American opposition to this procedure.[1]

The OAS condemned Trujillo, agreed that all members sever diplomatic relations with the Dominican Republic, that a partial interruption of economic relations be imposed, and that arms trade with the Dominican Republic be suspended. The OAS transmitted its resolution to the United Nations under Article 54, which was merely a formality since the OAS had already decided upon its course of action and since Security Council authorization of such measures should have been granted prior to their final application.

The Soviet Union did not seem to share the OAS Council's view that actions against the Dominican Republic had only to be reported and did not require Security Council authorization. The Soviet delegation requested a Security Council meeting to specifically approve the sanctions, a maneuver which greatly surprised the Security Council members. In a draft resolution, the Soviet Union argued that diplomatic and partial economic sanctions were "enforcement action" under Article 53, which must be validated by the Security Council.[2] This was the first occasion on which Article 53 was used and interpreted by a United Nations member to assert the authority of the Security Council to approve or disapprove measures adopted by regional organizations.

During the Security Council meetings held on September 8 and 9 to discuss the Soviet Union's assertion, the guilt or innocence of the Dominican government was not at issue; nobody questioned that the Trujillo government warranted the sanctions imposed on it by the OAS and everybody agreed that the Security Council should endorse them. The Soviet Union, however, along with Poland, made reference to the larger implications of the OAS resolution. They broadly interpreted enforcement action in Article 53 as including sanctions of an economic, political, and diplomatic nature even if they were adopted individually by member countries of a regional organization. The two representatives of the Soviet Union and Poland argued that the ultimate responsibility of the Security Council to approve or disapprove, invalidate or reconsider, annul or revise measures adopted by regional organizations was being threatened by the OAS's failure to get prior Security Council authorization. They argued that such actions would ultimately assign to the Council the role of passive observer in matters relating to the maintenance of international peace and security. Clearly, the real concern of the Soviet Union in making this accusation was not the Dominican Republic but Cuba. By establishing the precedent that Security Council approval was required for

OAS enforcement action, the Soviet Union hoped to prepare for OAS actions with regard to Cuba.

The United States was aware of the Soviet Union's strategy and took pains to assert that the United States would reject any attempt of the Communist bloc to make use of the political, economic, or social situation of the American states to intervene in the Western Hemisphere; the implication here was that Cuba was indeed next.[3] United States action when the Dominican case was being discussed at the Security Council was intended to thwart realization of the Soviet goals. The United States tried to persuade the Security Council members that the relation between the United Nations and regional organizations should be "so flexible as to permit these agencies to take effective action . . . without necessarily bringing the problem before a world forum."[4] Specifically, the United States interpreted enforcement action in Article 53 in a constricting way, arguing that Security Council authorization was needed only when regional organizations adopted measures involving the use of armed force and that, according to Article 54, the Security Council should simply be informed of the measures which did not involve the use of force. The United States also stated that the OAS's sanctions were carried out unilaterally by individual countries exercising their sovereign rights. In sum, the United States tried to question the applicability of Article 53 to the situation and was joined in this interpretation by Italy and Great Britain. Moreover, Britain strongly adhered to the United States interpretation that the responsibilities of the OAS toward the United Nations were adequately discharged through the submission of a letter of information to the United Nations.

The constricting interpretation of Article 53 offered by the United States was a recent one, stemming from its tactical opposition to Soviet aims. At the San Francisco Conference, for instance, the United States had endorsed a broadening interpretation of Article 53 which viewed enforcement action as including measures falling short of military action,[5] and more recently, at the OAS's Sixth Meeting of Consultation, which had adopted sanctions against Trujillo, Secretary of State Herter had used this same interpretation (stating that the diplomatic and economic sanctions contemplated against the Dominican Republic were enforcement action which needed Security Council authorization) to oppose sanctions against the Dominican Republic.

Argentina and Ecuador, Latin American members of the Security Council, backed the United States in its constricting interpretation of Article 53. They held that only regional measures amounting to armed force were subject to Security Council ratification. Like Italy and Great Britain, they attempted to base their positions on a general principle of regional autonomy rather than on the literal text of Article 53. Ceylon's delegate added that measures short of military action were enumerated in Article 41, thus providing the United States and other Security Council members with a distinctly legal basis to support their interpretation of Article 53.

To oppose the Soviet draft proposal, Argentina and Ecuador, along with the United States, sponsored a resolution recommending that the Security Council "take note" of the OAS measures; the proposal carefully avoided mentioning the United Nations-OAS relationship regarding enforcement action, and did not even refer to Article 53. This draft was given voting priority over the Soviet draft and was adopted by nine votes, with Poland and the Soviet Union abstaining.

The Security Council debate was far from conclusive since it left the United Nations' role in regard to enforcement action and Article 53 largely undetermined. The substantive decision as to which type of measures was going to be considered enforcement action was highly controversial, not only in view of the legal issues involved, but also because of its political implications. Legally, it was important to decide if only those measures involving the use of armed force were to be authorized by the Security Council, or if all kinds of political, economic, and diplomatic sanctions (in addition to the use of armed force) required such authorization. Politically, such a decision involved the degree of control the Security Council was to exercise over regional organizations: Would they be supervised by the Security Council or left completely free to adopt all kinds of nonmilitary sanctions? The latter possibility would give regional organizations a tremendous amount of political power that could be used to bring about the downfall of regimes disliked by the rest of the members of the organization. In view of the Council's unwillingness to specifically define enforcement action, many members who were inclined to a compatible perspective interpreted the resolution as not setting a firm precedent but leaving the door open for a future determination on the issue. Moreover, there seemed to be little difference between approval and "taking note"; to some members of the Council besides the Soviet Union and Poland, "taking note" in effect meant acceptance or at least a lack of clear opposition.[6]

Incompatible regionalists, led by the United States, interpreted the adoption of the resolution as a victory. No obstacle to regional organizations had been created, since the need for Security Council authorization for measures falling short of military action was not clearly asserted. They felt that since the United Nations did not strictly define enforcement action, there were grounds to conclude that this term in Article 53 covered only such actions as would not normally be legitimate for any individual member to adopt except on the basis of a Security Council authorization.

Behind the semantic subtleties of the "take note" clause debated by the Soviet Union and the United States, lay the significant issue of the compatibility or incompatibility of regional organizations in the field of enforcement action and the adoption of nonmilitary sanctions. Technically speaking, "taking note" could be interpreted either as Security Council approval of a regional course of action or as complete avoidance of a specific definition of enforcement action, which would leave regional organizations with virtually complete freedom of action. The practical consequences of this Security Council action, leaving the issue of universal priority in such a vague state, were not immediately felt in the United Nations-OAS relationship. They were to become evident in the course of future events developing around the interpretation and actual application of sanctions and enforcement action by the OAS.

CUBA III (1962)

The trend towards regional incompatibility in the OAS continued into 1960, when the Seventh Meeting of Consultation's Declaration of San Jose indirectly disapproved the growing ties between Cuba and the Soviet Union (see above) by condemning extracontinental intervention and the acceptance of such aid by an American state.[7] In many ways this action established the groundwork for Cuba's condemnation in 1962 since it specifically categorized a certain type of conduct as a "delict" (a wrong or illegal act) in the Inter-American System.[8] If at one point a particular kind of behavior was defined as an offense, it could at a later point become the basis of a sanction, since sanctions generally condemn a delict that has been committed or a legal obligation that has been disregarded.[9]

Later efforts to condemn Soviet-Cuban ties were made by Peru, who on October 16, 1961, attempted to have the OAS Council convoke a new Meeting of Consultation to deal with Cuba as a Communist threat to the hemisphere. Peru's note argued (1) that the Cuban government was guilty of violating human rights, (2) that Cuba had been incorporated into the Sino–Soviet bloc, and (3) that Cuba was instigating Communist subversion and promoting revolutions against Latin American governments and democratic institutions. Opposition headed by Mexico succeeded both in postponing a Council decision on convoking such a meeting and in sending the

Peruvian request to the Inter-American Peace Committee for study. In November, Colombia sent to the OAS Council a new request for a Conference of Ministers of Foreign Relations on the basis of Article 6 of the Rio Treaty. The Eighth Meeting of Consultation was convoked, as the Colombian document suggested, to deal with threats to hemispheric peace "that might arise" from extracontinental intervention and to decide what action should be taken "if they occur." Extracontinental subversion aiming at the overthrow of legitimately established governments was the major threat to be defined here in order to prepare the groundwork for the later application of security measures.

Mexico and Chile headed a group which questioned the legal basis for calling this meeting. They argued (1) that the element of urgency required by the Rio Treaty was lacking; and (2) that the Rio Treaty authorized the convokation of a Meeting of Consultation only when a dangerous situation existed and not when one might exist. However, on December 4, 1961, the majority voted in favor of holding the requested conference. Mexico and Cuba voted against, while Argentina, Bolivia, Brazil, Chile, and Ecuador abstained.

Active bilateral and multilateral diplomatic consultation among those favoring the holding of the meeting took place to reach an agreement on the way Cuba should be condemned and the sanctions that should be imposed before the conference convened. These consultations were numerous, especially among Central American governments, as well as among military and rightist regimes, all of which were interested in obtaining collective support for the diplomatic and economic policies that they had unilaterally adopted against Cuba. But, in spite of their efforts, there was actually no change in the attitudes of those governments already opposed to holding the meeting and opposed to sanctioning Cuba from the time the meeting was announced to the moment when it began at Punta del Este on January 22, 1962. Disagreements over interpretations of the Rio Treaty which had occurred at the outset between the United States and Latin American countries, as well as among Latin Americans themselves, continued throughout the conference.

As its main sources of information, the conference relied on a report submitted by the Inter-American Peace Committee (initiated early in October, 1961, after the Peruvian request mentioned earlier) and on a United States State Department White Paper on Cuba. The first one attempted to prove the identification of Cuba itself with the Sino-Soviet bloc but admitted the committee's inability to conduct an exhaustive investigation on the charges of Cuban subversive activities in the Western Hemisphere. The State Department's White Paper intended to do both and effectively prove the existence of a situation calling for collective measures. Its case rested on two points: (1) the Cuban government had become an appendage of the Communist; and (2) Cuba was a beachhead for the Sino-Soviet bloc in the Western Hemisphere, serving the objectives of "international Communism."

Inasmuch as agreement could not be reached between the two groups of countries (the one opposing sanctions against Cuba and the other favoring them), efforts were concentrated on emphasizing the points on which all of them agreed, such as incompatibility of Marxism-Leninism with the principles of the Inter-American System. The countries which had challenged the legal competence of a meeting convoked to consider *potential* threats also opposed the application of diplomatic and economic sanctions against Cuba by challenging the legality of the procedures employed to apply such sanctions, the nature of the sanctions, and the capacity of the meeting itself to decide on sanctions. In view of this opposition, the United States had to lower its demands for economic, political, and diplomatic sanctions and to work instead for the expulsion of Cuba from the OAS. But once the United States had decided upon this in order to avoid a split among OAS members, assent of those Latin American governments favoring strong sanctions against Cuba had to be obtained.

The compromise formula of expelling Cuba from the OAS ran into major difficulties. Opponents argued: (1) that Article 6 of the Rio Treaty was not applicable to this situation since an actual danger to the peace of the Americas did not exist; (2) that, even in the event that sanctions could be legally imposed, only those measures listed in Article 8 of the same treaty could be applied to Cuba (among which expulsion from the OAS was not mentioned); and (3) that nowhere in the OAS constitutional documents was the organization granted the power to suspend or exclude a member.

Nevertheless, some points were finally agreed upon. The OAS members decided that Communism was incompatible with the Inter-American System and that action, such as the establishment of a Special Consultative Committee of experts on security to advise countries on specific measures, should be taken against the subversive actions of "international Communism" in the Western Hemisphere. Initially, it was decided that Cuba be excluded from participating in the Inter-American Defense Board. After heated debate, however, a resolution was passed by a divided vote holding that Cuba "as a consequence of repeated acts" had placed itself outside of the Inter-American System; with this Cuba was virtually expelled from the OAS. Mexico, Brazil, Chile, Ecuador, and Bolivia refused to vote in favor of the resolution against Cuba.[10]

In the General Assembly in February, 1962, Cuba accused the United States of diplomatic and economic aggression and referred to the results of the Eighth Meeting of Consultation as proof of United States hostility towards Cuba. Cuba called for a reconsideration of the United Nations-OAS relationship, arguing that the Meeting of Consultation itself, as well as the procedures by which the expulsion was decided, were illegal. To be sure, the Cuban government did not seem to care very much about its participation in the OAS, but its expulsion presented an opportunity to criticize the United States and the OAS and to insist upon United Nations action. Up until this time it had customarily been held in international law that expulsion, as opposed to voluntary withdrawal, from an international organization was an enforcement measure. Furthermore, expulsion was seen as a sanction, for it was expressly initiated in order to condemn the violation of the constitutional documents of an international organization.

Coincidentally, at the time Cuba appealed to the General Assembly to complain about United States policies and its expulsion from the OAS, the First Committee was considering an earlier (August, 1961) Cuban complaint against the United States, as well as a joint Czechoslovakian-Romanian draft resolution which exhorted the United States to put an end to its intervention in Cuban domestic affairs and called for a peaceful settlement of the differences between the two states. The First Committee carefully studied Cuban complaints during the course of its twelve meetings between February 5 and 15. During these meetings, Cuba primarily emphasized its earlier complaints about the United States' threat of unilateral intervention and the pressures the United States exerted upon the Latin American countries to force them to break diplomatic and economic relations with Cuba.[11] It referred frequently to the Bay of Pigs invasion to corroborate its charges. But on this occasion Cuba did not make any formal complaint concerning the results of the Eighth Meeting of Consultation in particular, nor did it ask the General Assembly to discuss the legality of such action, rather, Cuba just included it in the list of complaints it presented as examples of the United States' hostile policies. Thus, while Cuba took advantage of the opportunity to insist on the General Assembly's universal responsibility vis-à-vis the OAS, the Cuban charges were more oriented toward a criticism of aggressive United States policies than to the legality of the OAS measures per se.

At these twelve meetings of the General Assembly's First Committee, the countries of the Soviet bloc supported Cuba in its accusation of United States intervention. But the Latin

Americans, especially those more incompatibly oriented, were particularly sensitive to accusations aiming at the legality of OAS actions rather than to complaints of United States intervention in Cuba. As a result, they attempted to defend OAS jurisdiction against what they considered as its invasion of it by the United Nations. They supported Cuba's expulsion from the OAS on the grounds of the political incompatibility of the Cuban system with the democratic beliefs of the OAS and of Cuba's own actions, by which it effectively placed itself outside the Inter-American System. On the other hand, the majority of the United Nations' members, especially the Asian and African countries, felt that Cuba's charges against the United States were vague and without substantial evidence. But, on the issue of the illegality of the Punta del Este resolution of expulsion, Cuban views drew considerable support among the more compatibly oriented United Nations members who were fearful of the dangerous precedents of regional independence the OAS might set.[1 2]

Despite the support Cuba received on the question of its expulsion, no action was taken by the United Nations. At the meetings of the First Committee, and later at the Plenary Assembly of February 20, neither the draft presented jointly by Czechoslovakia and Romania, nor a second draft resolution introduced late in the plenary meeting by Mongolia,[1 3] achieved the required majority. At this point the General Assembly dropped the Cuban accusation from its agenda. Cuba was clearly not satisfied and new efforts were planned to gain United Nations support for its position.

Cuba went to the Security Council demanding that it consider United States efforts to promote the adoption of enforcement action at the Punta del Este meeting of the OAS in January as a prelude to a large-scale invasion. Cuba called for an immediate Security Council meeting which would insist both on a broadening interpretation of Article 53 and on the need to consider measures adopted at Punta del Este as enforcement action requiring Security Council authorization.[14] It seemed that Cuba became aware of her past mistakes and realized that her case would be more successful if she emphasized the illegality of the Punta del Este resolution vis-à-vis the United Nations Charter, rather than making a political case against the United States.

On February 27, 1962, the Security Council studied this new Cuban complaint and discussed it extensively before adopting the agenda. Only the Soviet Union, Ghana, Romania, and the United Arab Republic voted in favor of placing the Cuban appeal on the agenda. The rest of the Security Council members opposed the measure on the grounds that (1) Cuba was abusing United Nations procedures since its complaint had already been exhaustively discussed by the General Assembly; (2) the Dominican Republic case in 1960 set the precedent that it was not necessary or appropriate for the Security Council to either approve or disapprove resolutions or actions of this kind taken by the OAS (at that time the council simply took note of the actions which were duly reported to it according to Article 54); and (3) that there should be a constricting interpretation of the term "enforcement action" to include only those measures involving the use of force.

The Soviet Union objected to such an interpretation of the 1960 Dominican case and stated that each country had its own specific interest or problems, that each presented a unique case. The Soviet Union's delegate also admonished the Latin American countries for establishing a dangerous precedent which could be used against them and for embarking on a course which would destroy the United Nations by usurping the prerogatives of the Security Council.

This, however, was not the end of the matter. Since, in the previous Security Council meetings, some of the members charged Cuba with having propaganda objectives and therefore refused to consider the case, Cuba decided to limit its complaint to juridical questions. On March 2 and 8 Cuba asked the Security Council to request an advisory opinion of the

International Court of Justice on the following questions
related to Article 53: (1) Should a regional organization, such
as the OAS, adjust its activities to the purposes and principles
of the United Nations? (2) Did the United Nations Charter
allow the OAS to take "enforcement action" under Article 53
without Security Council authorization? (3) Did "enforcement
action" mentioned in Article 53 include measures in Article
41, and to what extent? (4) Did the OAS Charter provide for
the expulsion of its members because of their system of
government? (5) Could the OAS Charter and the Rio Treaty
prevail over United Nations provisions? (6) Was the Resolution of Punta del Este in agreement with United Nations
provisions?[15] It is noteworthy that the Cuban government
elaborated these questions in such a way that, going from the
general to the particular issue, the International Court of
Justice would be very likely inclined to assert, first, the
primacy of universal organs, as well as a broadening interpretation of enforcement action under Article 53, and second,
that compatible links should prevail between the United
Nations and the OAS.

By this time, none of the Security Council members
opposed placing the Cuban complaint on the agenda and
Cuba's request became the subject of the next six meetings.[16]
Cuba, Ghana, Romania, and the Soviet Union tried to establish Security Council authority in determining the validity of
the OAS's sanctions against Cuba. They criticized the OAS's
resolution in terms of the organization's own constitution—for
instance, the OAS Charter did not provide for the expulsion
of a member, and the fact that the legal basis for the Eighth
Meeting of Consultation was also questioned by several Latin
American countries. Furthermore, they attacked the resolution on the grounds of their incompatibility with United
Nations provisions.

While Cuba was trying to convince the Security Council
members of the need for an advisory opinion by the International Court of Justice, the United States consistently main-

tained that there was no need for such a clarification. The United States once again argued that the Dominican case in 1960 had established the precedent that the Security Council should only "take note" and not authorize nonmilitary sanctions adopted by the OAS; the responsibilities of the OAS were satisfied when it reported its action to the United Nations in accordance with Article 54. Adlai E. Stevenson also criticized the Soviet Union's desire to use its veto on the Security Council as a means of extending its influence into the Western Hemisphere as well as into Africa and Asia. He compared Soviet action in this case to Soviet attempts to establish a "troika" for the office of the Secretary General which, in Stevenson's view, would have subjected the entire Secretariat to the Soviet veto. It is not unlikely that the United States' position was motivated by the fact that the International Court of Justice, which relies on legal and nonpolitical considerations for its decisions, would probably not favor the United States' constricting interpretations of Article 53.

In the vote on the Cuban request for judicial consideration, Britain, Chile, China, France, Ireland, and Venezuela supported the United States and rejected the Cuban measure. Romania and the Soviet Union voted in favor, the United Arab Republic abstained. Ghana did not vote, in order to protest the techniques used to prevent Cuba's participation in the last crucial moments of the debate; Cuba was not allowed to participate in the Security Council discussions once the issue was being voted, as a consequence of a procedural technicality defended by the United States and some other members. A separate vote taken on the section of the Cuban draft resolution which questioned whether enforcement action could include the measures contemplated in Article 41 (measures not involving the use of armed force) was also defeated by a vote of seven to four.

Although the final votes, and the conflicting explanations and interpretations given them by the Security Council members, were inconclusive, since the Security Council had actually rejected a petition to have the issue clarified by the International Court of Justice, the overall outcome of the meetings seemed to substantiate the proposition, advanced somewhat vaguely during the Dominican case of 1960, that the United Nations should not be permitted to block regional enforcement action of this kind. The refusal to submit Cuba's question to the International Court of Justice indicated that incompatible political considerations weighed heavily and forced the Security Council to be generally unwilling to question the OAS's competence to take measures against any of its members without Security Council authorization. It is clear that by adopting this attitude the Security Council pragmatically diminished its universal authority.

As a consequence of the ambiguity surrounding the Security Council's actions, the OAS effectively acquired a new basis from which it could continue its drive against Cuba. Based on Article 6 of the Rio Treaty, a Ninth Meeting of Consultation was held in Washington, D.C., from July 21 to 26, 1964, whose formal aim was to study Venezuelan charges of Cuban aggression. In actuality, although it was not explicitly stated in the official documents, the meeting was convened in order to persuade, or to force, those countries still maintaining diplomatic relations or economic ties with Cuba (Mexico, Uruguay, Chile, and Bolivia) to align themselves with the inter-American policy of isolating Cuba from the rest of the hemisphere. The meeting as a whole condemned Cuba and recommended that OAS members sever diplomatic, consular, and commercial relations, as well as air and sea communication, with it; only Mexico, Chile, Bolivia, and Uruguay demurred.[17] This time, the Cuban government, assuming that the balance of forces in the Security Council would render worthless any effort on behalf of compatible regionalism, did not present the result of the new OAS action to the United Nations. In addition, dissensions against OAS policies by Latin

Americans still maintaining relations with Cuba had diminished. The OAS's drive to isolate Cuba was almost completely successful since Chile finally severed diplomatic relations with Cuba on August 11, 1964, Bolivia on August 21, and Uruguay on September 9, 1964. Mexico alone, among all the members of the OAS, has maintained relations with Cuba.

Mexico has refused to cut its ties with Cuba, arguing that the Rio Treaty was not applicable to the case brought by Venezuela in 1964 against Cuba because there was no convincing proof of the threats allegedly posed by Cuba to Venezuela. Mexico has further argued that the Rio Treaty did not envisage the application of such measures in situations of the kind Venezuela described. Mexico has been rejecting OAS bids to sever diplomatic relations with Cuba in the face of a provision of the Rio Treaty stating that all measures adopted by the required majority, except the use of force, are binding upon all members. [18] It has politely circumvented OAS and United States political pressures and has repeatedly insisted that, like Cuba, it will obey only a decision of the International Court of Justice clarifying its alleged obligation to sever diplomatic relations with Cuba.[19]

It is unlikely that either the United States or the other Latin Americans who voted for the resolution of the Ninth Meeting of Consultation would be willing to take the question to the International Court of Justice. Mexico has placed the burden of proving the legality of OAS resolutions on the OAS's members themselves and has avoided initiating proceedings in the International Court of Justice, a course which would probably prove more embarrassing for many Latin American countries who are especially concerned with the domestic political implications of any international stand they assume. By avoiding positive action, Mexico's position was maintained intact without precipitating a split among OAS members.[20]

CUBA IV (MISSILE CRISIS 1962)

After the Security Council had discussed the Cuban request for an advisory opinion of the International Court of Justice in March, 1962, United States-Cuban relations continued to deteriorate. Cuba's growing military ties with the Communist bloc led, on October 1962, to one of the most serious international crises of the entire postwar period. Despite its regional origin in United States-Cuban relations, the Cuban Missile Crisis, as it is often referred to, represented a global rather than a regional confrontation.

On October 14, 1962, United States U-2 reconnaissance flights over Cuban territory verified that active work was being carried out to install Soviet nuclear ballistic missiles on the western end of Cuba, which were likely to become operational in two weeks. The Soviet Union had never before placed nuclear missiles in a country within what may be considered the United States' zone of vital interest. Missiles of this kind could easily reach Washington, Dallas, Cape Canaveral, St Louis, and all SAC bases and cities in-between. They were clearly being prepared for use as a sort of nuclear blackmail against the United States, since they effectively doubled Soviet striking capacity against American targets.

In the United States, several alternative responses were carefully considered. Finally, despite its disadvantages, the President and his advisors decided to establish a blockade designed to stop further shipments of offensive weapons into Cuba and, hopefully, to force the removal of the missiles already there.[21] There were several reasons for choosing the blockade as a means of retaliation. A blockade was clearly a more limited, low-key military action than an air strike or an invasion, and offered the Soviet Union the choice of avoiding a direct military clash by keeping its ships and airplanes away. Since it could be initiated without a shot being fired, it seemed less likely to precipitate an immediate military response from the Soviet Union. [22] However, since a blockade was legally related to a declared war, legal experts in the State Department foresaw objections from United Nations jurists. Blockade, a tactic closely associated with Berlin, seemed also likely to cause a new Berlin blockade in response to the Cuban one. It was therefore decided to avoid the term blockade and to substitute "quarantine" for it. Quarantine was a less belligerent term than blockade and more applicable to what was seen as an act of peaceful self-preservation.

Deputy Attorney Nicholas deB. Katzenbach and the legal advisors of the State Department were called by the president and his political and military advisers to study the legal basis of the quarantine and to derive its legal justification. It was concluded that legal justification could be obtained only through OAS approval of the measure and a later presentation to the United Nations as a fait accompli. On October 22, President Kennedy, in a radio and television address, disclosed the existence of Soviet offensive weapons in Cuba and announced the United States' intention to establish a quarantine around Cuba very shortly. "Hoping to obtain OAS endorsement, he [Kennedy] deliberately obscured this question [that the United States had already decided to institute the blockade, at this point without OAS approval, because national security was directly involved] in the speech by a call for unspecified OAS action and an announcement of the blockade and other steps in 'the defense of our own security and of the entire Western Hemisphere.' "[2][3] Following the advice of Adlai E. Stevenson and the legal consultants in the State Department, the actual establishment and proclamation of the quarantine was delayed so that the OAS might have the opportunity to sanction it, thus providing the United States with a regional support for a United Nations presentation of the measures it had adopted.

That same day, October 22, Latin American ambassadors in Washington were summoned by the Secretary of State. The United States asked the OAS Council to hold an emergency meeting of the Organ of Consultation on October 23, as provided in Article 39 of the OAS Charter.[24] Edwin M. Martin, United States Assistant for Latin American Affairs, spent the night before the Meeting of Consultation briefing the OAS ambassadors in order to avoid Latin American resentment against the United States for its unilateral actions. On the following day, Secretary of State Dean Rusk invoked the security resolution of Punta del Este and the Rio Treaty[25] and offered a resolution which was beyond all previous agreements of the OAS. The Council of the OAS resolved:

> 1. *To call for the immediate dismantling and withdrawal from Cuba of all missiles and other weapons with an offensive capability;*
>
> 2. *To recommend that the Member States, in accordance with Article 6 and 8 of the Inter-American Treaty of Reciprocal Assistance, take all measures individually and collectively, including the use of armed force, which they may deem necessary to assure that the government of Cuba cannot continue to receive from the Sino-Soviet powers military material and related supplies which may threaten the peace and security of the continent and to prevent the missiles in Cuba with offensive capability from ever becoming an active threat to the peace and security of the continent;*
>
> 3. *To inform the Security Council of the United Nations of this Resolution in accordance with Article 54 of the Charter of the United Nations and to express the hope that the Security Council will, in accordance with the draft resolution introduced by the United States, disptach United Nations observers to Cuba at the earliest moment;*
>
> 4. *To continue to serve provisionally as Organ of Consultation and to request the Member States to keep the Organ of Consultation duly informed of measures taken by them in accordance with paragraph two of this resolution.*[26]

The unanimous support given by Latin Americans to the United States in the OAS temporarily obscured the divergence of views between the United States and some Latin Americans who were universally or compatibly inclined, such as, in particular, Mexico.[27] Despite widespread anti-United States feelings, the Latin American governments showed that they were not neutral when continental interests as a whole were concerned. However, there were some cracks in the solid Latin American front. Mexico, Brazil, and Bolivia had abstained from voting on the sentence of the United States' resolution that authorized the use of armed force, especially where armed force was proposed in order to "prevent the missiles in Cuba with offensive capability from ever becoming an active threat to the peace and security of the Continent." They felt that the resolution should not be used to justify an armed attack on Cuba after the current crisis had passed. Rather, they wanted to put themselves on record as supporting the United States only in its efforts to meet the immediate situation but not in its general policy toward Castro. It was apparent they felt that this particular sentence might commit them to support a United States invasion of Cuba in an effort to counteract whatever potential danger Cuba presented.

United States political objectives in convoking a meeting of the Organ of Consultation were accomplished by the passing of the United States resolution. The OAS gave collective support to the measure, which the United States was already prepared to carry out unilaterally. Any other course of action would have surely proved unsuccessful. Had the United States attempted to obtain Security Council approval before that of the OAS, the Soviet Union would certainly have vetoed the proposal. The next alternative might then have been to go to the General Assembly (under the principle of the Uniting for Peace Resolution first used during the Korean War). However, at the time, the good will lost as a result of the Bay of Pigs invasion, and the sympathy for Cuba on the part of a number of governments, would have made United States success problematic. The United Nations action could hardly have resulted in the kind of action that, at that moment, was urgently needed by the United States.[28] If the effort had still failed in the General Assembly, the United States might then have imposed the embargo independently or through the OAS. However, this would have been clearly embarrassing in light of a previous, unsuccessful effort to obtain United Nations approval of an equivalent action.

Another alternative, also discarded, envisaged turning to the United Nations General Assembly after the OAS had endorsed the United States' position. Here, since the majority would be unfavorably inclined to any unilateral action, the United States would be forced to make concessions to get the necessary majority for passage. At the precise moment a response was being considered this was impossible since the minimum demands of the United States were the dismantling of the missile sites and verification of Cuba's compliance. Clearly, the majority of the new nations would not accept enacting a collective intervention, let alone giving the United States a mandate to independently enforce an OAS decision. What Dean Acheson provided for President Truman in the Korean War—General Assembly endorsement—Stevenson was unable to procure for Kennedy. His best hope was to present OAS action as a fait accompli to the Security Council to "inform" the Council of United States actions, and to obtain a propaganda success by branding the Russian maneuver a threat to peace. This was the tactic the United States followed at the United Nations when its case was considered late in the afternoon of October 23. Some problems, however, arose in the timing of the strategy. The OAS's resolution, which actually established the strongest legal basis for United States action, was passed while the action in the Security Council was well under way. Stevenson had to be notified and given the text of the Resolution while he was addressing the Security Council. For the most part, during the Security Council meeting from October 23 to 25, Stevenson avoided juridical arguments and focused on political issues, accusing the Soviet

Union of posing a grave threat to the Western Hemisphere and to the peace of the world.

In view of the political and military emergency, which at the time could hardly be influenced by legal opinion, the Security Council treated the case as another phase of the cold war between the United States and the Soviet Union and not as an issue of regionalism versus universalism. In the course of the crisis the whole question of the definition of enforcement action in Article 53 was largely obscured. Under normal circumstances the OAS-United States action would have stirred up a jurisdictional battle of considerable proportions. On this occasion, however, since the case was taken to both organizations, calling upon them to avert a possible nuclear conflict, some jurisdictional aspects were overlooked. The jurisdictional quarrel faded into the background as the two organizations tried to join hands to help find a way out of the dilemma.[29] In particular, since the measures adopted by the OAS on United States initiative openly mentioned the use of armed force, it was not in the United States' interest in the Security Council to even mention previous American arguments in the Dominican and Cuban cases that associated enforcement action with the use of force.

Although the situation intimately involved the issue of enforcement action in Article 53 and its regional or universal implications, this provision was seldom cited in the meetings of the Security Council. Actually, when legal arguments were used by Security Council members, either to criticize or to support United States action, these revolved more around Article 2, paragraph 4, than Article 53. Article 2 (4), which stated:

> *All members shall refrain in their international relations from the threat or use of force against the territorial integrity or political independence of any state, or in any other manner inconsistent with the Purposes of the United Nations.*

was more widely referred to in connection with the quarantine than the provisions in Chapter VII or even Article 51. Only Ghana's delegate, Quaison-Sackey, criticized the United States' tacit contention that the measures ratified by the OAS did fall exclusively within the competence of the regional body. He defended the priority of the United Nations over regional organizations and termed the United States action an enforcement action, inadmissible without the prior authorization of the Security Council according to the terms of Article 53.[30]

The crisis, at the same time, had unforeseen consequences for the strengthening of the mediatory-diplomatic role of the Secretary General. When the nonaligned countries, especially from Asia and Africa, found themselves impotent as mediators in this confrontation of the superpowers, they decided to give moral and diplomatic backing to the mediatory role of the Secretary General. Involvement of the Secretary General in the crisis was decisive and was replaced only by direct communication between the Soviet Union and the United States. The crisis abated when Khrushchev promised to allow United Nations observers to verify the dismantling of the missile sites and Kennedy assured the Soviet Union that it would lift the blockade and that it would not undertake or tolerate attacks on Cuba by other states. It was in view of the agreement between the Soviet Union and American leaders that the Security Council ended its consideration of the case on October 25. The interest of the United Nations was maintained through the good offices of the Secretary General, which remained available throughout the diplomatic communications that lasted until the crisis had completely ended.

Although, in fact, the United States and the Soviet Union were left free to negotiate between themselves, the United Nations, through the Secretary General, kept a watchful vigilance over the matter. There were some obstacles in effecting the original Khrushchev-Kennedy agreement, and negotiations dragged on until January, 1963. Castro was not interested in an international inspection by the United Nations to verify the dismantling of the missile sites and he demanded exaggerated terms for his acceptance which even the visits of Anastas I. Mikoyan, Soviet first deputy premier, and Secretary General U Thant could not soften. In spite of these problems, suitable solutions were finally worked out accommodating both the United States' and the Soviet Union's demands. Instead of United Nations inspection, American aerial reconnaisance served as the means of verification and the United States in turn refrained from invasion and took measures in the spring of 1963 to prevent attacks from United States territory by Cuban refugees.

After the crisis, wide-ranging legal claims were made by the United States in support of the measures it had adopted during October, 1962. The legal advisers of the State Department developed, ex post facto, a more elaborate legal framework to justify the quarantine than the one presented to the Security Council or the OAS at the height of the crisis.[31]

The legal basis of United States arguments relied heavily on the legal and political precedents established by the 1960 Dominican case and the January-March, 1962, Cuban case, both of which tended to reinforce the authority of regional organizations to take autonomous coercive action to settle regional disputes. In the first place, United States advisers interpreted that, as a result of the discussion of the Cuban case in January-March, 1962, the Security Council accepted the fact that the measures not involving the use of armed force (Article 41) did not require authorization by the Security Council when applied by regional organizations and that such measures are not enforcement action for the purposes of Article 53. In the second place, United States legal advisers interpreted the Security Council action in the 1960 Dominican case as conclusively affirming that if an action by regional organizations were voluntarily carried out by its individual members it could not be termed illegal by the Security Council and did not require its prior authorization. Therefore, as in 1960, complete or partial interruption of economic relations and severance of diplomatic relations were not illegal measures in the United States' view because they could be taken voluntarily and unilaterally by United Nations members who were also members of a regional organization, without a decision of the Security Council; such measures did not derive their lawfulness from a Security Council authorization or fall under any provision of the charter itself.

With these precedents supplying an important legal basis, the main arguments were further elaborated. The first argument maintained that the quarantine was a coercive action, not an exercise in collective self-defense (Article 51), and not equivalent to an enforcement action under Article 53. In the proclamation of the quarantine and in President Kennedy's speech announcing it, specific reference to self-defense against armed attack under Article 51 of the United Nations Charter was deleted.

We no longer live in a world where only the actual firing of weapons represents a sufficient challenge to a nation's security to constitute maximum peril. Nuclear weapons are so destructive, and ballistic missiles are so swift, that any substantially increased possibility of their use or any sudden change in their deployment may well be regarded as a definite threat to peace.[32]

As a matter of fact, the United States rejection of the self-defense argument in effect meant turning down a course of action that might have given wider legal justification to the quarantine.[33]

The second main argument utilized by advisers in the State Department was that the use of force or the threat to use force by a regional organization could be justified on the ground that it was a voluntary action which did not require Security Council authorization. If a regional organization did not make the resort to armed force mandatory for its members but merely recommended it, there was no question of conflict of obligation; only compulsory employment of armed force on the part of OAS members was contrary to the United Nations and the OAS charters. The counterarguments stated (1) that if states band together in a regional organization whose constitution contains a provision such as the one contained in Article 20 of the Rio Treaty—members are not required to use armed force without its consent even if voted by the necessary two-thirds majority—they still cannot resort to armed force in circumstances in which it would be illegal, according to the United Nations Charter, for each one of them if they were not associated; and (2) that the recommendatory aspect is nothing more than a procedural device, irrelevant to Article 53, which emphasizes the kind of mandate issued in a regional organization and not the way it was arrived at.[34]

The third main argument of State Department legal advisers held that the quarantine was in strict compliance with the Rio Treaty: a collective action adopted by a regional organization designed to deal with a situation detrimental to the security of the Inter-American System caused by a member of that system. The sequence of the actions followed during October, 1962, backed up this argument. First, on October 22 the president's speech outlined the building of offensive missiles sites in Cuba and the Soviet Union's participation; second, on October 23, the OAS's decisions depicted the situation as one falling within Article 6 of the Rio Treaty (a danger to peace occasioned by an aggression which is not an armed attack) and recommended the measures enumerated in Article 8 of the same Rio Treaty, including the use of armed force; and third, on October 24, the quarantine proclamation was issued based on the OAS's resolution. Critics challenged this position on the basis of the fact that another part of the same Rio Treaty, Article 1, prohibits "the resort or the threat or the use of force in any manner inconsistent with the provisions of the Charter of the United Nations or of this Treaty."

A fourth argument also used by United States advisers to justify the quarantine was drawn from an expanding interpretation of the competence of regional organizations under Article 52 which actually exaggerated the overall competence of regional organizations in view of the Security Council's inability to cope with the task of adopting politically sound decisions. It was argued that "the Cuban quarantine marked an assumption of increased responsibility by a regional organization. Accompanying a decline in the affirmative authority of the Security Council it should not be surprising to find also some contradiction in the Security Council's negative authority to preclude action by other bodies."[35] It was also said that "the paralysis of the Security Council has led to a reliance on alternative peace-keeping institutions."[36] In other words, if the Security Council was unable to perform its duties, it should not be permitted to create obstacles to the development of a strong regional organization that would assume the burden of the Security Council's tasks in maintaining international peace and security. This argument was equally criticized and opposed as unsound, because action by regional organizations, according to the United Nations Charter, must under any circumstance, be consistent with the purposes and principles of the United Nations.

In sum, the actual crisis passed without serious attention being devoted to the ultimate universal and regional implications of the developing United Nations-OAS relationship. The ex post facto attempts by the United States to cite the legality of the action were not very useful in clarifying the legal basis of regional organizations when they in effect legitimized the limited use of force by its members without Security Council authorization; it was clear that the quarantine needed a more satisfactory legal basis than that which had been advanced by its official advocates.

From the political point of view, the Cuban quarantine turned out to be a skilful move: it gave the United States the assurance that no offensive missile sites would be installed by the Soviet Union in the Western Hemisphere; the Soviet Union saved face and, relative to the United States, appeared as a peace loving power; Castro was left somewhat safer politically and militarily, and the Latin Americans felt that the United States had taken them into account before acting unilaterally. From the legal point of view, the fact that the case was brought to the Security Council and, in a sense, settled through Soviet Union-United States agreement initiated within the United Nations framework and with the help of the Secretary General, avoided a direct confrontation of the two powers and the legal positions on regionalism each advocated. As a result, the major question of the nature of regional incompatibility in the adoption of enforcement action was not faced in a straightforward manner.

DOMINICAN REPUBLIC II (1965)

The OAS had pragmatically achieved, in the course of the cases just described, a de facto independence from United Nations control in the adoption of enforcement measures. Yet, despite the fact that the United States' actions in October, 1962, were based on an OAS resolution authorizing the use of military force, the OAS, up to this point, had never gone beyond simply approving the use of force; it had never engaged itself officially in the actual execution of any measure which involved the use of military force. New developments in Latin America and new political pressures brought about by United States policies soon changed this situation and brought the OAS into an active role as coordinator of peace-keeping activities where military force was prevalent. This initially occurred in April, 1965, with the crisis provoked by the United States intervention in the Dominican Republic.

Since the beginning of 1965, the stability of the military government in the Dominican Republic was threatened by the strength of popular as well as military forces favorable to the return to power of President Juan Bosch who had been ousted by a military coup in 1962. In the midst of the political and military turmoil provoked by the clash of these two factions seeking power in the Dominican Republic—the military group opposed to Bosch and to what they considered his leftist inclinations and the rebel group, or "constitutionalists," advocating the return to a constitutional rule and the reinstallation of the Bosch government—the United States dispatched marine forces to the Dominican Republic on April 28, 1965, ostensibly "to protect the lives of United States citizens living there," but actually to prevent the seizure of power by leftist forces favorable to Bosch.[37]

Criticism in the Western Hemisphere and the world compelled the United States to call for OAS action as well. Therefore, following this United States appeal, on April 30, 1965, the OAS Council convoked and immediately called for the Tenth Meeting of Consultation of the Ministers of Foreign Affairs in Washington D.C. This Meeting of Consultation made the OAS formally assume collective responsibility of the developments in the Dominican Republic, but left effective command of the entire situation to the United States. Meanwhile, despite Latin American popular and official criticisms, the United States continued to increase its military forces, and to intervene in the domestic affairs of the Dominican Republic.[38] At the Tenth Meeting of Consultation, the majority was critical of the United States' lack of willingness to consult with the OAS beforehand and its military buildup in the Dominican Republic. Many Latin American ambassadors felt that the United States, in bringing to the OAS a fait accompli, was using the OAS as a shield against criticisms from Europe, the Soviet bloc, and nonaligned countries of Asia and Africa. However, in spite of the fact that some Latin American countries, such as Mexico, did not want to cooperate in "rendering honest"[39] the act of United States intervention, OAS members, for the most part, followed a policy which avoided an open condemnation of the United States. On the contrary, the OAS did in fact serve as the means by which the United States could protect itself against outside criticism of its Dominican intervention.

At the OAS Meeting of Consultation, several courses of action were considered until finally, on May 1, 1965, the majority agreed upon Mexico's proposal to install a five-member committee to investigate the situation and submit a report. Almost immediately, the United States, in a continuing effort to divert world criticism to the OAS as a whole, began to insist that the Meeting of Consultation consider the United States troops sent to the Dominican Republic as the basis of an inter-American force. This suggestion was accepted on May 6, 1965, by the majority, which included the Dominican military junta representative. Mexico, Chile, Ecuador, and Peru were opposed and Venezuela abstained. In actuality, however, only nominal military forces were sent much later by some Latin American countries, especially Brazil and Costa Rica. The United States kept political and military command of the operations, for which the OAS was being held responsible in the Dominican Republic.

OAS lack of effectiveness in dealing with this delicate situation, despite its facade of independent action, was soon noticeable. Activities of the OAS were frequently criticized by both factions of the Dominican war, each of which at one point requested the removal of Secretary General Jose A. Mora to express their disagreement over what each faction considered the weak or strong involvement of the OAS. Equally criticized in most political and diplomatic circles all around the world was the failure of the OAS to restore peace and to restrain United States activities in the rebel-controlled zone of the Dominican capital, which violated ceasefire agreements painfully achieved by the Red Cross, the head of the Peace Corps, and the Vatican's representative to the Dominican Republic. The United States itself did not seem to rely heavily on the OAS and often either bypassed it or disregarded it politically and diplomatically. For instance, without consulting with the OAS, United States advisers, McGeorge

Bundy and Thomas Mann, were sent separately to help select the head of a provisional Dominican government.[40]

While the OAS was trying to present itself as in command of the situation and the United States was continuing to give full assistance to the military faction of the Dominican civil strife, the United Nations, at the request of the Soviet Union and Cuba, had since May 1, 1965, been engaged in discussing the United States' presence in the Dominican Republic. This time, however, the United States was unable to secure its usual backing from the members of the Security Council, as several nations outside the Soviet bloc were sharply critical of United States action. Uruguay sided with other Security Council members in its criticism of United States policies and seemed even more disposed to defend the Security Council's jurisdiction than previous Latin American members of the Security Council had ever been. The Uruguayan delegate strongly criticized the so-called Johnson doctrine: this doctrine held that even though a revolution in any Western Hemisphere country might constitute a domestic problem, it ceased to be simply an internal problem and became subject to hemispheric action and to United States involvement when its object was to establish a Communist regime. Uruguay was also among those Security Council members who criticized the establishment of an international force at the regional level. Another change of position occurred with France, who at this time seemed inclined to follow a universalist stand; it criticized United States actions and the assertions of OAS competence and favored entrusting the responsibility for the problem to the Security Council. The Ivory Coast, Malaysia, and Jordan shared similar views in defense of the Security Council's primary competence.

The Security Council met approximately thirty times between May 3 and July 26, 1965, to consider this crisis. As was expected, the United States asserted that it was "prudent and constructive" to allow the OAS to deal with the problem. The United States frequently mentioned Article 33 of the

United Nations Charter to remind the Security Council that efforts aiming at finding solutions to disputes by peaceful means included the resort to regional agencies. In the United States' view, this article described the procedures and priorities envisaged by the United Nations and the OAS Charter to deal with disputes of local nature. Only Bolivia[41] and the United Kingdom supported the United States in its defense of OAS competence. By defending incompatible regionalism in the adoption of enforcement action to this extent, the United States' real political objective of not permitting the establishment of another Communist government in the Western Hemisphere became manifest. It was clear that the United States had called the OAS in the Dominican case merely to summon the resources of the entire hemisphere to this task.

Cuba and the Soviet Union were the only countries who tried to draw Security Council attention to Article 53 of the United Nations Charter, charging that the OAS had violated that article in installing an inter-American force. But surprising as it may seem, then as well as later, little attention was given to this aspect of the crisis. United Nations efforts were oriented towards sending observers to the Dominican Republic who could inform the Security Council about developments in that country,[42] rather than focusing attention upon the jurisdictional aspects of the crisis. In the long run, attempts by Cuba, the Soviet Union, France, Uruguay, and Jordan to condemn the United States in varying degrees and to extend the power of the United Nations observer in the Dominican Republic (José A. Mayobre) were unsuccessful. A consistent United Nations universalist policy vis-à-vis the OAS failed to materialize.

United Nations observation activities in the Dominican Republic were very restricted; the situation was controlled exclusively by the OAS and particularly through the United States' dominance of the inter-American force. One of the OAS's most notorious attempts to put an end to the conflict was the installing of a three-man commission, headed by

United States Ambassador to the OAS Elsworth Bunker, and including Brazilian and Salvadorean representatives, to seek a political solution to the crisis. However, OAS attempts to bring peace to the Dominican Republic were largely unsuccessful. For many weeks the situation remained chaotic, due to OAS inability to impose a political and military solution and to United States problems in establishing an acceptable government.[43]

Finally, Hector García Godoy, Bosch's former minister of foreign affairs, became provisional president and pledged to hold free elections. The caretaker Dominican government carried out its promise and elections were held in early 1966. Bosch was defeated by a right-wing candidate, Joaquín Balaguer, former president and puppet of Trujillo, during an electoral campaign in which it seemed clear that everyone wanted peace. Bosch could not guarantee that peace, in spite of his popular support, since the military's dislike for his policies forecast new problems. To all intents and purposes, the Balaguer government turned out to be the best bet for a peaceful compromise.

Once again, as in the Cuban Missile Crisis, a crisis situation, and the need to bring about a politically workable solution as soon as possible, meant that very little attention was given to the jurisdictional aspects of the question, the issues of universalism and regionalism, the nature of regional compatibility. The onrush of events obscured the underlying issues. During the Cuban Missile Crisis the OAS authorized the use of military force by the United States, an assumption of power that was hardly contested in the Security Council due to the emergency conditions and the threat of a nuclear war. As a result, the OAS's exaggerated expectations of complete regional autonomy were nurtured and soon after applied to another emergency situation which was seen as threatening the Western Hemisphere with extracontinental intervention. This time, coercive measures adopted by the OAS not only authorized the use of military force by one member against another, but institutionalized the use of such force for all its members through the establishment of an international force at the regional level without authorization of the Security Council.

CONCLUSIONS

The sequence of cases analyzed in this chapter marks a continuum in the trend toward regional incompatibility. Measures went from diplomatic sanctions and economic boycott (in the 1960 Dominican case and in the January-March, 1962, Cuban case) to the use of armed force (in the October, 1962, Cuban Missile Crisis) and the establishment of peace-keeping operations at the regional level (in the 1965 Dominican crisis). Except for the Dominican case of 1960, Security Council authorization was neither requested nor given for measures adopted by the OAS.

Clearly, political considerations were responsible for much of what has ensued. All four cases share the feature of being examples of crisis situations which have obscured the underlying issues involved and in so doing subjected the charter to the strain of an incompatible interpretation with only limited support from the international community. The incompatibility of the OAS, resulting from this strain in the last decade and a half, in effect represented a political victory for the United States rather than a tribute to the efficacy of international organizations, either universal or regional. But this victory was not without its costs; the success of the United States in getting the necessary votes for its policies as quickly as possible has been offset in each instance by the resentment created.

Nevertheless there are differences among the cases described, particularly in terms of the legal debate over the regional provisions of the United Nations Charter. For example, the 1960 Dominican case and the January-March, 1962, Cuban case were discussed in the United Nations under the framework of Article 53, while in the Cuban Missile

Crisis, and in the 1965 Dominican affairs, Article 53 was seldom mentioned. Later, discussions focused on Article 2 (4) and the first three paragraphs of Article 52. Action by the United Nations in the 1965 Dominican crisis consisted of the sending of an observer, and, in the Cuban Missile Crisis, the involvement of the Secretary General. While in both cases the OAS sanctioned collective intervention, in the first the OAS was consulted beforehand, while in the second the OAS faced a fait accompli.

The effective power of Article 53 to control OAS regional activities in the adoption of enforcement action in each one of these cases was pragmatically minimized, if not eliminated, for the OAS either completely disregarded United Nations primacy or took steps to avoid United Nations control. In actual fact, the OAS monopolized all stages of peaceful settlement of disputes of countries within its area, in addition to the application of sanctions and the establishment of peacekeeping operations. Provisions of the United Nations Charter which assign a monopoly of such measures to the universal organization for the purpose of safeguarding the needs and interests of the members appear to have been more or less relegated to the background.

Some universally inclined observers have argued that the Security Council did assert its jurisdiction in these cases. It has been said that the Security Council "took note" of the action against the Dominican Republic in 1960, that the same body heard and then rejected the Cuban bid for an advisory opinion of the International Court of Justice, that the Secretary General's involvement in the Cuban Missile Crisis was the turning point of the crisis, and that in the Dominican crisis of 1965 the Security Council studied the case and sent an observer. All these arguments conclude optimistically that, as a result, the United Nations' universal competence was confirmed and that the United States' battle to make the Security Council recognize the primacy of the OAS suffered significant setbacks. However, the outcome of each one of the four cases does not actually allow for such an enthusiastic universal interpretation. On the contrary, realistically speaking, one may affirm without exaggeration that the four rounds were won by the incompatible regionalists. Incompatible regionalists were largely justified in viewing the Dominican case of 1960 and the failure of Cuba's efforts to have Article 53 defined by the International Court of Justice as practical confirmations of OAS exclusive jurisdiction. Also, because of the biases of OAS members against United Nations involvement, and the United States predominance in OAS activities in the Dominican Republic, including the inter-American force, incompatible regionalists were able to keep the role of the United Nations' observer in the Dominican Republic in 1965 to a minimum.

Going beyond the organizational level to the more general political context, the issue of regional compatibility or incompatibility can be seen on the already long list of disagreements and tensions in Soviet-American relations. In addition, the discussion of these regional-universal issues and of regional incompatibility has exacerbated some procedural problems of the United Nations' general practice, especially in those instances where complaining countries not represented in the Security Council have not been granted a hearing and have been forced to present their views through the Soviet Union delegation. Invariably, Soviet presentation of the views of other nations is taken by the United States and Western countries as a proof of the Communist affiliations of a government. But the placement of these issues in the battlefield of the cold war has essentially distorted them; each side has championed a given position in an effort to enhance its relative position vis-à-vis the other. Moreover, in effect, the alignment of the superpowers on either side has escolated the debates and often tied them to crisis situations. The Soviet Union has abandoned its traditional negative position with respect to the authority of international organizations and has assumed the role of defender of a strong and effective United

Nations. By so doing, the Soviet Union has placed the United States in the embarrassing position of opposing a vigorous and expansive role of the United Nations. With the Latin Americans lending uncertain support, the United States has come to assume the leadership of the battle for regional incompatibility. Although the United States has tried to justify such a course of action by arguing that it is attempting to avoid the Soviet veto, the fact that the use of the veto blocks the Security Council's execution of functions entrusted to it by the charter does not justify a group of countries taking over that function.

In addition, the issue of regional incompatibility here again entails important consequences for the relations between large and small states, and in particular the United States and the Latin American states. The United Nations is still the only forum where world political forces converge and the only place where they can be balanced. It provides the context where complaints of small and middle-sized countries against big powers can be considered without the exclusive control of one over the other. Regional forums, as the past two chapters have shown, do not guarantee the effective and equal participation of all members in the organization's activities. Indeed, more often than not, one power clearly dominates the actions of all the others.

More important, in terms of international relations as a whole, is the effect of the OAS's example on other regional organizations throughout the world. The use of force, even under collective regional authorization, runs the grave risk of triggering a chain reaction of wider proportions. Although the United Nations Charter itself has withstood formal modifications despite the incompatible interpretations of this period, the same license taken by the OAS on the grounds of expediency could be and has been claimed by other regional organizations.

In July, 1964, for example, the Organization of African Unity (OAU) went beyond a United Nations resolution regarding restrictions on air and sea transport to South Africa and Portugal and called for the denial of the rights of aircraft or ships en route to or coming from South Africa or Portugal. In addition, it is not unlikely that, in view of the political situation in most of the African countries, the OAU, might very well in the future, regard the right to intervene for or against the suppression of a rebellion in, let us say Ghana or the Congo. An example of NATO's incompatibility can be cited when, in 1964, the United Kingdom considered the possibility of asking NATO to undertake the peace-keeping operations in Cyprus to prevent Soviet intervention. President Makarios refused to accept such a plan and it was eventually discarded.

Furthermore, examples of regional incompatibility can also be found within the Soviet bloc. In 1956, the Soviet repression of the Hungarian revolution prompted the United Nations to consider the possibility of intervening. This proposal was dispensed with when the Russian-installed Hungarian government rejected every move for United Nations inquiry, including a visit by the Secretary General, under the privilege of domestic jurisdiction. The Warsaw Treaty members helped keep the United Nations aside when they insisted that the international implications of the rebellion concerned only Hungary's allies. To some extent, the Soviet government used the Warsaw Treaty provisions to find excuses for its unilateral intervention.

In addition, the Middle East is in danger of becoming the stage of an incompatible regional action. There are some precedents along this line: in May, 1948, after the declaration of independence by Israel, forces of Arab countries contended that their military activities were taken in accordance with the Arab League. At that time, although the United States and other Security Council members objected, the Security Council never discussed the issue seriously. However, in their constant quarrels with Israel, the Arab countries might well in the future come up with a stronger case for the autonomy of the

Arab League and its right to take action against Israel, now that the way has been paved by the OAS. Nor is it impossible that, in Asia, a China-centered regional organization will be set up at some future time claiming independence from the United Nations.

The continuum towards regional incompatibility in the adoption of enforcement action was exhibited in three main areas: (1) in the application of sanctions falling short of military action, (2) in the use of force, and (3) in the establishment of peace-keeping operations. Each of these measures represents a relatively high level of coercion. As a result, it is only logical that the authority for their use was intended to reside in a universal organization subject to the approval or disapproval of the nations of the world. The usurpation of these functions by a strictly regional organization is thus highly incompatible with the purposes for which the United Nations was set up.

The necessity of reporting and getting prior Security Council authorization for nonmilitary sanctions was ignored by OAS members despite the fact that this kind of sanction was particularly coercive for small countries in areas dominated by a big power. Considerable evidence in the modern international community supports the view that diplomatic and financial sanctions should be treated as enforcement action under Article 53 and therefore subject to United Nations control. The solution to the Dominican Republic case in 1960, that the Security Council should only take note of such measures, was far from conclusive. The assertion that the Security council take note of such measures introduces a note of uncertainty into the original United Nations concepts, which were to some extent compatibly oriented. The decision of the Security Council to take note, without approving or disapproving regional enforcement measures falling short of military action, turned out to be an especially important precedent for the OAS. Later, it was actually used as the basis upon which to reject the Cuban request for an advisory opinion by the International Court of Justice and to stress the fact that the United Nations should not block regional action. Such pragmatic reductions in the scope of enforcement actions—removing measures falling short of military action from the traditional concept of coercive measures—narrowed the circumstances in which Security Council authorization was required under Article 53.

But OAS members, however, went considerably further. The use of force was authorized by the OAS in October, 1962, during the Cuban Missile Crisis and was actively carried out by the United States through the establishment of an air and naval blockade. The United Nations was presented with the fait accompli that the OAS had already granted the United States the power to establish the quarantine—for which Security Council authorization was neither sought nor given. Due to the emergency of the situation, the Security Council avoided the juridical issue and the political implications of such an action. Later, as a result of its success in this instance, the OAS organized peace-keeping operations on its own, again without prior authorization by the Security Council, during the Dominican crisis of 1965.

Clearly, the seriousness of enforcement actions (military as well as nonmilitary) requires that they receive prior authorization in the United Nations. Yet several distinctions may be made in an attempt to reach, or at least suggest, a solution to the problem of regional incompatibility in this field. Due to the intensity of the action, it can be concluded that the use of military force should be authorized only by the Security Council and should not be initiated against the approval of one or more of the great powers. Since measures falling short of military action are less likely to create serious conflicts, it seems reasonable to propose that such an authorization may be given by the General Assembly. This would make regional organizations more likely to accept the requirement of prior approval. It would also seem to be acceptable to the big powers because of the worldwide support that such measures could draw from a majority in the General Assembly. How-ever, under the present circumstances, the actual possibility of this alternative looks rather dim. The OAS's members are reluctant to seek approval from the General Assembly because of the voting power of the African and Asian members. Latin Americans have even labeled this strength the *aplanadora,* the steam roller which gets policies endorsed or rejected by the Afro-Asian group through the General Assembly by sheer weight of numbers, crushing all opposition.[44]

Finally, peace-keeping has to be considered on a different level of coercion than ordinary military operations. Peace-keeping is a concept that was pragmatically introduced in the United Nations to meet deficiencies in the system of collec-tive security but not designed to substitute for it. Thus, because of its novelty and lack of clear definition, it is especially important that peace-keeping operations be made to comply with certain requisites already established in the prac-tice of the United Nations itself. While peace-keeping opera-tions vary from one situation to another, there are some conditions that may be devised for their satisfactory function-ing, such as the consent of the parties involved, the voluntary contributions of the members, balanced control by the Secur-ity Council, de facto control by the Secretary General and the self-imposed restriction on the use of force only in cases of self-defense.[45] It is apparent that its pacifying functions are more similar to policing functions than to traditional military ones. Therefore, if the requisites established by the United Nations are met and peace-keeping operations do not become coercive, authorization for regional organizations to establish such operations could be sought in the General Assembly. The General Assembly could then grant its approval only if the regional body which initiates and controls the operation is not biased against one or more of its members, especially the one or ones to which the operation is directed. Unfortunately, not only the OAS, but most of the regional organizations func-tioning nowadays, fall short of meeting this requirement.

More frequently than not, regional organizations are more interested in the final political outcome than in the impartial solution of a problem.

In sum, it can be shown that regional incompatibility cannot be justified either logically—in terms of the essential functions of regional and universal organizations—or politically—in terms of the actual power relationships of the postwar world. Even if it is agreed that regionalism is a "halfway house in a time when single nations are no longer viable and the world is not ready to become one,"[46] and that the lack of world unity and understanding will make necessary the resort to halfway measures for a long time, it is vital not to lose sight of the long-range goals of universal organizations and world order. If recourse to solutions that are essentially incompatible is used exclusively, ignoring the broader aspirations of the international community, international organizations run the risk of being left straddled awkwardly between two worlds, a world of ideals and a world of power politics, bridged only by a succession of pragmatic improvisations to meet a series of unanticipated crises.

Clearly, the current political situation provides obstacles to reversing this trend. Naturally, the major powers, the United States included, will prefer the handling of cases in the regional forums, which they dominate with less difficulty than the world organization. In a regional forum they essentially retain their capacity for unilateral decision-making on fundamental matters, and, in many instances, regional organizations provide valuable face-saving devices for a big power's action which cannot be obtained easily at the United Nations. For instance, the United States' cavalier disregard for the OAS during the 1965 Dominican crisis, when it acted before consulting with the OAS, had to be masked by assigning a regional responsibility for the action; the "legitimacy of multilateralization"[47] had to be sought in order to face the United Nations' and world's criticisms. The 1965 Dominican crisis, and to a certain extent the Cuban Missile Crisis, proved that the United States will act unilaterally and will disregard OAS principles most cherished by Latin Americans whenever the OAS does not provide the United States with support for its policies against Communist penetration in the Western Hemisphere.[48]

In its hemispheric context, the United States' policy of containment of Communism disassociates the military security problem from the deeper hemispheric problems of social, political, and economic development. It fails to recognize the more basic threats to security posed by demands for social change and political recognition. It disregards the fact that the OAS is not seen by Latin Americans as a rubber stamp for United States policies. Latin Americans view the major function of the OAS as mitigation, even if it is only by giving the appearance of prior consultation, of the inevitable subordination of their interests to those of the United States. For the Latin Americans, the OAS exists fundamentally as a device through which they can persuade the United States to exercise self-restraint in the use of its enormous power. Frequently, any United States reference to collective intervention revives among Latin Americans the fear of United States intervention more than of Communist intrusion. In fact, they are more afraid of the shepherd than of the wolf.

If only to redress the political balance between the United States and the Latin American states, and between all major powers and smaller powers, the primacy of the United Nations must be reinforced. In order to accomplish this, nations faced with apparent threats to world peace and security must turn more and more often to universal organs rather than seeking pragmatic and essentially ad hoc solutions at the regional level. Here, due to the unequal distribution of power among members of regional organizations, whatever political balance exists depends upon the self-restraint of the predominant power rather than on concrete institutional safeguards. Thus, as this analysis has shown, while actual political trends have been promoting the opposite tendencies, political exigencies, the requirement of a peaceful and just world community, demand the creation of compatible regional organizations and a predominant universal one.

NOTES

CHAPTER 1

1. The only changes in the United Nations Charter, amendments to Articles 22, 27, and 61 (adopted by the General Assembly on December 17, 1965, effective August 31, 1965) are circumscribed to enlarge the membership of the Security Council and the Economic and Social Council. They also changed the number of votes required in the Security Council on procedural and substantive matters.

2. Article 102 of the OAS Charter states that none of its provisions should be construed as impairing the rights and obligations of the members under the UN Charter.

3. Presently the OAS has more than twenty-one members. The phrase was coined popularly in Latin America before Cuba's expulsion from the OAS in 1962 and before the recent admission of new members into the OAS.

CHAPTER 2

1. Robert E. Sherwood, ROOSEVELT AND HOPKINS, pp. 785-790; Ruth B. Russell, A HISTORY OF THE UNITED NATIONS CHARTER: THE ROLE OF THE UNITED STATES, 1940-1945, pp. 98-101.

2. Romain Yakemtchouk, "Le régionalisme et l'ONU," pp. 406-410; Sherwood, ROOSEVELT AND HOPKINS, pp. 717-718.

3. Cordell Hull, THE MEMOIRS OF CORDELL HULL, pp. 1626-1627; Sumner Wells, WHERE ARE WE HEADING? p. 24.

4. Welles, WHERE ARE WE HEADING? pp. 23-24 and THE TIME FOR

DECISION, pp. 377-378.

5. As quoted in Russell, THE UNITED NATIONS CHARTER, p. 107.

6. A brief summary of Winston Churchill's and the British views is available in Hull, MEMOIRS, pp. 1740-1642. See also Russell, THE UNITED NATIONS CHARTER, pp. 102-105, 114-115.

7. Sherwood, ROOSEVELT AND HOPKINS, p. 786.

8. Hull, MEMOIRS, p. 1643.

9. Ibid., p. 1640.

10. Ibid., pp. 1645-1646.

11. Russell, THE UNITED NATIONS CHARTER, pp. 116-121.

12. Ibid., p. 96.

13. Hull, MEMOIRS, p. 1645.

14. The United States Senate interpreted and accepted the content of the proposals as pure and straightforward universalism. See debates, especially Warren B. Austin and Homer Ferguson in CONGRESSIONAL RECORDS, vol. 91, pt. 1, pp. 470-472.

15. See Yakemtchouk, L'ONU: LA SECURITE REGIONALE ET LE PROBLEME DU REGIONALISME, pp. 59-64; Hanna Saba, "Les accords régionaux dans la Charte de l'ONU," pp. 662-663.

16. Alvin Z. Rubinstein, THE SOVIETS IN INTERNATIONAL ORGANIZATION, p. 3.

17. Welles, WHERE ARE WE HEADING? p. 26.

18. Their enthusiasm for American participation at this time contrasts very starkly with their later position (see Chapter IV).

19. Hull, MEMOIRS, p. 164. See also Arthur P. Whitaker, INTER-AMERICAN AFFAIRS, 1943, pp. 45-47; and J. Lloyd Mecham, "The integration of the inter-American security system into the United Nations," pp. 181-182.

20. Whitaker, THE WESTERN HEMISPHERE IDEA: ITS RISE AND DECLINE, p. 171.

21. Hull, MEMOIRS, pp. 1709-1710.

22. Laurence Duggan, THE AMERICAS: THE SEARCH FOR HEMISPHERE SECURITY, p. 107.

23. Welles, WHERE ARE WE HEADING? pp. 24, 210-211. Welles is probably referring in the last paragraph to Latin American reluctance to go along with the United States' attitudes toward Argentina.

24. The first one held after the Columbus Day Celebration was on October 26, 1944. A second one was held on November 9, and a third on December 29. Later, in 1945, they met on January 5, 26, and 31, and February 5 and 9. See Alfred A. Volpe, "Latin America at San Francisco: the aims, attitudes and accomplishments of Latin America at the United Nations Conference on International Organization, San Francisco, April 25 - June 26, 1945," pp. 51-60.

25. Mecham, "The inter-American security system," pp. 184-185.

26. Duggan, THE AMERICAS, p. 108.

27. Welles, WHERE ARE WE HEADING? pp. 34-35, 211.

28. See Duggan, THE AMERICAS, pp. 108-109 and Hull, MEMOIRS, p. 1678 for two different versions of this incident. See also Russell, THE UNITED NATIONS CHARTER, p. 556.

29. Quoted in Samuel Guy Inman, INTER-AMERICAN CONFERENCES, 1826-1954: HISTORY AND PROBLEMS, p. 216.

30. Galo Plaza, "Latin America's contribution to the United Nations," pp. 153-155.

31. Hull, MEMOIRS, pp. 1405-1408.

32. Yet membership in this international organization was never implied in a narrow sense. It was agreed that at least two of the Soviet republics would be accepted as original members. At the San Francisco Conference, Latin Americans were able to use this circumstance as an argument in their struggle for Argentina's admission. See Leland M. Goodrich, THE UNITED NATIONS, p. 86 and Sherwood, ROOSEVELT AND HOPKINS, pp. 854-857.

33. Volpe, "Latin America at San Francisco," pp. 215-225; Sherwood, ROOSEVELT AND HOPKINS, pp. 875-877.

34. This belief was further strengthened by another incident, which occurred on April 26 over the conference's presidency, and which once again aligned Latin America with the United States. Mexican Foreign Minister Ezequiel Padilla, acting as spokesman for the Latin American group, defended United States presidency as the application of a customary diplomatic rule that always granted the country serving as host for a conference the right to the presidency. Molotov, supported by Eden, proposed a rotating presidency of the sponsoring governments. Exasperated over the Latin American position, Molotov attacked the Mexican delegate's views and called the Latin American countries puppets of the United States. These Soviet attacks antagonized Latin American attitudes toward the Soviet Union even more than the issue of Argentina, which was to be discussed next. See Arthur H. Vandenberg, Jr. (ed.), THE PRIVATE PAPERS OF SENATOR VANDENBERG, pp. 179-181.

35. Hull, MEMOIRS, p. 1680.

36. Welles, WHERE ARE WE HEADING? pp. 211-214; Vandenberg, PAPERS OF SENATOR VANDENBERG, pp. 181-183; United Nations, CONFERENCE ON INTERNATIONAL ORGANIZATION, vol. 1, pp. 344-358; John A. Houston, LATIN AMERICA IN THE UNITED NATIONS, pp. 27-29. (Documents of the United Nations Conference in San Francisco on International Organization will be hereinafter referred to as UNCIO.)

37. For these views see Whitaker, "Development of American regionalism: the Organization of American States," pp. 129-130; Welles, WHERE ARE WE HEADING? pp. 41-42; H. G. Nicholas, THE UNITED NATIONS AS A POLITICAL INSTITUTION, p. 9; Daniel S. Cheever and Field H. Haviland, ORGANIZING FOR PEACE, pp. 64-65; Victor Andrès Belaunde, LA CONFERENCIA DE SAN FRANCISCO, pp. 22-23.

CHAPTER 3

1. UNCIO, vol. 12, p. 857.

2. For these views, see the Australian, Belgian, and Bolivian delegations' statements. UNCIO, vol. 12, pp. 668-670.

3. See UNCIO, Terms of Reference of Committee III/4, vol. 12, pp. 764-784, and Interim Report to Committee III/4 on the Work of Subcommittee III/4/A, vol. 12, pp. 833-837. See also Romain Yakemtchouk, L'ONU, LA SECURITE REGIONALE ET LE PROBLEME DU REGIONALISME, pp. 73, 105.

4. For a distinction between arrangements and agencies see Hans Kelsen, THE LAW OF THE UNITED NATIONS: A CRITICAL ANALYSIS OF ITS FUNDAMENTAL PROBLEMS, p. 319.

5. Ibid., p. 324.

6. Ibid., pp. 434-435.

7. This interpretation was given by Leland M. Goodrich and Edvard Hambro, THE CHARTER OF THE UNITED NATIONS: COMMENTARY AND DOCUMENTS, p. 314.

8. Ward P. Allen, "Regional arrangements and the United Nations," pp. 926-927.

9. Kelsen, THE LAW OF THE UNITED NATIONS, pp. 436-437.

10. Goodrich and Hambro, THE CHARTER OF THE UNITED NATIONS, p. 314.

11. Fear, especially among the members of the Soviet delegation, that the universalist basis of the maintenance of peace and security would be threatened by any substantial decentralization of authority was probably behind the adoption of this last paragraph in Article 52. See Victor Andrés Belaunde, LA CONFERENCIA DE SAN FRANCISCO, p. 88.

12. UNCIO, vol. 12, pp. 686-687.

13. Allen, "Regional arrangements and the United Nations," pp. 926-927.

14. The travaux préparatoires of the conference support the contention that "enforcement action" was broadly interpreted, including military and nonmilitary coercion. See report of H. Boncour, UNCIO, Commission III/3, Section II, vol. 12, p. 508.

15. Kelsen, THE LAW OF THE UNITED NATIONS, pp. 786-787. In two draft plans for the charter, the United States included economic, commercial, and financial measures within the category of enforcement action. See Inis L. Claude, Jr., "The OAS, the UN and the United States," p. 50.

16. See Pierre Vellas, LE REGIONALISME INTERNATIONALE ET L'ONU, pp. 38-48. The exception covered the Treaty of Alliance between the Soviet Union and the United Kingdom, signed at London on May 26, 1942; the Agreement of Friendship and Mutual Assistance between the Soviet Union and Czechoslovakia, signed at Moscow on December 12, 1942; the Treaty of Alliance and Mutual Assistance between the Soviet Union and France, signed at Moscow on December 12, 1944; the Treaty of Friendship and Alliance between the Soviet Union and the Republic of China, signed at Moscow on August 15, 1945; the Treaty of Friendship and Alliance between France and the United Kingdom, signed at Dunkirk on March 14, 1947; and the treaties of mutual assistance concluded by the Soviet Union and the states of Eastern Europe. See Goodrich and Hambro, THE CHARTER OF THE UNITED NATIONS, pp. 316-317. See also W. W. Kulski, "The Soviet system of collective security as compared with the Western system"; Claude, SWORDS INTO PLOWSHARES, p. 108; John F. Dulles, WAR OR PEACE, p. 90

17. UNCIO, Fifth Meeting of Committee III/4, June 8, 1945, vol. 12, p. 702.

18. The joint proposal of the four sponsoring governments was very similar to an earlier amendment separately presented by France, which proposed, in addition to paragraph 2 of the corresponding regional provisions of the Dumbarton Oaks Proposals, a provision to the effect that authorization not be requested for measures of an urgent nature provided for in treaties of mutual assistance of which the Security Council had been advised, subject, however, to an obligation to give an account to the Council of the measures taken. UNCIO, Terms of Reference of Committee III/4, vol. 12, p. 777.

19. Arthur H. Vandenberg, Jr. (ed.), THE PRIVATE PAPERS OF SENATOR VANDENBERG, pp. 187-188.

20. Ibid., p. 189.

21. Ibid., p. 191.

22. Dulles, WAR OR PEACE, p. 91.

23. The origins of this provision are in an Australian proposal that measures regional or otherwise, taken in self-defense, should be permissible if the Security Council failed either to authorize such action or to take action itself. However, a Turkish project was the first one to mention collective aspects of self-defense. See Yakemtchouk, L'ONU, LA SECURITE REGIONAL, pp. 110-111; UNCIO, Terms of Reference of Committee III/4, vol. 12, p. 781. The United States explained that the article was an amalgamation of the projects of amendments offered by Australia, Czechoslovakia, France, Turkey, and the Latin American states. See Ruth B. Russell, A HISTORY OF THE UNITED NATIONS CHARTER: THE ROLE OF THE UNITED STATES, 1940-1945, p. 703.

24. Vandenberg, PAPERS OF SENATOR VANDENBERG, p. 192.

25. Ibid. The United States delegation had its quarters at the Fairmont Hotel. The penthouse was occupied by Secretary Stettinius and many important decisions were reached there.

26. John F. Dulles (WAR OR PEACE, p. 92) recalls that one vivid impression of that meeting was "Senator Connally, standing half crouched, with arms outstretched, and shouting to a circle of Latin American diplomats: 'You must trust the United States.'"

27. Ibid.

28. Vandenberg, PAPERS OF SENATOR VANDENBERG, p. 197; Dulles, WAR OR PEACE, p. 92; Russell, THE UNITED NATIONS CHARTER, p. 701.

29. UNCIO, vol. 12, pp. 682-684.

30. Ibid. pp. 680-682.

31. Ibid.

32. This interpretation that an international treaty was necessary seems to have been favored by the Latin Americans and the United States. See below the section on the Rio Treaty, signed in 1947.

33. For a detailed description of these ambiguities in Article 51 see Yakemtchouk, L'ONU, LA SECURITE REGIONALE, pp. 120-130; Goodrich, "Regionalism and the United Nations," pp. 9-12; Covey Oliver, THE INTER-AMERICAN SECURITY SYSTEM AND THE CUBAN CRISIS, pp. 13-14; J. E. S. Fawcett, "Intervention in international law: a study of some recent cases, " pp.

359-369; Asbjorn Eide, "Peace-keeping and enforcement by regional organizations."

The "Uniting for Peace" resolution may also have had some effects in these contexts. The General Assembly could intervene if the Security Council would be paralyzed by a veto. See Gerhard Behr, "Regional organizations; a United Nations problem," pp. 174-175.

CHAPTER 4

1. Ronald M. Stromberg, COLLECTIVE SECURITY AND AMERICAN FOREIGN POLICY, p. 237.

2. Phillip E. Jacob and Alexine L. Atherton, THE DYNAMICS OF INTERNATIONAL ORGANIZATION, p. 112.

3. D. W. Bowett, SELF-DEFENSE IN INTERNATIONAL LAW, p. 219.

4. Only eight countries declared the war on the Central Powers: Brazil, Cuba, Costa Rica, Guatemala, Haiti, Honduras, Nicaragua, and Panama; five severed diplomatic relations: Peru, Bolivia, Uruguay, Ecuador, and the Dominican Republic; while seven remained neutral: Argentina, Chile, Colombia, Mexico, El Salvador, Venezuela, and Paraguay. The belligerents and those that severed diplomatic relations, except Costa Rica and the Dominican Republic, were represented at Versailles, and, except Ecuador, signed and ratified the peace treaty as original members. The neutrals were invited to adhere almost immediately, except Mexico, who joined the league later.

5. ARTICLE 10. *The Members of the League undertake to respect and preserve against external aggression the territorial integrity and existing political independence of all Members of the League. In case of any such aggression or in case of any threat or danger of such aggression the Council shall advise upon the means by which this obligation shall be fulfilled.*

6. ARTICLE 21. *Nothing in the Covenant shall be deemed to affect the validity of international engagements, such as the treaties of arbitration or regional understandings such as the Monroe Doctrine, for securing the maintenance of peace.*

7. John H. Spencer, "The Monroe Doctrine and the League Covenant," pp. 411-413; Pierre Vellas, LE REGIONALISME INTERNATIONALE ET L'ONU, pp. 11-16; J. M. Yepes, "Les accords régionaux et le droit internationale," p. 258. For relations between Articles 10 and 21 see Arfa Mirza Riza Khan, L'ARTICLE 10 DU PACTE DE LA SOCIETE DES NATIONS: LES ACCORDS DE LOCARNO ET LE DESARMEMENT; David Hunter Miller; THE DRAFTING OF THE COVENANT; Vladislao Mirkovitch, DES RAPPORTS ENTRE L'ARTICLE 10 ET L'ARTICLE 21 DU PACTE DE LA SOCIETE DES NATIONS; Philip Marshall Brown, "Mexico and the Monroe Doctrine."

8. Brown, "The Monroe Doctrine and the League of Nations," pp. 207-208.

9. For a detailed description of these incidents see Bryce Wood, THE UNITED STATES AND LATIN AMERICAN WARS, 1932-1942.

10. See Wood, THE MAKING OF THE GOOD NEIGHBOR POLICY.

11. Arthur P. Whitaker, THE WESTERN HEMISPHERE IDEA: ITS RISE AND DECLINE, p. 24.

12. Erich Hula, "Pan Americanism: its utopian and realistic elements." This Argentinian view prevailed during the war and after.

13. Gordon Connell-Smith, THE INTER-AMERICAN SYSTEM, p. 97.

14. Whitaker, THE WESTERN HEMISPHERE IDEA, p. 157.

15. Hula, "Pan Americanism," p. 130

16. Connell-Smith, THE INTER-AMERICAN SYSTEM, p. 95.

17. J. Lloyd Mecham, THE UNITED STATES AND INTER-AMERICAN SECURITY, 1889-1960, p. 188.

18. Connell-Smith, THE INTER-AMERICAN SYSTEM, p. 113.

19. Hula, "Pan Americanism," p. 131.

20. When the conference met, nine Central American and Caribbean countries (Costa Rica, Cuba, the Dominican Republic, Guatemala, Haiti, Honduras, Nicaragua, Panama, and El Salvador) had declared war on the Axis powers, while Colombia, Mexico, and Venezuela had severed diplomatic relations with them. The remaining Latin American countries had proclaimed their nonbelligerence but had affirmed their faith in the principle of continental solidarity.

21. Whitaker, THE WESTERN HEMISPHERE IDEA, p. 172.

22. Donald M. Dozer, ARE WE GOOD NEIGHBORS? p. 225.

23. The tremendous dollar credits accumulated by Latin America during the war could not be used because they had to be spent in the United States at inflated prices. For all practical purposes they became valueless.

24. This plan was later enforced during the San Francisco Conference by promises of President Truman and Secretary Stettinius to convoke a conference immediately after the United Nations conference to negotiate such a treaty.

25. Connell-Smith, THE INTER-AMERICAN SYSTEM, p. 141.

26. Shortly before the Argentine elections, United States Ambassador Spruille Braden engaged in an open criticism of Juan Domingo Perón, presidential candidate. The United States government issued a Blue Book giving an account of Perón's Facist inclinations in an effort to discredit him before the elections. Nationalist Argentinians resented such intervention in their domestic affairs and voted for him anyhow. Contrary to what was subsequently expected, when the conference finally met, the Argentine delegation did cooperate satisfactorily with the other delegations in the drafting and signing of the treaty.

27. All the Latin American republics were represented except for Nicaragua, who was not officially admitted because the revolutionary government that had recently seized power in that country had not been recognized by many of the participants, and Ecuador, who was not asked to sign the treaty because of a change of government that occurred while the conference was taking place.

28. Some distinctions were made as to the process to be followed if aggression took place in or outside the regional safety belt. See Article 3, paragraph 3, of the Rio Treaty.

29. The Organ of Consultation could be either a Meeting of Foreign Ministers or the Governing Board of the Pan-American Union (later transformed into the OAS Council).

30. *ARTICLE 8. For the purposes of this Treaty, the measures on which the Organ of Consultation may agree will comprise one or more of the following: recall of chiefs of diplomatic missions; breaking of diplomatic relations; breaking of consular relations; partial or complete interruption of economic relations; or of rail, sea, air, postal, telegraphic, telephonic, and radiotelephonic or radiotelegraphic communications; and use of armed force.*

31. For an analysis of the Inter-American Treaty of Reciprocal Assistance see Antonio Gómez Robledo, LA SEGURIDAD COLECTIVA EN EL CONTINENTE AMERICANO; Ward P. Allen, "The Inter-American Treaty of Reciprocal Assistance"; George A. Finch, "The inter-American defense treaty"; Norberto A. Frontini, "El Pacto de Rio de Janeiro y el Pacto del Atlantico"; Gómez Robledo, "El Tratado de Rio"; Joseph L. Kunz, "The Inter-American Treaty of Reciprocal Assistance"; Connell-Smith, THE INTER-AMERICAN SYSTEM, pp. 195-196.

32. See Whitaker, "Development of American regionalism: the Organization of American States," p. 135; Daniel S. Cheever and Field H. Haviland, ORGANIZING FOR PEACE, pp. 826-827; Arthur H. Vandenberg, Jr. (ed.) THE PRIVATE PAPERS OF SENATOR VANDENBERG, pp. 400, 419-420; John F. Dulles, WAR OR PEACE, pp. 94-99, 204-207.

33. Leland M. Goodrich, THE UNITED NATIONS, pp. 169-170.

34. Samuel Guy Inman, INTER-AMERICAN CONFERENCES, 1826-1954: HISTORY AND PROBLEMS, p. 226.

35. Ibid., p. 227. Marshall recognized that the United States was giving its primary economic aid to Europe, whose rehabilitation was more important for the rest of the world than that of any other region. The Truman administration, inspired particularly by Secretary of Commerce Averell Harriman, had been sponsoring programs to foster private United States capital investments in Latin America, in spite of the fact that most of the countries of the area preferred government loans because they draw a lower interest and therefore make a smaller drain in their foreign exchange holdings. See Donald M. Dozer, ARE WE GOOD NEIGHBORS? p. 244.

36. Connell-Smith, THE INTER-AMERICAN SYSTEM, p. 152.

37. The inter-American conference that was scheduled to meet after the Rio Conference was postponed five different times and became one of Washington's main difficulties in inter-American relations. It was held finally in December, 1954, and did not live up to Latin American expectations. See Inman, INTER-AMERICAN CONFERENCES, p. 234.

38. Miguel S. Wionczek, "Latin American Free Trade Association," pp. 24-25; by the same author, "La actitud de los Estados Unidos frente al problema de la integración económica de América Latina"; Minerva Morales M., "Política económica de los Estados Unidos en la América Latina."

39. Great Britain, France, and the Netherlands, besides Canada and the Latin Americans, are members of ECLA.

40. These views about Marshall were expressed by Inman, INTER-AMERICAN CONFERENCES, p. 234.

41. Ibid., p. 35.

42. This was transformed from the old Governing Board of the Pan-

American Union into a standing permanent committee of the representatives of all the American republics. Its functions are outlined mainly in Articles 39 and 40.

43. It should be noted that no mention is made here of the General Assembly. For an opinion on this lack of mention see Connell-Smith, THE INTER-AMERICAN SYSTEM, p. 216.

44. Ibid., p. 210.

45. Ibid., p. 214.

46. United Nations Secretary Trygve Lie attended the Rio Conference in 1947 as United Nations representative and Byron Price, Lie's representative, had been at the Ninth Inter-American Conference.

CHAPTER 5

1. Lincoln P. Bloomfield, THE UNITED NATIONS AND UNITED STATES FOREIGN POLICY: A NEW LOOK AT THE NATIONAL INTEREST, p. 247.

2. Edgar S. Furniss, "A re-examination of regional arrangements," p. 84.

3. The cases considered here are Costa Rica-Nicaragua, 1948-1949, 1955-1956, Haiti-Dominican Republic, 1949, 1949-1950, 1963, Honduras-Nicaragua, 1957, Panama, 1959, Nicaragua, 1959, Dominican Republic, 1959, Bolivia-Chile, 1962, Venezuela-Dominican Republic, 1961.

4. Neale Ronnings, LAW AND POLITICS IN INTER-AMERICAN DIPLOMACY, pp. 64-65.

5. Investigating or mediating committees have been established to carry out OAS responsibilities in every individual instance. They do not have a permanent stand and their performance usually ends when the cases are solved or when an agreement is reached between the parties of a conflict. Participation in these committees varies from one instance to the other but, frequently, representatives of big, or middle-sized, and respected powers in the OAS are elected to serve in these ad hoc committees.

6. The Inter-American Peace Committee began its work during the war in 1940 to settle inter-American disputes. (See above, Chapter IV, on the Second Meeting of Consultation.) Its functions and its role are not specifically mentioned in the OAS Charter and thus it can be argued that its role is primarily an informal one. In 1956 the OAS Council established a specialized and informal mediation process for its activities. It is permanent, but its involvement in disputes is not compulsory; the conflicting parties have to approve its mediation. It is comprised of representatives of five member states, each of whom is elected for a period of five years, with only one of its members elected each year. Its site is in Washington, D.C., but it can meet somewhere else whenever the situation requires. See the Pan-American Union, ESTATUTO DE LA COMISION INTERAMERICANA DE PAZ, pp. 1-4.

7. This kind of committee of observation and investigation (different from the Inter-American Peace Committee, which is a permanent body) is established by the Organ of Consultation to work on every specific dispute. The number of

representatives and number of members vary from one situation to another and they do not have a permanent stand; they are just appointed for the time the dispute lasts.

8. For instance, Mexican Ambassador Vicente Sánchez Gavito's performance during the settlement of the dispute between Nicaragua and Honduras (1957) helped to carry out the decision of the International Court of Justice which put an end to their border dispute.

9. For a detailed description of the cases and the ways in which they were solved by the OAS see David W. Wainhouse et al., INTERNATIONAL PEACE OBSERVATION: A HISTORY AND FORECAST, pp. 106-214; the Pan-American Union, TRATADO INTERAMERICANO DE ASISTENCIA RECIPROCA: APLICACIONES, vols. I and II.

10. This was done when the Special Committee for the Caribbean was created in 1950 to handle Haiti's and the Dominican Republic's complaints against aggressive activities of their neighbors.

11. The Venezuela-Dominican Republic ease is an exception in that it was taken to the Security Council at a Soviet request in an effort to gain Security Council approval of OAS sanctions against the Dominican Republic. Another exception occurred when, during the Haitian-Dominican Republic dispute in 1963, Haiti sought Security Council support, but later agreed to the OAS handling of the case. These cases will be considered later.

12. The United Fruit Company lost 234,000 acres of its holdings of 300,000 acres on the Pacific coastland, and 174,000 acres on the Caribbean coast. Compensation in the form of bonds was offered. International Railways of Central America was expropriated after prolonged wage and labor disputes.

13. The United States government had refused the sale of arms to Guatemala and tried without avail to impede the purchase of arms by Guatemala from other countries. The arms were acquired in Poland and Czechoslovakia and delivered by a Swedish freighter. Guatemala justified the purchase by stating that it had to defend itself against groups of exiles that were threatening to regain control of the country. United States Secretary of State Dulles considered that Guatemala had a military establishment three to four times the size of its neighbors'. See J. E. S. Fawcett, "Intervention in international law: a study of some recent cases," pp. 372-374.

14. Security Council Official Records, Document S/2988, April 15, 1953. (These records will be hereinafter referred to as SCOR.)

15. SCOR, Document S/3233, June 19, 1954.

16. SCOR, Document S/PV, 675th Meeting of the Security Council, June 29, 1954, p. 16.

17. SCOR, Document S/3236, June 20, 1954.

18. Inis L. Claude, Jr., "The OAS, the UN and the United States," p. 24.

19. The action of this committee started on June 17, 1954 as a consequence of a Guatemalan request.

20. SCOR, Document S/3247, June 24, 1954.

21. SCOR, Document S/PV, 676th Meeting of the Security Council, June 25, 1954, p. 30.

22. Ibid., p. 32.

23. Claude, "The OAS, the UN and the United States," p. 28.

24. For a view on this uncertainty see United Nations, REPERTORIO DE LA PRACTICA SEGUIDA POR LOS ORGANOS DE LAS NACIONES UNIDAS, Vol. II, pp. 464-474.

25. See, for example, British views in SCOR, Document S/PV, 676th Meeting of the Security Council, June 25, 1954, p. 15.

26. OAS Official Records, Comisión Interamericana de Paz, Document CIP.119/54.

27. General Assembly Official Records, Ninth Session, 485th Plenary Session, October 1, 1954, p. 148. (These records will be hereinafter referred to as GAOR.)

28. GAOR, Ninth Session, 481st Plenary Meeting, September 28, 1954, p. 98.

29. GAOR, Ninth Session, 488th Plenary Meeting, October 4, 1954, p. 174.

30. GAOR, Ninth Session, Annual Report of the Secretary General on the Work of the Organization, July, 1953, to June 30, 1954, Supplement 1, p. xi.

31. SCOR, Document S/4378, July 11, 1960. Cuba also invoked Articles 24, 34, 35 (1), and 36 of the United Nations Charter.

32. This turned out to be the Seventh Meeting of Consultation, held in San Jose, Costa Rica, from August 22 to 29, 1960, shortly after the Sixth Meeting, which lasted from August 16 to 20, and at which the Venezuelan complaint against the Dominican Republic was discussed. This latter case will be analyzed in the next chapter.

33. SCOR, Document S/4395, July 19, 1960.

34. See Lucien Nizard, "La question cubaine devant le Conseil de Sécurité."

35. Ronning, LAW AND POLITICS IN INTER-AMERICAN DIPLOMACY, p. 78.

36. GAOR, Fifteenth Session, 872nd Plenary Meeting, September 26, 1960, p. 125.

37. SCOR, Document S/4565, November 29, 1960.

38. GAOR, Document A/BUR/SR, 131st Meeting of the General Committee, October 25, 1960.

39. SCOR, Documents S/4605, December 31, 1960, and S/4611, January 4, 1961.

40. This committee was to include representatives of Mexico, Venezuela, Brazil, Colombia, Chile, and Costa Rica; its main role (if explicitly requested to do so by the parties of a conflict) was to mediate in controversies occurring between members of the OAS.

41. *The New York Times,* April 28, 1960.

42. See GAOR, Fifteenth Session, Documents A/C.1/276 and A/C.1/SR, 1154th Meeting of the First Committee, April 18, 1961. Also, Luis Padilla Nervo, "Presencia de México en las Naciones Unidas: el caso de Cuba."

43. Claude, "The OAS, the UN and the United States," p. 41.

44. *The New York Times,* April 25 and 28, 1966.

45. See especially GAOR, Fifteenth Session, Document A/4832, September 5, 1961; GAOR, Sixteenth Session, Document A/C.1/847, October 12, 1961.

46. See Amitai Etzioni, "U.S. did the right thing in the wrong way,"

Washington Post, June 13, 1965; SCOR, Documents S/4992, November 21, 1961, and S/PV, 980th to 983rd Security Council Meetings, November 22 to November 28, 1961; Gordon Connell-Smith, THE INTER-AMERICAN SYSTEM, p. 176.

47. Interviews with Ambassador Luis Quintanilla, Mexico City, 1964.

48. Frederick B. Pike, "Guatemala, the United States and Communism in the Americas," pp. 258-260.

49. See Dwight D. Eisenhower, MANDATE FOR CHANGE, 1953-1956, pp. 420-427. See also *The New York Times,* April 28, 1965 and May 5, 1965; *Daily News,* May 7, 1965; and information presented on the NBC program, "The Science of Spying," May 4, 1965.

50. Asbjorn Eide, "Peace-keeping and enforcement action," p. 126.

51. Similar incompatible trends appear to be developing in other regional organizations, in particular the Organization of African Unity. See Patricia Berko Wild, "The Organization of African Unity and the Algerian-Moroccan border conflict: a study of new machinery for peace-keeping and for peaceful settlement of disputes among African states," especially p. 30.

52. The party or parties calling upon an international organization, regional or universal, are expected to be quite aware of the legal, as well as the political, forces predominant in the international organization under whose jurisdiction they choose to place their complaints.

53. See *The New York Times,* June 27, 1967, for a description of these negotiations.

CHAPTER 6

1. See Jerome Slater, "The United States, the Organization of American States and the Dominican Republic"; Minerva Morales M., ASPECTOS POLITICOS DEL SISTEMA INTERAMERICANO, chap. V.

2. SCOR, Documents S/4477, September 5, 1960 and S/4481, September 7, 1960.

3. SCOR, Documents S/PV, 893rd Meeting, September 9, 1960, p. 9 and S/PV, 895th Meeting, September 9, 1960, pp. 1-2.

4. SCOR, Document S/PV, 893rd Meeting, September 8, 1960, p. 12.

5. See Inis L. Claude, Jr., "The OAS, the UN and the United States," pp. 50-51.

6. SCOR, Document S/PV, 893rd Meeting, September 8, 1960.

7. This meeting had been called as a result of an offer by the Soviet prime minister (on July 9, 1960) to assist Cuba in case of invasion. See Morales M., ASPECTOS POLITICOS DEL SISTEMA INTERAMERICANO, pp. 151-152.

8. This was expressed by Chilean diplomat, Enrique Bernstein Carabantes, in "Punta del Este y las erróneas interpretaciones de un tratado"; by Mexican diplomats, Isidro Fabela, in "La Sexta y Séptima Reuniones de Cancilleres ante el derecho positivo internacional," and Antonio Gómez Robledo, "La crisis actual del Sistema Interamericano."

9. For this point on international delicts see Hans Kelsen, THE LAW OF THE UNITED NATIONS: A CRITICAL ANALYSIS OF ITS FUNDAMENTAL PROBLEMS, p. 706.

10. For an analysis on the controversial points of the Punta del Este Conference see the excellent study by C. Neal Ronning, PUNTA DEL ESTE: THE LIMITS OF COLLECTIVE SECURITY IN A TROUBLED HEMISPHERE; and the Pan-American Union, OCTAVA REUNION DE CONSULTA DE MINISTROS DE RELACIONES EXTERIORES: ACTAS Y DOCUMENTOS. See also Gordon Connell-Smith, THE INTER-AMERICAN SYSTEM, pp. 177-178.

11. GAOR, Sixteenth Session, Documents A/C.1/SR, 1231st to 1243rd Meetings of the First Committee, February 5 to 15, 1962, pp. 369-438.

12. See, for example, Ghana's, Ceylon's, and Morocco's views. GAOR, Sixteenth Session, Documents A/C.1/SR, 1328th, 1240th, and 1241st Meetings, February 13 and 14, 1962.

13. GAOR, Sixteenth Session, Document A/PV, 1105th Meeting, February 20, 1960.

14. SCOR, Documents S/5080, February 22, 1962.

15. SCOR, Documents S/5083, March 2, 1962; S/5086, March 8, 1962; S/5095, March 20, 1962.

16. SCOR, Documents S/PV, 922nd to 998th Meetings, March 14 to 23, 1962.

17. Pan-American Union, NOVENA REUNION DE CONSULTA DE MINIS-TROS DE RELACIONES EXTERIORES: ACTAS Y DOCUMENTOS.

18. See Arthur P. Whitaker, "Cuba's intervention in Venezuela: a test for the OAS," p. 535.

19. *The New York Times,* August 4, 1964.

20. For research of this Mexican attitude, I am indebted to Mrs. Linda L. Hoeschler and the fine paper which she prepared on the basis of documents and interviews with several Mexican diplomats and officials in the Mexican Foreign Office.

21. Several arguments were used against the blockade: (1) that it could not neutralize weapons already in Cuba; (2) that it could not bring enough pressure on the Soviet Union to remove those weapons; (3) that it could not interfere and stop the work at the bases enabling the missiles to become operational; (4) that it would seem unjustifiable to United States allies who were sensitive to freedom of the seas; and (5) that United States adversaries might well regard it as an illegal blockade, in violation of the United Nations Charter, and therefore feel free to defy it.

22. Theodore C. Sorensen, KENNEDY, p. 776.

23. Ibid., p. 788.

24. *ARTICLE 39. The Meeting of Consultation of Ministers of Foreign Affairs shall be held in order to consider problems of an urgent nature and common interest to the American States, and to serve as the Organ of Consulta-tion.*

25. The Eighth Meeting of Consultation, held in 1962 at Punta del Este, had established a Special Consultative Committee on Security Against Subversive Action of International Communism to counteract threats or acts of aggression, subversion or other dangers to the peace and security of the Western Hemisphere. It was also argued that Articles 6 and 8 of the Rio Treaty could be used to justify the quarantine.

26. Only the Uruguayan ambassador abstained, as he had not received instructions from his government. Uruguayan consent arrived the next day. The Bolivian ambassador voted affirmatively although unable to receive instructions from his government due to a bad telephone communication. See *The New York Times Supplement,* "The Cuban crisis," November 3, 1962; Arthur M. Schlesinger, Jr., A THOUSAND DAYS: JOHN F. KENNEDY IN THE WHITE HOUSE, pp. 744-745; and Henry M. Pachter, COLLISION COURSE: THE CUBAN MISSILE CRISIS AND COEXISTENCE, p. 29.

27. Some Latin Americans dissented at the Eighth Meeting of Consultation from OAS policies vis-a-vis the United Nations when Cuba was expelled from the OAS and when some issues involving Article 53 arose (see above).

28. This can also explain why secrecy was maintained and none of the allies was consulted. They might not have gone along with the chosen style of action and consultation would have meant a loss of precious time. See Schlesinger, A THOUSAND DAYS, p. 741.

29. Francis O. Wilcox, "Regionalism and the United Nations," p. 801.

30. For these views of Ghana's delegate see SCOR, Document S/PV, 1024th Meeting, October 24, 1962.

31. These arguments were presented through the unofficial writings of Abram Chayes, "Law and the quarantine in Cuba," and Leonard C. Meeker, "Defensive quarantine and the law."

32. Quoted by Sorensen, KENNEDY, p. 789, with this purpose and in relation to possible uses of Article 51.

33. Possibly a broadening interpretation of Article 51 could have been used to include the anticipatory measures and the preventive nature of United States action in view of the destructive power of nuclear weapons installed in Cuba, even if there was not an armed attack. The quarantine was carefully calculated to ward off the threatened danger while reducing to a minimum the possibility of the crisis leading to war.

34. Arguments criticizing United States legal advisers' views can be found in G. I. A. D. Draper, "Regional arrangements and enforcement action," and in John W. Halderman, "Regional enforcement measures and the United Nations."

35. Meeker, "Defensive quarantine and the law," pp. 519-520.

36. Chayes, "Law and the quarantine in Cuba," p. 556.

37. It had been proved that no foreigners were killed until after the marines arrived. See Bryce Wood's letter to *The New York Times,* June 13, 1965.

38. The United States considered the conflict a case of civil strife which necessitated the establishment of a 'neutral zone around the embassies of Latin American countries. Arguments initially used by the United States to justify the intervention protecting the lives of United States citizens were dropped by the president and United States officials as soon as the marines began to assist the military junta leaders and to accuse the rebel group of Communist infiltration. See Max Frankel, "Secret US report details policy in Dominican Republic," *The New York Times,* November 14, 1965, p. 1.

39. This term, first used by Mexican Ambassador Rafael de la Colina, became popular at the OAS meeting and in Latin American political and diplomatic circles. The word is *cohonestar* in Spanish.

40. Some Latin American governments in the OAS were strongly opposed to any effort to establish a provisional government since this was considered a flagrant intervention in the domestic affairs of the Dominican Republic.

41. At the request of Bolivia, thirteen Latin American representatives to the United Nations sent a letter to the Security Council endorsing the OAS's exclusive handling of the crisis.

42. Frequently, reports about the crisis sent by United Nations observers to the Security Council contradicted the reports submitted by the OAS Council.

43. Different views on the crisis can be obtained in Tad Szulc, DOMINI-CAN DIARY; and John Bartlow Martin; OVERTAKEN BY EVENTS: THE DOMINICAN CRISIS FROM THE FALL OF TRUJILLO TO THE CIVIL WAR.

44. See *The New York Times,* June 26, 1967.

45. See Marina and Lawrence S. Finkelstein, COLLECTIVE SECURITY, pp. 260-265.

46. Quoted by Wilcox, "Regionalism and the United Nations," p. 811.

47. Connell-Smith, THE INTER-AMERICAN SYSTEM, p. 341.

48. Up to this point, Latin American lack of unity, political homogeneity, and leadership has generally rendered the United States able to use its influence with enough governments to prevent a "Latin American alliance" from ever becoming a majority in the OAS.

REFERENCES

Allen, Ward P. (1947) "The Inter-American Treaty of Reciprocal Assistance." Department of State Bulletin 27, 438: 983-987.
——— (1946) "Regional arrangements and the United Nations." Department of State Bulletin 14, 361: 923-927.
Behr, Gerhard (1965) "Regional organizations: a United Nations problem." American Journal of International Law 49, 2: 166-184.
Belaunde, Victor Andrés (1945) LA CONFERENCIA DE SAN FRANCISCO. Lima: Ediciones Lumen.
Bloomfield, Lincoln P. (1960) THE UNITED NATIONS AND UNITED STATES FOREIGN POLICY: A NEW LOOK AT THE NATIONAL INTEREST. Boston: Little, Brown.
Bowett, D. W. (1964) SELF-DEFENSE IN INTERNATIONAL LAW. New York: Frederick A. Praeger.
Brown, Philip Marshall (1932) "Mexico and the Monroe Doctrine." American Journal of International Law 26, 1: 117-121.
——— (1920) "The Monroe Doctrine and the League of Nations." American Journal of International Law 14, 2: 207-210.
Carabantes, Enrique Bernstein (1962) "Punta del Este y las erróneas interpretaciones de un tratado." Foro Internacional 2, 4: 518-534.
Chayes, Abram (1963) "Law and the quarantine in Cuba." Foreign Affairs 41, 4: 550-558.
Cheever, Daniel S. and Field H. Haviland (1954) ORGANIZING FOR PEACE: Boston: Houghton Mifflin.
Claude, Inis L., Jr. (1964) "The OAS, the UN and the United States." International Conciliation, no. 547 (March): 1-67.
——— (1959) SWORDS INTO PLOWSHARES. New York: Random House.
Connell-Smith, Gordon (1966) THE INTER-AMERICAN SYSTEM. London: Oxford University Press.

Dozer, Donald M. (1961) ARE WE GOOD NEIGHBORS? Gainesville: University of
    Florida Press.
Draper, G. I. A. D. (1964) "Regional arrangements and enforcement action."
    Revue Egyptiènne de Droit International, vol. 20: 1-44.
Duggan, Laurence (1949) THE AMERICAS: THE SEARCH FOR HEMISPHERE
    SECURITY. New York: Holt Publishing.
Dulles, John F. (1950) WAR OR PEACE. New York: Macmillan.
Eide, Asbjorn (1966) "Peace-keeping and enforcement by regional organizations."
    Journal of Peace Research, no. 2: 125-145.
Eisenhower, Dwight D. (1963) MANDATE FOR CHANGE, 1953-1956. New York:
    Doubleday.
Etzioni, Amitai (1965) "U.S. did the right thing in the wrong way." Washington
    Post (June 13).
Fabela, Isidro (1960) "La Sexta y Séptima Reuniones de Cancilleres ante el
    derecho positivo internacional." Cuadernos Americanos 112, 6: 9-27.
Fawcett, J. E. S. (1961) "Intervention in international law: a study of some recent
    cases." Recueil des Cours, tome 103, vol. 2: 344-423.
Finch, George A. (1947) "The inter-American defense treaty." American Journal
    of International Law 41, 4: 863-866.
Finkelstein, Marina and Lawrence S. Finkelstein (1966) COLLECTIVE SECUR-
    ITY. San Francisco: Chandler Publishing.
Frontini, Norberto A. (1949) "El Pacto de Rio de Janeiro y el Pacto del
    Atlántico." Cuadernos Americanos 48, 6: 33-39.
Furniss, Edgar S. (1955) "A re-examination of regional arrangements." Columbia
    Journal of International Affairs 9, 2: 78-89.
Gómez Robledo, Antonio (1962) "La crísis actual del Sistema Interamericano."
    Foro Internacional 3, 1: 25-61 and 3, 2: 176-208.
——— (1960) "El Tratado de Rio." Foro Internacional 1, 1: 47-81.
——— (1960) LA SEGURIDAD COLECTIVA EN EL CONTINENTE AMERI-
    CANO. Mexico City: National University Press.
Goodrich, Leland M. (1959) THE UNITED NATIONS. New York: Crowell Pub-
    lishing.
——— (1949) "Regionalism and the United Nations." Columbia Journal of Inter-
    national Relations 3, 2: 5-20.
——— and Edvard Hambro (1949) THE CHARTER OF THE UNITED NATIONS:
    COMMENTARY AND DOCUMENTS. Boston: World Peace Foundation.
Halderman, John W. (1963) "Regional enforcement measures and the United
    Nations." Georgetown Law Journal, vol. 52 (Fall): 89-118.
Houston, John A. (1956) LATIN AMERICA IN THE UNITED NATIONS. New
    York: Carnegie Endowment for International Peace.
Hula, Erich (1942) "Pan Americanism: its utopian and realistic elements." Pp.
    125-146 in Henry P. Jordan (ed.) PROBLEMS OF POST WAR RECON-
    STRUCTION. Washington, D.C.: American Council on Public Affairs.
Hull, Cordell (1948) THE MEMOIRS OF CORDELL HULL. New York: Mac-
    millan.
Inman, Samuel Guy (1965) INTER-AMERICAN CONFERENCES, 1826-1954:

HISTORY AND PROBLEMS. Washington, D.C.: University Press of Washington, D.C.

Jacob, Phillip E. and Alexine L. Atherton (1965) THE DYNAMICS OF INTERNATIONAL ORGANIZATION. Homewood, Ill.: Dorsey Press.

Kelsen, Hans (1950) THE LAW OF THE UNITED NATIONS: A CRITICAL ANALYSIS OF ITS FUNDAMENTAL PROBLEMS. New York: Frederick A. Praeger.

Khan, Arfa Mirza Riza (1932) L'ARTICLE 10 DU PACTE DE LA SOCIETE DES NATIONS: LES ACCORDS DE LOCARNO ET LE DESARMEMENT. Paris: Académie Diplomatique Internationale, Séances et Travaux.

Kulski, W. W. (1950) "The Soviet system of collective security as compared with the Western system." American Journal of International Law 44, 3: 453-476.

Kunz, Joseph L. (1948) "The Inter-American Treaty of Reciprocal Assistance." American Journal of International Law 42, 1: 111-121.

Martin, John Bartlow (1966) OVERTAKEN BY EVENTS: THE DOMINICAN CRISIS FROM THE FALL OF TRUJILLO TO THE CIVIL WAR. New York: Doubleday.

Mecham, J. Lloyd (1963) THE UNITED STATES AND INTER-AMERICAN SECURITY, 1889-1960. Austin: University of Texas Press.

――― (1947) "The integration of the inter-American security system into the United Nations." Journal of Politics 9, 2: 178-196.

Meeker, Leonard C. (1963) "Defensive quarantine and the law." American Journal of International Law 57, 3: 515-524.

Miller, David Hunter (1928) THE DRAFTING OF THE COVENANT. New York: G. P. Putnam.

Mirkovitch, Vladislao (1932) DES RAPPORTS ENTRE L'ARTICLE 10 ET L'ARTICLE 21 DU PACTE DE LA SOCIETE DES NATIONS. Paris: Editions Internationales.

Morales M., Minerva (1964) "Política económica de los Estados Unidos en la América Latina." Foro Internacional 4, 3: 394-428.

――― (1962) ASPECTOS POLITICOS DEL SISTEMA INTERAMERICANO. Mexico City: National University Press.

Nervo, Luis Padilla (1961) "Presencia de México en las Naciones Unidas: el caso de Cuba." Cuadernos Americanos 116, 3: 72-86.

Nicholas, H. G. (1959) THE UNITED NATIONS AS A POLITICAL INSTITUTION. London: Oxford University Press.

Nizard, Lucien (1962) "La question cubaine devant le Conseil de Sécurité." Revue Général de Droit International Public, tome 66: 486-545.

Oliver, Covey (1962) THE INTER-AMERICAN SECURITY SYSTEM AND THE CUBAN CRISIS. Hammarskjold Forum Series. New York: Association of the Bar of the City of New York.

Pachter, Henry M. (1963) COLLISION COURSE: THE CUBAN MISSILE CRISIS AND COEXISTENCE. New York: Frederick A. Praeger.

Pan-American Union (1964) NOVENA REUNION DE CONSULTA DE MINISTROS DE RELACIONES EXTERIORES: ACTAS Y DOCUMENTOS. Washington, D.C.: Pan-American Union.

——— (1964) TRATADO INTERAMERICANO DE ASISTENCIA RECIPROCA: APLICACIONES. Washington, D.C.: Pan-American Union.

——— (1963) OCTAVA REUNION DE CONSULTA DE MINISTROS DE RELACIONES EXTERIORES: ACTAS Y DOCUMENTOS. Washington, D.C.: Pan-American Union.

——— (1956) ESTATUTO DE LA COMISION INTERAMERICANA DE PAZ. Washington, D.C.: Pan-American Union.

Pike, Frederick B. (1955) "Guatemala, the United States and Communism in the Americas." Review of Politics 17, 2: 232-261.

Plaza, Galo (1946) "Latin America's contribution to the United Nations." International Conciliation, no. 419 (March): 150-157.

Ronning, C. Neale (1963) LAW AND POLITICS IN INTER-AMERICAN DIPLOMACY. New York: John Wiley.

——— (1963) PUNTA DEL ESTE: THE LIMITS OF COLLECTIVE SECURITY IN A TROUBLED HEMISPHERE. New York: Carnegie Endowment for International Peace.

Rubinstein, Alvin Z. (1964) THE SOVIETS IN INTERNATIONAL ORGANIZATION. Princeton: Princeton University Press.

Russell, Ruth B. (1958) A HISTORY OF THE UNITED NATIONS CHARTER: THE ROLE OF THE UNITED STATES, 1940-1945. Washington, D.C.: Brookings Institution.

Saba, Hanna (1953) "Les accords régionaux dans la Charte de l'ONU." Recueil des Cours, tome 80, vol. 1: 635-727.

Schlesinger, Arthur M., Jr. (1967) A THOUSAND DAYS: JOHN F. KENNEDY IN THE WHITE HOUSE. New York: Fawcett Crest.

Sherwood, Robert E. (1950) ROOSEVELT AND HOPKINS. New York: Harper.

Slater, Jerome (1964) "The United States, the Organization of American States and the Dominican Republic." International Organization 18, 2: 268-291.

Sorensen, Theodore C. (1966) KENNEDY. New York: Bantam Books.

Spencer, John H. (1936) "The Monroe Doctrine and the League Covenant." American Journal of International Law 30, 3: 400-413.

Stromberg, Ronald M. (1963) COLLECTIVE SECURITY AND AMERICAN FOREIGN POLICY. New York: Frederick A. Praeger.

Szulc, Tad (1966) DOMINICAN DIARY. New York: Dell Publishing.

United Nations (1956) REPERTORIO DE LA PRACTICA SEGUIDA POR LOS ORGANOS DE LAS NACIONES UNIDAS. New York: United Nations.

——— (1945) CONFERENCE ON INTERNATIONAL ORGANIZATION. San Francisco: United Nations.

Vandenberg, Arthur H., Jr. [ed.] (1952) THE PRIVATE PAPERS OF SENATOR VANDENBERG. Boston: Houghton Mifflin.

Vellas, Pierre (1948) LE REGIONALISME INTERNATIONALE ET L'ONU. Paris: Editions Pédone.

Volpe, Alfred A. (1950) "Latin America at San Francisco: the aims, attitudes and accomplishments of Latin America at the United Nations Conference on International Organization, San Francisco, April 25 - June 26, 1945." Ph.D. dissertation, Stanford University.

Wainhouse, David W. et al. (1966) INTERNATIONAL PEACE OBSERVATION: A HISTORY AND FORECAST. Baltimore: John Hopkins Press.

Wells, Sumner (1946) WHERE ARE WE HEADING? New York: Harper.

––– (1944) THE TIME FOR DECISION. New York: Harper.

Whitaker, Arthur P. (1964) "Cuba's intervention in Venezuela: a test for the OAS." Orbis 8, 3: 530-535.

––– (1954) THE WESTERN HEMISPHERE IDEA: ITS RISE AND DECLINE. Ithaca: Cornell University Press.

––– (1951) "Development of American regionalism: the Organization of American States." International Conciliation, no. 469 (March): 123-164.

––– (1943) INTER-AMERICAN AFFAIRS, 1943. New York: Columbia University Press.

Wilcox, Francis O. (1965) "Regionalism and the United Nations." International Organization 9, 3: 789-812.

Wild, Patricia Berko (1966) "The Organization of African Unity and Algerian-Moroccan border conflict: a study of new machinery for peace-keeping and for peaceful settlement of disputes among African states." International Organization 20, 1: 18-36.

Wionczek, Miguel S. (1965) "Latin American Free Trade Association." International Conciliation, no. 551 (January).

––– (1962) "La actitud de los Estados Unidos frente al problema de la integración económica de América Latina." Comercio Exterior (January): 3-4.

Wood, Bryce (1966) THE UNITED STATES AND LATIN AMERICAN WARS, 1932-1942. New York: Columbia University Press.

––– (1961) THE MAKING OF THE GOOD NEIGHBOR POLICY. New York: Columbia University Press.

Yakemtchouk, Romain (1955) L'ONU, LA SECURITE REGIONALE ET LE PROBLEME DU REGIONALISME. Paris: Editions Pédone.

––– (1955) "Le régionalisme et l'ONU." Revue de Droit International Publique, tome 49: 406-422.

Yepes, J. M. (1947) "Les accords régionaux et le droit internationale." Recueil des Cours, tome 71, vol. 2: 235-341.